1992

BAD BLOOD

BAD BLOOD

The Tuskegee Syphilis Experiment

JAMES H. JONES

THE FREE PRESS
A Division of Macmillan Publishing Co., Inc.
NEW YORK

Collier Macmillan Publishers
LONDON

The Free Press
A Division of Macmillan Publishing Co., Inc.
866 Third Avenue, New York, N.Y. 10022

Collier Macmillan Canada, Inc.

First Free Press Paperback Edition 1982

Library of Congress Catalog Card Number: 80-69281

Printed in the United States of America

printing number paperback

        8 9 10

printing number hardcover

1 2 3 4 5 6 7 8 9 10

Library of Congress Cataloging in Publication Data

Jones, James H. (James Howard)
     Bad blood.

     Bibliography: p.
     Includes index.
        1. Human experimentation in medicine—Alabama—
Macon County—History. 2. Tuskegee Syphilis Study.
3. Syphilis—Research—Alabama—Macon County—His-
tory. 4. Syphilis—Alabama—Macon County—History.
5. Afro-American men—Diseases—Alabama—Macon
County—History. I. Tuskegee Institute. II. Title.
(DNLM: 1. Blacks—Alabama. 2. Human Experimentation.
3. Syphilis. WG 160 J77b)
R853.H8J66   1981   364.1'42   80-69281
ISBN 0-02-916670-5   AACR2
ISBN 0-02-916690-X pbk.

for Linda

Contents

Acknowledgments

I have incurred many debts in writing *Bad Blood*. I first came across materials on the Tuskegee Study in 1969 while investigating another topic in the National Archives. Needless to say, I did not know that the experiment was still going on then. When Jean Heller broke the story in 1972, I was as shocked as everyone else, but I knew exactly where to go to initiate research on the topic.

Work began in 1972 while I was a Kennedy Fellow in the Interfaculty Program in Bioethics at Harvard University, a program jointly sponsored by the Joseph P. Kennedy, Jr., Foundation and the National Endowment for the Humanities. The directors of the program, William J. Curran, Arthur J. Dyck, and Stanley Joel Reiser, were encouraging and congenial hosts. I learned a great deal about medical ethics from discussions with other fellows, especially Norman Fost, M.D.

I appreciate the courteous help I received from the professional staff of the Francis A. Countway Library of Medicine of the Harvard Medical School. I also wish to acknowledge the assistance of the staff of the National Archives, especially Albert H. Leisinger, Jr., who shared his incomparable knowledge of the Archives. Over the years that followed, Al's warm friendship supported my efforts to complete the manuscript.

In 1974 and 1975 I worked closely with Fred Gray, the civil rights attorney who brought the class action suit on behalf of the men in the Tuskegee Study. We labored side by side probing legal and medical records and preparing the case for trial. I much admired his courage and devotion to his clients and I am indebted to him for giving me total access to his files, including important materials from the Tuskegee Institute's Archives.

Thanks to a second fellowship from the Joseph P. Kennedy, Jr., Foundation, I held a six-month appointment in 1975 as senior research scholar at the Center for Bioethics of the Kennedy Institute of Ethics at Georgetown University. There I met the late André Hellegers, who served with distinction as the director of the Kennedy Institute. A brilliant and wonderfully vital man, he had a gift for asking penetrating questions, for seeing the best in other people, and for making them feel good about themselves. He was a source of constant encouragement and inspiration. I also wish to thank Eunice Kennedy Shriver and Sargent Shriver for their personal interest and support.

Several colleagues at the Kennedy Institute read and criticized the four chapters I wrote during my tenure there. I am grateful to LeRoy Walters, Roy Branson, and Richard McCormick for their help. James F. Childress deserves special thanks for his valuable criticism of the manuscript and for the good humor with which he suffered my numerous forays into his office to chatter about one point or another. I learned much from every conversation with this gifted scholar. Thanks are also due for research assistance to Donna Churchill and Sue Johe, and to Mary Baker and Carol Hetler for excellent typing of drafts and oral histories. The library staff at the Institute was most helpful, particularly Doris Goldstein, who filled my numerous requests for articles from the National Library of Medicine. I also appreciate the aid of the staff of the National Library of Medicine for locating countless articles from medical journals and for supplying the photographs of the Public Health Service officers whose portraits appear in this book.

I received invaluable legal assistance from the Covington and Burling law firm of Washington, D.C. In 1975 my efforts to gain total access to the records of the Tuskegee Study were impeded by the Justice Department. Only after Charles A. Miller, a senior partner of Covington and Burling, agreed to take my case *pro bono* and instituted a Freedom of Information Act inquiry on my behalf did the Justice Department withdraw its opposition.

Archival materials acquired a new meaning in the light of conversations with the participants in the study. This book would not have been possible without oral history. As a result of the efforts of Fred Gray, several survivors overcame their newly acquired suspicion of white researchers from Washington, D.C., and graciously consented to talk with me. I wish to thank Frank Douglas Dixon, Carter Howard, Charles Pollard, Herman Shaw, and Bill Williams. I am also grateful to the following former Public Health Service officers who agreed to talk with me: William J. Brown, M.D.; John R. Heller, M.D.; Sidney Olansky, M.D.; and David Sencer, M.D.

I owe an enormous debt to Eunice Rivers Laurie for spending several days with me and helping me to see the experiment through her eyes. More than any other principal of the Tuskegee Study, she increased my tolerance for ambiguity.

Peter Buxtun kindly agreed to answer my queries about his extraordinary role in ending the experiment. He has offered much encouragement to get the story told. The same is true of Jean Heller, who shared both her memories and her extensive files on the study.

Despite the onerous work loads required of its professional staff, the National Endowment for the Humanities granted me a six-month leave of absence in 1975. Moreover, my colleagues at the Endowment bolstered my efforts to complete the study. I wish to thank, in particular, Richard Blum, Daniel Mayers, Michael Roman, Morton Sosna, and Dorothy Wartenberg. As fellow humanists who earn their living as bureaucrats, they affirmed my struggle to remain a historian.

My work has benefited from the comments of numerous scholars and friends. Richard Abrams proved my most incisive critic, and debates with him helped sharpen many of the arguments in *Bad Blood*. John W. Cooke and Philip R. Muller, two old and dear friends, wrote detailed notes on the manuscript and saved me from numerous errors. Jack also scouted materials for me at the Fisk University Archives. I appreciate the special consideration I received from the professional staff there. Thanks are also due to Benjamin Benford for research in local newspapers in Tuskegee, Alabama.

I learned a great deal from James Reed, who shared his impressive knowledge of the social history of medicine with me. James T. Patterson offered keen comments on the entire manuscript and was especially helpful with chapters three and eleven. Joan Scott offered an insightful critique of an early draft of the manuscript and gave me timely encouragement along the way. William A. Tisdale, M.D., provided technical assistance and advice on the medical issues treated in *Bad Blood*. Ann Collins Nelson worked many hours giving valuable bibliographic assistance and her efforts sustained me greatly. For reading and commenting on all or parts of the manuscript, I wish to thank: Willard B. Gatewood, Jr., Gerald N. Grob, Timothy Gunn, Darlene Hine, R. Christian Johnson, Robert Kehoe, August Meier, J. Kenneth Morland, James Powell, Martin Ridge, Sheldon Rothblatt, Barbara Gutmann Rosenkrantz, Todd L. Savitt, Marion Torchia, and Regina Wolkoff.

I would like to offer a special word of thanks to Charles E. Smith, Vice President of Macmillan Publishing Company. Charlie sensed immediately the experiment's importance and offered me financial support and enormous encouragement.

A word of thanks is also due Michael Sander, my editorial supervisor at the Free Press.

Three important women in my life gave me loving support: my sister, Ann Grosse; my mother, Mildred Mackey; and my grandmother, Jewel Jones.

My children hastened my efforts to complete the manuscript. David was impervious; Jessica was demanding; and Laura was impatient.

Finally, my greatest debt is to Linda Auwers, my wife. We alone know how much she contributed.

A Note on Spelling and Punctuation

In order to avoid cluttering the text with notes to verify accuracy, the following rules have been followed. The original capitalization of "Negro" has been used without noting the use of the small "n" in the bulk of the early quotes. The transition in social attitudes toward blacks can be traced in the switch from the lower-case to the upper-case letter in these documents. The spelling and punctuation recorded by the Charles Johnson Team for the interviews in *Shadow of the Plantation* have been preserved. They attempted to record the dialect of the people of Macon County. Standard spelling and punctuation have been used for my own interviews.

BAD BLOOD

CHAPTER 1

"A Moral Astigmatism"

I N late July of 1972, Jean Heller of the Associated Press broke the story: for forty years the United States Public Health Service (PHS) had been conducting a study of the effects of untreated syphilis on black men in Macon County, Alabama, in and around the county seat of Tuskegee. The Tuskegee Study, as the experiment had come to be called, involved a substantial number of men: 399 who had syphilis and an additional 201 who were free of the disease chosen to serve as controls. All of the syphilitic men were in the late stage of the disease when the study began.[1]

Under examination by the press the PHS was not able to locate a formal protocol for the experiment. Later it was learned that one never existed; procedures, it seemed, had simply evolved. A variety of tests and medical examinations were performed on the men during scores of visits by PHS physicians over the years, but the basic procedures called for periodic blood testing and routine autopsies to supplement the information that was obtained through clinical examinations. The fact that only men who had late, so-called tertiary, syphilis were selected for the study indicated that the investigators were eager to learn more about the serious complications that result during the final phase of the disease.

The PHS officers were not disappointed. Published reports on the experiment consistently showed higher rates of mortality and morbidity among the syphilitics than the controls. In fact, the press reported that as of 1969 at least 28 and perhaps as many as 100 men had died as a direct result of complications caused by syphilis. Others had developed serious syphilis-related heart conditions that may have contributed to their deaths.[2]

The Tuskegee Study had nothing to do with treatment. No new drugs were tested; neither was any effort made to establish the efficacy of old forms of treatment. It was a nontherapeutic experiment, aimed at compiling data on the effects of the spontaneous evolution of syphilis on black males. The magnitude of the risks taken with the lives of the subjects becomes clearer once a few basic facts about the disease are known.

Syphilis is a highly contagious disease caused by the *Treponema pallidum*, a delicate organism that is microscopic in size and resembles a corkscrew in shape. The disease may be acquired or congenital. In acquired syphilis, the spirochete (as the *Treponema pallidum* is also called) enters the body through the skin or mucous membrane, usually during sexual intercourse, though infection may also occur from other forms of bodily contact such as kissing. Congenital syphilis is transmitted to the fetus in the infected mother when the spirochete penetrates the placental barrier.

From the onset of infection syphilis is a generalized disease involving tissues throughout the entire body. Once they wiggle their way through the skin or mucous membrane, the spirochetes begin to multiply at a frightening rate. First they enter the lymph capillaries where they are hurried along to the nearest lymph gland. There they multiply and work their way into the bloodstream. Within days the spirochetes invade every part of the body.

Three stages mark the development of the disease: primary, secondary, and tertiary. The primary stage lasts from ten to sixty days starting from the time of infection. During this "first incubation period," the primary lesion of syphilis, the chancre, appears at the point of contact, usually on the genitals. The chancre, typically a slightly elevated, round ulcer, rarely causes personal discomfort and may be so small as to go unnoticed. If it does not become secondarily infected, the chancre will heal without treatment within a month or two, leaving a scar that persists for several months.[3]

While the chancre is healing, the second stage begins. Within six weeks to six months, a rash appears signaling the development of secondary syphilis. The rash may resemble measles, chicken pox, or any number of skin eruptions, though occasionally it is so mild as to go unnoticed. Bones and joints often become painful, and circulatory disturbances such as cardiac palpitations may develop. Fever, indigestion, headaches, or other nonspecific symptoms may accompany the rash. In some cases skin lesions develop into moist ulcers teeming with spirochetes, a condition that is especially severe when the rash appears in the mouth and causes open sores that are viciously infectious. Scalp hair may drop out in patches, creating a "moth-eaten" appearance. The greatest proliferation and most widespread distribution of spirochetes throughout the body occurs in secondary syphilis.[4]

Secondary syphilis gives way in most cases, even without treatment, to a period of latency that may last from a few weeks to thirty years. As if by magic, all symptoms of the disease seem to disappear, and the syphilitic patient does not associate with the disease's earlier symptoms the occasional skin infections, periodic chest pains, eye disorders, and vague discomforts that may follow. But the spirochetes do not vanish once the disease becomes latent. They bore into the bone marrow, lymph glands, vital organs, and central nervous systems of their victims. In some cases the disease seems to follow a policy of peaceful coexistence, and its hosts are able to enjoy full and long lives. Even so, autopsies in such cases often reveal syphilitic lesions in vital organs as contributing causes of death. For many syphilitic patients, however, the disease remains latent only two or three years. Then the delusion of a truce is shattered by the appearance of signs and symptoms that denote the tertiary stage.

It is during late syphilis, as the tertiary stage is also called, that the disease inflicts the greatest damage. Gummy or rubbery tumors (so-called gummas), the characteristic lesions of late syphilis, appear, resulting from the concentration of spirochetes in the body's tissues with destruction of vital structures. These tumors often coalesce on the skin forming large ulcers covered with a crust consisting of several layers of dried exuded matter. Their assaults on bone structure produce deterioration that resembles osteomyelitis or bone tuberculosis. The small tumors may be absorbed, leaving slight scarred depressions, or they may cause wholesale destruction of the bone, such as the horrible mutilation that occurs when nasal and palate bones are eaten away. The liver may also be attacked; here the result is scarring and deformity of the organ that impede circulation from the intestines.

The cardiovascular and central nervous systems are frequent and often fatal targets of late syphilis. The tumors may attack the walls of the heart or the blood vessels. When the aorta is involved, the walls become weakened, scar tissue forms over the lesion, the artery dilates, and the valves of the heart no longer open and close properly and begin to leak. The stretching of the vessel walls may produce an aneurysm, a balloonlike bulge in the aorta. If the bulge bursts, and sooner or later most do, the result is sudden death.

The results of neurosyphilis are equally devastating. Syphilis is spread to the brain through the blood vessels, and while the disease can take several forms, the best known is paresis, a general softening of the brain that produces progressive paralysis and insanity. Tabes dorsalis, another form of neurosyphilis, produces a stumbling, foot-slapping gait in its victims due to the destruction of nerve cells in the spinal cord. Syphilis can also attack the optic nerve, causing blindness, or the eighth cranial nerve, inflicting deafness. Since nerve cells lack regenerative power, all such damage is permanent.

The germ that causes syphilis, the stages of the disease's development, and the complications that can result from untreated syphilis were all known to medical science in 1932—the year the Tuskegee Study began.

Since the effects of the disease are so serious, reporters in 1972 wondered why the men agreed to cooperate. The press quickly established that the subjects were mostly poor and illiterate, and that the PHS had offered them incentives to participate. The men received free physical examinations, free rides to and from the clinics, hot meals on examination days, free treatment for minor ailments, and a guarantee that burial stipends would be paid to their survivors. Though the latter sum was very modest (fifty dollars in 1932 with periodic increases to allow for inflation), it represented the only form of burial insurance that many of the men had.

What the health officials had told the men in 1932 was far more difficult to determine. An officer of the venereal disease branch of the Center for Disease Control in Atlanta, the agency that was in charge of the Tuskegee Study in 1972, assured reporters that the participants were told at the beginning that they had syphilis and were told what the disease could do to them, and that they were given the opportunity to withdraw from the program any time and receive treatment. But a physician with firsthand knowledge of the experiment's early years directly contradicted this statement. Dr. J. W. Williams, who was serving his internship at Andrews Hospital at the Tuskegee Institute in 1932 and assisted in the experiment's clinical work, stated that neither the interns nor the subjects knew what the study involved. "The people who came in were not told what was being done," Dr. Williams said. "We told them we wanted to test them. They were not told, so far as I know, what they were being treated for or what they were not being treated for." As far as he could tell, the subjects "thought they were being treated for rheumatism or bad stomachs." He did recall administering to the men what he thought were drugs to combat syphilis, and yet as he thought back on the matter, Dr. Williams conjectured that "some may have been a placebo." He was absolutely certain of one point: "We didn't tell them we were looking for syphilis. I don't think they would have known what that was."[5]

A subject in the experiment said much the same thing. Charles Pollard recalled clearly the day in 1932 when some men came by and told him that he would receive a free physical examination if he appeared the next day at a nearby one-room school. "So I went on over and they told me I had bad blood," Pollard recalled. "And that's what they've been telling me ever since. They come around from time to time and check me over and they say, 'Charlie, you've got bad blood.'"[6]

An official of the Center for Disease Control (CDC) stated that he understood the term "bad blood" was a synonym for syphilis in the black community. Pollard replied, "That could be true. But I never heard no such thing. All I knew was that they just kept saying I had the bad blood—they never mentioned syphilis to me, not even once." Moreover, he thought that he had been receiving treatment for "bad blood" from the first meeting on, for Pollard added: "They been doctoring me off and on ever since then, and they gave me a blood tonic."[7]

The PHS's version of the Tuskegee Study came under attack from yet another quarter when Dr. Reginald G. James told his story to reporters. Between 1939 and 1941 he had been in-volved with public health work in Macon County—specifically the diagnosis and treatment of syphilis. Assigned to work with him was Eunice Rivers, a black nurse employed by the Public Health Service to keep track of the participants in the Tuskegee Study. "When we found one of the men from the Tuskegee Study," Dr. James recalled, "she would say, 'He's under study and not to be treated.'" These encounters left him, by his own description, "distraught and disturbed," but whenever he in-sisted on treating such a patient, the man never returned. "They were being advised they shouldn't take treatments or they would be dropped from the study," Dr. James stated. The penalty for being dropped, he explained, was the loss of the benefits that they had been promised for participating.[8]

Once her identity became known, Nurse Rivers excited con-siderable interest, but she steadfastly refused to talk with re-porters. Details of her role in the experiment came to light when newsmen discovered an article about the Tuskegee Study that appeared in *Public Health Reports* in 1953. Involved with the study from its beginning, Nurse Rivers served as the liai-son between the researchers and the subjects. She lived in Tus-kegee and provided the continuity in personnel that was vital. For while the names and faces of the "government doctors" changed many times over the years, Nurse Rivers remained a constant. She served as a facilitator, bridging the many bar-riers that stemmed from the educational and cultural gap be-tween the physicians and the subjects. Most important, the men trusted her.[9]

As the years passed the men came to understand that they were members of a social club and burial society called "Miss Rivers' Lodge." She kept track of them and made certain that they showed up to be examined whenever the "government doctors" came to town. She often called for them at their homes in a shiny station wagon with the government emblem on the front door and chauffeured them to and from the place of examination. According to the *Public Health Reports* article, these rides became "a mark of distinction for many of the men who enjoyed waving to their neighbors as they drove by." There was nothing to indicate that the members of "Miss Rivers' Lodge" knew they were participating in a deadly serious experiment.[10]

Spokesmen for the Public Health Service were quick to point out that the experiment was never kept secret, as many newspapers had incorrectly reported when the story first broke. Far from being clandestine, the Tuskegee Study had been the subject of numerous reports in medical journals and had been openly discussed in conferences at professional meetings. An official told reporters that more than a dozen articles had appeared in some of the nation's best medical journals, describing the basic procedures of the study to a combined readership of well over a hundred thousand physicians. He denied that the Public Health Service had acted alone in the experiment, calling it a cooperative project that involved the Alabama State Department of Health, the Tuskegee Institute, the Tuskegee Medical Society, and the Macon County Health Department.[11]

Apologists for the Tuskegee Study contended that it was at best problematic whether the syphilitic subjects could have been helped by the treatment that was available when the study began. In the early 1930s treatment consisted of mercury and two arsenic compounds called arsphenamine and neoarsphenamine, known also by their generic name, salvarsan. The drugs were highly toxic and often produced serious and occasionally fatal reactions in patients. The treatment was painful and usually required more than a year to complete. As one CDC officer put it, the drugs offered "more potential harm for the patient than potential benefit."[12]

PHS officials argued that these facts suggested that the experiment had not been conceived in a moral vacuum. For if the state of the medical art in the early 1930s had nothing better than dangerous and less than totally effective treatment to offer, then it followed that, in the balance, little harm was done by leaving the men untreated.[13]

Discrediting the efficacy of mercury and salvarsan helped blunt the issue of withholding treatment during the early years, but public health officials had a great deal more difficulty explaining why penicillin was denied in the 1940s. One PHS spokesman ventured that it probably was not "a one-man decision" and added philosophically, "These things seldom are." He called the denial of penicillin treatment in the 1940s "the most critical moral issue about this experiment" and admitted that from the present perspective "one cannot see any reason that they could not have been treated at that time." Another spokesman declared: "I don't know why the decision was made in 1946 not to stop the program."[14]

The thrust of these comments was to shift the responsibility for the Tuskegee Study to the physician who directed the experiment during the 1940s. Without naming anyone, an official told reporters: "Whoever was director of the VD section at that time, in 1946 or 1947, would be the most logical candidate if you had to pin it down." That statement pointed an accusing finger at Dr. John R. Heller, a retired PHS officer who had served as the director of the division of venereal disease between 1943 and 1948. When asked to comment, Dr. Heller declined to accept responsibility for the study and shocked reporters by declaring: "There was nothing in the experiment that was unethical or unscientific."[15]

The current local health officer of Macon County shared this view, telling reporters that he probably would not have given the men penicillin in the 1940s either. He explained this curious devotion to what nineteenth-century physicians would have called "therapeutic nihilism" by emphasizing that penicillin was a new and largely untested drug in the 1940s. Thus, in his opinion, the denial of penicillin was a defensible medical decision.[16]

A CDC spokesman said it was "very dubious" that the participants in the Tuskegee Study would have benefited from penicillin after 1955. In fact, treatment might have done more harm than good. The introduction of vigorous therapy after so many years might lead to allergic drug reactions, he warned. Without debating the ethics of the Tuskegee Study, the CDC spokesman pointed to a generation gap as a reason to refrain from criticizing it. "We are trying to apply 1972 medical treatment standards to those of 1932," cautioned one official. Another officer reminded the public that the study began when attitudes toward treatment and experimentation were much different. "At this point in time," the officer stated, "with our current knowledge of treatment and the disease and the revolutionary change in approach to human experimentation, I don't believe the program would be undertaken."[17]

Journalists tended to accept the argument that the denial of penicillin during the 1940s was the crucial ethical issue. Most did not question the decision to withhold earlier forms of treatment because they apparently accepted the judgment that the cure was as bad as the disease. But a few journalists and editors argued that the Tuskegee Study presented a moral problem long before the men were denied treatment with penicillin. "To say, as did an official of the Center for Disease Control, that the experiment posed 'a serious moral problem' after penicillin became available is only to address part of the situation," declared the *St. Louis Post-Dispatch*. "The fact is that in an effort to determine from autopsies what effects syphilis has on the body, the government from the moment the experiment began withheld the best available treatment for a particularly cruel disease. The immorality of the experiment was inherent in its premise."[18]

Viewed in this light, it was predictable that penicillin would not be given to the men. *Time* magazine might decry the failure to administer the drug as "almost beyond belief or human compassion," but along with many other publications it failed to recognize a crucial point. Having made the decision to withhold treatment at the outset, investigators were not likely to experience a moral crisis when a new and improved form of treatment was developed. Their failure to administer penicillin resulted from the initial decision to withhold all treatment. The only valid distinction that can be made between the two acts is that the denial of penicillin held more dire consequences for the men in the study. The *Chicago Sun Times* placed these separate actions in the proper perspective: "Whoever made the decision to withhold penicillin compounded the original immorality of the project."[19]

In their public comments, the CDC spokesmen tried to present the Tuskegee Study as a medical matter involving clinical decisions that may or may not have been valid. The antiseptic quality of their statements left journalists cold, prompting an exasperated North Carolina editor to declare: "Perhaps there are responsible people with heavy consciences about their own or their organizations' roles in this study, but thus far there is an appalling amount of 'So what?' in the comments about it." ABC's Harry Reasoner agreed. On national television, he expressed bewilderment that the PHS could be "only mildly uncomfortable" with an experiment that "used human beings as laboratory animals in a long and inefficient study of how long it takes syphilis to kill someone."[20]

The human dimension dominated the public discussions of the Tuskegee Study. The scientific merits of the experiment, real or imagined, were passed over almost without comment. Not being scientists, the journalists, public officials, and concerned citizens who protested the study did not really care how long it takes syphilis to kill people or what percentages of syphilis victims are fortunate enough to live to ripe old age with the disease. From their perspective the PHS was guilty of playing fast and loose with the lives of these men to indulge scientific curiosity.[21]

Many physicians had a different view. Their letters defending the study appeared in editorial pages across the country, but their most heated counterattacks were delivered in professional journals. The most spirited example was an editorial in the *Southern Medical Journal* by Dr. R. H. Kampmeir of Vanderbilt University's School of Medicine. No admirer of the press, he blasted reporters for their "complete disregard for their abysmal ignorance," and accused them of banging out "anything on their typewriters which will make headlines." As one of the few remaining physicians with experience treating syphilis in the 1930s, Dr. Kampmeir promised to "put this 'tempest in a teapot' into proper historical perspective."[22]

Dr. Kampmeir correctly pointed out that there had been only one experiment dealing with the effects of untreated syphilis prior to the Tuskegee Study. A Norwegian investigator had reviewed the medical records of nearly two thousand untreated syphilitic patients who had been examined at an Oslo clinic between 1891 and 1910. A follow-up had been published in 1929, and that was the state of published medical experimentation on the subject before the Tuskegee Study began. Dr. Kampmeir did not explain why the Oslo Study needed to be repeated.

The Vanderbilt physician repeated the argument that penicillin would not have benefited the men, but he broke new ground by asserting that the men themselves were responsible for the illnesses and deaths they sustained from syphilis. The PHS was not to blame, Dr. Kampmeir explained, because "in our free society, antisyphilis treatment has never been forced." He further reported that many of the men in the study had received some treatment for syphilis down through the years and insisted that others could have secured treatment had they so desired. He admitted that the untreated syphilitics suffered a higher mortality rate than the controls, observing coolly: "This is not surprising. No one has ever implied that syphilis is a benign infection." His failure to discuss the social mandate of physicians to prevent harm and to heal the sick whenever possible seemed to reduce the Hippocratic oath to a solemn obligation not to deny treatment upon demand.[23]

Journalists looked at the Tuskegee Study and reached different conclusions, raising a host of ethical issues. Not since the Nuremberg trials of Nazi scientists had the American people been confronted with a medical *cause célèbre* that captured so many headlines and sparked so much discussion. For many it was a shocking revelation of the potential for scientific abuse in their own country. "That it has happened in this country in our time makes the tragedy more poignant," wrote the editor of the *Philadelphia Inquirer*. Others thought the experiment totally "un-American" and agreed with Senator John Sparkman of Alabama, who denounced it as "absolutely appalling" and "a disgrace to the American concept of justice and humanity." Some despaired of ever again being able to hold their heads high. A resident of the nation's capital asked: "If this is true, how in the name of God can we look others in the eye and say: 'This is a decent country.'"[24]

Perhaps self-doubts such as these would have been less intense if a federal agency had not been responsible for the experiment. No one doubted that private citizens abused one another and had to be restrained from doing so. But the revelation that the Public Health Service had conducted the study was especially distressing. The editor of the *Providence Sunday Journal* admitted that he was shocked by "the flagrant immorality of what occurred under the auspices of the United States Government." A curious reversal of roles seemed to have taken place in Alabama: Instead of protecting its citizens against such experiments, the government was conducting them.[25]

Memories of Nazi Germany haunted some people as the broader implications of the PHS's role in the experiment became apparent. A man in Tennessee reminded health officials in Atlanta that "Adolf Hitler allowed similar degradation of human dignity in inhumane medical experiments on humans living under the Third Reich," and confessed that he was "much distressed at the comparison." A New York editor had difficulty believing that "such stomach-turning callousness could happen outside the wretched quackeries spawned by Nazi Germany."[26]

The specter of Nazi Germany prompted some Americans to equate the Tuskegee Study with genocide. A civil rights leader in Atlanta, Georgia, charged that the study amounted to "nothing less than an official, premeditated policy of genocide." A student at the Tuskegee Institute agreed. To him, the experiment was "but another act of genocide by whites," an act that "again exposed the nature of whitey: a savage barbarian and a devil."[27]

Most editors stopped short of calling the Tuskegee Study genocide or charging that PHS officials were little better than Nazis. But they were certain that racism played a part in what happened in Alabama. "How condescending and void of credibility are the claims that racial considerations had nothing to do with the fact that 600 [all] of the subjects were black," declared the *Afro-American* of Baltimore, Maryland. That PHS officials had kept straight faces while denying any racial overtones to the experiment prompted the editors of this influential black paper to charge "that there are still federal officials who feel they can do anything where black people are concerned."[28]

The *Los Angeles Times* echoed this view. In deftly chosen words, the editors qualified their accusation that PHS officials had persuaded hundreds of black men to become "human guinea pigs" by adding: "Well, perhaps not quite that [human guinea pigs] because the doctors obviously did not regard their subjects as completely human." A Pennsylvania editor stated that such an experiment "could only happen to blacks." To support this view, the *New Courier* of Pittsburgh implied that American society was so racist that scientists could abuse blacks with impunity.[29]

Other observers thought that social class was the real issue, that poor people, regardless of their race, were the ones in danger. Somehow people from the lower class always seemed to supply a disproportionate share of subjects for scientific research. Their plight, in the words of a North Carolina editor, offered "a reminder that the basic rights of Americans, particularly the poor, the illiterate and the friendless, are still subject to violation in the name of scientific research." To a journalist in Colorado, the Tuskegee Study demonstrated that "the Public Health Service sees the poor, the black, the illiterate and the defenseless in American society as a vast experimental resource for the government." And the *Washington Post* made much the same point when it observed, "There is always a lofty goal in the research work of medicine but too often in the past it has been the bodies of the poor . . . on whom the unholy testing is done."[30]

The problems of poor people in the rural South during the Great Depression troubled the editor of the *Los Angeles Times*, who charged that the men had been "trapped into the program by poverty and ignorance." After all, the incentives for cooperation were meager—physical examinations, hot lunches, and burial stipends. "For such inducements to be attractive, their lives must have been savagely harsh," the editor observed, adding: "This in itself, aside from the experiment, is an affront to decency." Thus, quite apart from the questions it raised about human experimentation, the Tuskegee Study served as a poignant reminder of the plight of the poor.[31]

Yet poverty alone could not explain why the men would cooperate with a study that gave them so little in return for the frightening risks to which it exposed them. A more complete explanation was that the men did not understand what the experiment was about or the dangers to which it exposed them. Many Americans probably agreed with the *Washington Post's* argument that experiments "on human beings are ethically sound if the guinea pigs are fully informed of the facts and danger." But despite the assurances of PHS spokesmen that informed consent had been obtained, the Tuskegee Study precipitated accusations that somehow the men had either been tricked into cooperating or were incapable of giving informed consent.[32]

An Alabama newspaper, the *Birmingham News*, was not impressed by the claim that the participants were all volunteers, stating that "the majority of them were no better than semi-

literate and probably didn't know what was really going on."
The real reason they had been chosen, a Colorado journalist
argued, was that they were "poor, illiterate, and completely at
the mercy of the 'benevolent' Public Health Service." And a
North Carolina editor denounced "the practice of coercing or
tricking human beings into taking part in such experiments."[33]

The ultimate lesson that many Americans saw in the Tuskegee Study was the need to protect society from scientific pursuits that ignored human values. The most eloquent expression
of this view appeared in the *Atlanta Constitution*. "Sometimes,
with the best of intentions, scientists and public officials and
others involved in working for the benefit of us all, forget that
people are people," began the editor. "They concentrate so totally on plans and programs, experiments, statistics—on ab-
stractions—that people become objects, symbols on paper, figures in a mathematical formula, or impersonal 'subjects' in a
scientific study." This was the scientific blindspot to ethical
issues that was responsible for the Tuskegee Study—what the
Constitution called "a moral astigmatism that saw these black
sufferers simply as 'subjects' in a study, not as human beings."
Scientific investigators had to learn that "moral judgment
should always be a part of any human endeavor," including
"the dispassionate scientific search for knowledge."[34]

Many editors attributed the moral insensitivity of PHS officers to the fact that they were bureaucrats, as well as scientists.
Distrust of the federal government led a Connecticut editor to
charge that the experiment stemmed from "a moral break-
down brought about by a mindless bureaucracy going through
repeated motions without ever stopping to examine the reason,
cause and effects." To a North Carolina editor, the experiment
had simply "rolled along of its own inhuman momentum with
no one bothering to say, 'Stop, in the name of human decency.'" In a sense, then, the government's scientific community itself became a casualty of the Tuskegee Study. The public's respect and trust were being eroded by doubts and
suspicions of the kind expressed by an editor in Utah who wondered "if similar or worse experiments could be occurring
somewhere in the bureaucratic mess."[35]

Medical and public discussions of the Tuskegee Study fell
off sharply within a few weeks, leaving many important questions unanswered. Why was the Public Health Service inter-

ested in studying syphilis in blacks, or were they using blacks
to study syphilis? Was the experiment good science? Did the
PHS doctors who began the study withhold therapy in the
1930s because they thought that treatment with salvarsan was
more harmful than the disease? Would penicillin have benefited the men when it became available in the 1940s? Or, for
that matter, was treatment for the men ever discussed in the
1930s or the 1940s? Why was the experiment conducted in Macon County? What health care was available to blacks there?
Why did the subjects cooperate with the study? Do inducements and ignorance tell the whole story? How did the participating doctors see themselves? Why did the Tuskegee Institute
and the Veterans Hospital in Tuskegee, both all-black facilities
in 1932, cooperate with the study? How could the experiment
last for forty years? Was there any opposition to the experiment before the story broke?

In order to answer these questions, it is necessary to place
the Tuskegee Study within its historical and institutional context, explaining how the experiment fits into the development
of the public health movement in the United States. The aura
of the kindly and priestly healer that surrounds physicians has
tended to blind the public to the fact that physicians are people. As people, they reflect the values and attitudes of their society. In Macon County, Alabama, the syphilitic men studied
were black; the Public Health Service directors and most of the
doctors who studied them were white. Hence, an overview of
the evolution of racial attitudes in American medicine is crucial to an understanding of the Tuskegee Study. The discussion
must begin in the nineteenth century, when the interaction between white physicians and black patients produced what
might be called "racial medicine."

CHAPTER 2

"A Notoriously Syphilis-Soaked Race"

MORE than a century ago, the eminent Boston physician Dr. Oliver Wendell Holmes noted that "medicine, professedly founded on observation, is as sensitive to outside influence, political, religious, philosophical, imaginative, as is the barometer to the atmospheric density." Few examples better illustrate this observation than the influence racial attitudes have exerted on the perception and response of white physicians to disease in blacks. Nineteenth-century physicians had ample opportunities to inject racial prejudice into their daily practices. Based more on tradition than science, medicine was a fragmented profession, divided into warring sects, each claiming to understand what caused illnesses and each prescribing its own treatments. The lack of agreement about the nature of illness produced different explanations for clinical phenomena. A rare point of agreement among the competing factions was that the health of blacks had to be considered separately from the health of whites.[1]

Like other white Americans of the nineteenth century, physicians were fascinated by the large number of ways in which black people appeared to be different. They were one of the first public groups to study blacks in a systematic manner; because they belonged to a profession that claimed to possess scientific knowledge about human beings, their views carried considerable weight. Physicians did not dissent as a group from white society's pervasive belief in the physical and mental inferiority of blacks. On the contrary, they did a great deal to bolster and elaborate racist attitudes. No difference between the races, real or imagined, went unnoticed, and topics such as the black's hair, facial features, posture and gait, odor, skin color, and cranium and brain size were emphasized repeatedly.

There was a compelling reason for this preoccupation with establishing physical and mental distinctions between the races, one that transcended the disinterested pursuit of empirical facts. Most physicians who wrote about blacks during the nineteenth century were southerners who believed in the existing social order. They justified slavery and, after its abolition, second-class citizenship by insisting that blacks were incapable of assuming any higher station in life. Too many differences separated the races. And here "different" unquestionably meant "inferior." Thus, medical discourses on the peculiarities of blacks offered, among other things, a pseudoscientific rationale for keeping blacks in their places.

Vociferous advocates of black inferiority such as Dr. Josiah Clark Nott of Mobile and Dr. Samuel A. Cartwright of New Orleans published numerous articles during the 1840s and 1850s on diseases and physical properties thought to be peculiar to blacks. Drs. Nott and Cartwright were merely the best known of a group of southern physicians who helped inflame the controversy over slavery. Among the diseases said to be unique to blacks were Cachexia Africana (dirt-eating) and Struma Africana ("Negro consumption"). Influenced by these physicians, slaveholders who wished to treat their bondsmen without benefit of professional help begged southern doctors to write medical manuals on the treatment of blacks. Their requests went unanswered. Instead, physicians simply continued to assert that blacks were medically inferior to whites without offering a plausible medical explanation based on racial differences. Their observations were perfect for polemics but useless for the care of sick blacks.[2]

Advocates of racial medicine argued that differences in natural immunity, degree of susceptibility, and relative severity of reaction to various diseases often separated the races. At times they were, in fact, recording what they observed, but in many instances racial prejudice influenced their views.

The medical discussion of malaria in blacks offers a case in point. In many instances blacks did appear to be less susceptible to the disease and seemed to suffer milder illnesses when they contracted it. But physicians extrapolated from individual cases to the entire race because they wished to defend slavery. By arguing that blacks were relatively immune to malaria, or suffered milder attacks, physicians created a medical sanction for sending blacks into the rice fields and canebrakes. In other words, they were helping to support the South's contention that the use of bondsmen to perform such unhealthy work was more humane than employing white laborers.[3]

Medical views of blacks were also used to answer the abolitionists. Drawing on the work of physicians, slaveowners argued that the "peculiar institution" provided a "hot house environment" for preserving the fragile health of an inferior race. They insisted that blacks could not survive without close supervision and constant medical attention. As proof they cited data from the Census of 1840 concerning free blacks living in the North. Now recognized as notoriously inaccurate and biased, the report purported to show a high incidence of mental and physical illness, accompanied by a declining birth rate and a rising death rate, among free blacks.[4]

Alleged differences between black and white patients seldom led to separate remedies or treatments for the same disease. Bleeding, a standard treatment employed by physicians who practiced during the age of heroic medicine (other treatments included purging and vomiting), was routinely inflicted upon blacks, despite the broadly held view that they could not tolerate the loss of blood as well as whites. There were, however, rare instances in which physicians differentiated treatment on the basis of race. A physician who was confronted with an outbreak of typhoid dysentary among slaves on a plantation in Jefferson County, Louisiana, observed that European methods of treatment did not work. "The poor negroes," he said, "treated like white men, continued to get sick and die." His solution was to lead the slaves from the plantation into the woods where he sought to create "an imitation of slave life," while treating them with sulphate of soda, elixir vitriol, slippery-elm water, and prickly-pear tea.[5]

Prescribing different remedies for blacks was the exception rather then the rule. In most instances, slaves received the same treatment as their masters. Apart from humanitarian considerations, the economic value of slaves made their health a matter of solicitous concern. Because physicians failed to produce a treatment manual for blacks, the only alternative was to apply white remedies to black patients. For routine ailments, masters treated their families and their slaves with identical home remedies; when serious illnesses made it necessary to call in professional help, the same physicians treated whites and blacks. Indeed, a sizable portion of the income of many southern physicians was derived from the care and treatment of slaves.[6]

When the Civil War erupted, physicians in both the North and South warned that freedom would mean extinction for blacks. While other groups discussed the future of the free blacks, physicians debated whether the race as such had a future. They saw the emancipation of the slaves as a watershed in black health, the chief result of which was likely to be a decline in health that was so drastic as to endanger the survival of the race. Most admitted (though some halfheartedly) that slavery had been an evil, but they argued that it had created a healthy race of people. Slavery had rescued blacks from disease-ridden jungles and placed them under a system that could offer the benefits of Western medicine. (Most physicians neglected to mention that blacks brought to the New World were exposed to white men's diseases.)

Physicians did not argue that slavery had altered the black man's physical inferiority or extreme susceptibility to many diseases, but they did contend that the South's "peculiar institution" had provided a benevolent system of total control in which the conditions necessary for the survival and prosperity of the race could be maximized. "Every owner took a dollar-and-cents view of his slave, had him housed, fed and clothed, and because it was in his interest to do so, just as he takes care of his horses and stock and property at this time; for death or injury or privation meant just so much loss of property," explained a South Carolina physician in 1891. He maintained that when slaves became ill, "they had the best medical skill that money could command."[7]

Though historically inaccurate, these beliefs enabled south-

erners to construct a benevolent view of slavery. One of the
most lamented results of freedom was the loss of control that
masters had exerted over black sexuality. Owners had devoted
special attention to the moral character of their slaves. They
believed that the sexual impulse in blacks was frighteningly
strong, but sin was sin even among slaves. Masters paid ministers to preach the fear of God and absolute submission to the
white man's moral code, and they carefully supervised premar-
ital contacts between the sexes. Since early marriage seemed
the best solution, masters exerted every effort to impress their
slaves with the sanctity of the institution. The ceremony, with
the master presiding, might be simple, but the bonds it created
were supposed to last for life. Extramarital affairs were neither
condoned nor permitted to go unpunished if discovered. Temp-
tation was removed from slaves' paths whenever possible by
strict prohibitions against night visits among slave cabins,
rules that also insured that chattels got enough rest. More
than moral character was at stake. Happy marriages produced
contented slaves, and contented slaves produced new slaves.[8]

By the turn of the twentieth century, many physicians, an-
thropologists, and popular writers had come to view emancipation as a veritable death sentence for blacks. A prime reason
for their concern was that the Ninth (1870), Tenth (1880), and
Eleventh (1890) Censuses contained alarming data. The Ninth
Census, for example, showed that the black population had increased at a slower rate than the white population between
1860 and 1870, a disturbing development since the opposite
had ususally been true before the war. While the Tenth Census
reversed this trend and placed the percentage increase in black
births ahead of white, pessimists were quick to note that these
apparent gains were reduced by a higher mortality rate among
the blacks. Moreover, when the Eleventh Census once again
showed the black birth rate to be lower than the white, many
predicted that the former race would become extinct. This
specter of a vanishing race was further supported when the nation's leading life insurance companies, led by Prudential, all
but refused to write policies for blacks.[9]

Like other intellectuals of the day, late-nineteenth-century
physicians were "social Darwinists" who had no difficulty
identifying blacks as the race least likely to triumph in the
struggle for survival. The black man was bound to follow the

red man down the path to extinction, for declining birth rates in the face of rising death rates had sealed the fate of both races.

Physicians also attempted to locate blacks in the nature-nurture controversy, an important scientific debate of the day. The crux of the debate was whether environment or heredity was responsible for racial development. The argument was quickly reduced in importance as physicians demonstrated the ease with which racist beliefs could whipsaw the black man between hereditary and environmental explanations of his inevitable demise. No one resolved the nature-nurture controversy more neatly than J. Wellington Byers, a Charlotte, North Carolina, physician. "The weakest members of the social body are always the ones to become contaminated," he explained, "and sooner or later succumb to the devitalizing forces of intemperance, disease, and crime and death. The Negro is peculiarly unfortunate," the doctor continued, "he has not only the inherent frailties of his nature to war against—instincts, passions and appetites; but also those nocuous, seductive, destroying influences that emanate from free institutions in a country of civil liberty."[10]

White physicians of the late nineteenth and early twentieth centuries blamed the decline in black health on self-destructive behavioral traits. In addition to discussions of weak constitutions and inherent susceptibility to disease, physicians hammered away at the black man's distaste for honest labor, fondness for alcohol, proclivity to crime and sexual vices, disregard for personal hygiene, ignorance of the laws of good nutrition, and total indifference to his own health. A standard feature of the vast majority of medical articles on the health of blacks was a sociomedical profile of a race whose members were rapidly becoming diseased, debilitated, and debauched, and had only themselves to blame.[11]

To some extent physicians merely echoed the arguments white middle-class Americans made against the poor regardless of race. Ethnicity, class, and life style were perceived as inseparable identifications. Middle-class Americans, imbued with the spirit of social Darwinism, tended to regard the lower classes, particularly recently arrived immigrants, as the "losers" in the struggle for survival. Poverty, sickness, disease, drunkenness, laziness, and immorality were all identified at one time or another with such groups as the "Irish race," the "Italian race," and the "Polish race." Though scientifically inaccurate, the nomenclature clearly illustrated the middle class's inability to distinguish among biology, culture, and environment.

By defining the black health problem in racial terms, physicians absolved themselves of responsibility for what they saw as the Negro's deterioration. Few were willing to ponder the responsibility that might fall to a profession whose members worked strictly on a fee-for-service basis and whose services were often beyond the reach of the poor. Attributing failure to the irresponsible victim was much easier on the professions's pride and permitted physicians to exercise a certain self-righteousness in their pronouncements. Some physicians of the day were overtly judgmental and spoke of blacks as having earned their illnesses as just recompense for wicked life-styles.

This preoccupation with personal responsibility for disease assured syphilis a prominent place in the medical discussion of black health. What better example of just retribution could be offered than the philanderer who contracted syphilis? Though the specific microbe that caused syphilis (the spirochete) was not isolated until 1905, physicians of the late nineteenth century expected such a discovery at any moment. The germ theory of disease had become widely accepted during their lifetimes, and they shared the world's excitement as the causative agents of such dread diseases as smallpox and cholera were discovered. Until a similar breakthrough occurred for syphilis, physicians could only wait, drawing what comfort they could from the knowledge that at least they understood how the disease was transmitted.

Physicians knew that syphilis was contracted through sexual intercourse, but the distinction between causative agent and means of transmittal often became blurred, especially when physicians wrote about syphilis in blacks. Here they tended to confuse a necessary cause with a sufficient cause, despite the knowledge that most men and women found it possible to copulate without contracting the disease. Since most sexual intercourse involved a willful, voluntary activity, physicians believed that the responsibility for any disease acquired during the act rested solely upon the individual. Their need to fix blame therefore blinded physicians to the critical problem of congenital syphilis. So great was their preoccupation with black sexual behavior that physicians completely ignored the plight of black infants who were born with the disease through no fault of their own.[12]

Few physicians managed to discuss the problem without revealing an inordinate fascination with black sexuality. Their writings both mirrored and augmented the public's stock of sexual stereotypes. They perpetuated the ancient myth that blacks matured physically at early ages and were more sexually active throughout their lives than whites. Blacks, they explained, had originated in a warm, tropical climate and were therefore closer on the evolutionary scale to man's bestial ancestors. Physicians pointed also to alleged anatomical and neurological differences. The formidable penis of the black man with its long prepuce offered greater opportunity for venereal infection. Moreover, personal restraints on self-indulgence did not exist, physicians insisted, because the smaller brain of the Negro had failed to develop a center for inhibiting sexual behavior.[13]

A striking parallel developed between the tone of race relations and the extent to which physicians attributed the incidence of syphilis among blacks to physical inferiority and sexual promiscuity as intrinsic racial characteristics. Agreement on the role of environment remained a constant. But while physicians agreed that blacks lived in conditions that were conducive to disease, they disagreed on the amount of responsibility blacks had to shoulder for their environment. When relations between the races were deteriorating and tense, physicians depicted blacks as the willing perpetrators of a ruinous life-style. As race relations improved, physicians presented blacks as the passive victims of a cruel environment.[14]

From the Civil War to about 1890, physicians discussed syphilis within the general context of the declining health of the black race. Syphilis was cited as only one of several diseases with debilitative effects in the black community. Disparaging comments about sexual immorality appeared occasionally but did not form a theme. The consensus among physicians was that blacks could be educated to adopt healthy habits of living but that any such progress would be slow.[15]

By the turn of the century, however, when race relations had sunk to their nadir, physicians became harsher in their

published views. While continuing to assert the inherent susceptibility of blacks to disease, they emphasized environment
and life-style as the principal factors behind the crisis in black
health. They criticized blacks for living in ignorant neglect of
the simple rules of personal and community hygiene, noting
with disgust the absence of pure water supplies and proper facilities for the disposal of human waste in black homes. Only
rarely was there a hint of compassion or sympathy in their
comments for the plight of the people whom they discussed.
Writing as though blacks were solely responsible for the socioeconomic conditions in which they lived, some even suggested
that disease held the ultimate solution to the race problem.[16]

In this atmosphere it was not surprising that physicians depicted syphilis as the quintessential black disease. Most practitioners no doubt agreed with an instructor in neurology at
Northwestern University who asserted that blacks contracted
syphilis because of their "ever-increasing low standards of sexual morality." The depths of these standards had become a
laughing matter to some members of the profession. "Morality
among these people is almost a joke, and only assumed as a
matter of convenience or when there is a lack of desire and
opportunity for indulgence," wrote Dr. Thomas W. Murrell, a
lecturer on syphilis and dermatology at the University College
of Medicine at Richmond, Virginia. "A negro man will not ab-
stain from sexual intercourse if there is the opportunity and no
mechanical obstruction," continued Dr. Murrell, for "his sexual
powers are those of a specialist in a chosen field." For a black
man "adultery and fornication is [sic] literally not regarded as
sin," Dr. Murrell concluded sardonically, adding, "In some
manner the negro has switched the Decalogue to suit his convenience and has made himself exempt from the seventh com-
mandment."[17]

Indeed, some physicians doubted that black men could control their sexual behavior. Dr. G. Frank Lydston, professor of
genito-urinary surgery and syphilology at the Chicago College
of Physicians and Surgeons, observed that the *furor sexualis* in
black men resembled sexual attacks in bulls and elephants in
intensity. The price that had to be paid for this frenzied behavior, however, made physicians stop short of envy. Noting that
there had to be a break in the skin for the spirochetes to enter
the body, a team of physicians from the United States Medical

Corps thought it entirely possible "that the negro's well-known sexual impetuosity may account for more abrasions of the integument [skin] of the sexual organs, and therefore more frequent infections than are found in the white race."[18]

With a consistency that was remarkable for Victorian gentlemen, physicians denied that black women were morally superior to black men. The double standard, it seemed, applied only to the white race. In the white race the chastity of respectable women reduced the agents of syphilis by nearly one-half, but the low moral standards of black women offered no resistance to the spread of the disease. Syphilis was "so prevalent among the men," asserted Dr. James McIntosh, "one can imagine what it was among the women, who had no virtue or chastity to protect them." The disease had infected men and women alike, the South Carolina physician concluded, "for with the utter lack of virtue and chastity so markedly characteristic of the race, there was nothing to prevent its indiscriminate spread."[19]

More than one colleague in the profession shared this assessment. "Virtue in the negro race is like 'angels' visits—few and far between,'" quipped Dr. Daniel D. Quillian of Athens, Georgia. "In a practice of sixteen years in the South," he added, "I have never examined a virgin over fourteen years of age." Three physicians affiliated with the University of South Carolina's Medical College reported more cases of syphilis among their female than male black patients, a fact they thought illustrated "the results of the extremely immoral relationship between the sexes of this people, as is also borne out by the admission of sexual indulgence from practically all of the unmarried women." A Georgia physician with a penchant for succinctness summed it up nicely: "The negro men love to frolic with the women; and the women love to frolic with the men; so they frolic."[20]

According to physicians, syphilitic blacks were extremely difficult to treat because they refused to take the disease seriously. Dr. E. M. Green, the director of the Georgia State Sanitarium for blacks, insisted that it was "impossible to impress upon the syphilitic Negro the gravity of the disease from which he suffers." Efforts to help syphilitic blacks, argued Dr. Eugene Corson of Atlanta, Georgia, were doomed to failure because blacks did not care if they caught or spread the disease. "This absolute indifference is a characteristic of the negro, not only as regards syphilis," the physician explained, "but of all diseases. He is simply concerned with the present moment of suffering, and not always concerned then." Dr. Corson attributed this indifference to "lack of development," and predicted that it would continue until the Negro could realize "the necessity of certain ideals." The root of the problem, argued a group of physicians from the Medical Department of Emory University, was that "the great majority of negroes look upon venereal infection as a rather trifling incident in life, something to be expected at rather an early age, and so long as this mental attitude is prevalent, it is difficult to impress upon these patients the necessity of treatment."[21]

Even when syphilitic blacks sought help, physicians complained that the Negro's ignorance and indifference to disease made effective treatment difficult, if not impossible. "In the years that I have practiced," wrote Dr. Henry McHatton of Macon, Georgia, "I have yet to see one [Negro] who would continue treatment for any venereal disease, either as a private patient in an out-door clinic, or a hospital, any longer than there was extreme discomfort to himself." Other physicians agreed. "Ignorance and uncleanliness have ever gone hand-in-hand with disease," explained a physician from Virginia, "and here ignorance will not permit a thorough treatment." Black people "come for treatment at the beginning and at the end," he continued, "but tell them not, though they look and feel well, that they are still diseased. Here ignorance rates science a fool." The source of the problem, argued Dr. Bruce McVey, was that black people did not understand the principle of scientific medicine, adding that a Negro "thinks where he is taking medicine and can not feel or see anything wrong . . . that the doctor is getting the better of his purse." The tragic result was that blacks, even those who could afford prolonged therapy, seldom remained under treatment long enough to be cured. Thus, the pessimism of the physician who wrote, "The only thing we can do is to give treatment, although we can have no heart in giving it." The same doctor predicted that "another fifty years will find an unsyphilitic negro a freak; unless some such procedure as vaccination comes to the relief of the race, and that in the hands of a compelling law." Short of a "quick fix" by science requiring no behavior changes by blacks, there was no hope for the race.[22]

Until scientists were able to develop an effective innoculation for syphilis, simple logic dictated a rigorous program of prophylaxis, but physicians doubted that such a program could succeed. The power of education, it seemed, simply fizzled before the strength of black libido. "From our knowledge of the negro," wrote Dr. Louis Wender, "we should be inclined to the opinion that a chance for an education or even its acquisition does not materially influence his well known sexual promiscuity." Other physicians concurred. "The prophylaxis of syphilis in the negro is especially difficult," Dr. H. H. Hazen explained, "for it is impossible to persuade the poor variety of negro that sexual gratification is wrong, even when he is in the actively infectious stage [of syphilis]." Moreover, Dr. Hazen thought it "probable that sex hygiene lectures will not have the slightest effect on this type."[23]

With prophylaxis doomed to failure and sexuality left unchecked, high rates of syphilis seemed inevitable. In lieu of hard data, physicians had to settle for individual observations. In other words, physicians reported what they saw and their estimates supported the general view that blacks had become, in the words of one doctor, "a notoriously syphilis-soaked race." Estimates placing the incidence of syphilis among adult blacks at less than twenty per cent were exceedingly rare, the consensus being that the true figure ran much higher. Dr. S. S. Hindman, a Georgia pathologist, suggested that 95 percent of the black population contracted syphilis at some point in their lives. Whether observations were based on private practices, asylum inmates, prison populations, or clinic patients, physicians assumed, if they did not prove, that rates were much lower among whites.[24]

If they thought that syphilis was more prevalent among blacks than whites, physicians were equally certain that the disease affected the races differently—that syphilis in blacks and whites did not produce identical clinical and pathological results. Doctors in the second half of the nineteenth century had debated whether whites and blacks were equally susceptible to syphilis, whether the disease affected both races with the same severity, and whether complications varied according to race. Discussants had based their reports on limited clinical observations, filtered through social attitudes that buttressed segregation. By World War I, these empirical observations had produced a medical consensus that the races were equally susceptible, and the disease affected both races severely. But well into the twentieth century physicians continued to believe that complications arising from syphilis differed according to race.[25]

Significantly, physicians had difficulties producing consistent and reliable observations documenting racial distinctions. Some saw one set of differences, while others cited another. Yet they persisted in the view that differences did exist. In 1921, Dr. Ernest Zimmerman published an extensive study based on 1,843 syphilitic patients observed at the charity clinic of the leading research institution in the country, The Johns Hopkins University. In his highly influential and often cited article, Dr. Zimmerman reported that bone and cardiovascular syphilis were much more common in blacks than whites, while, by contrast, whites suffered higher incidences of neural involvement. Such theories no doubt influenced many clinical diagnoses and stood as a powerful reminder of how racial attitudes could influence the medical profession's perceptions. Fortunately for black patients, however, twentieth-century doctors did not modify treatment according to race. Blacks were given the same therapy as whites.[26]

Disparaging statements about blacks as patients and the inability of education to improve their health fixed the responsibility for the state of black health solely on blacks themselves. A few physicians saw environment as the most important factor in the deterioration of black health, but even these dissenters often blamed blacks for dirty homes and poor child-rearing practices. No disease seemed more suited to blacks than syphilis, for physicians were certain that exaggerated libido and widespread sexual promiscuity had led to a high incidence of the disease among blacks.

The effect of these views was to isolate blacks even further within American society—to remove them from the world of health and to lock them within a prison of sickness. Whether by accident or design, physicians had come dangerously close to depicting the syphilitic black as the representative black. And as sickness replaced health as the normal condition of the race, something was lost from the sense of horror and urgency with which physicians had defined disease. The result was a powerful rationale for inactivity in the face of a disease, which by their own estimates, physicians believed to be endemic.

The gross exaggerations and virulent attitudes in the medical literature discussing syphilis in blacks declined after World War I as medical discussions became more quantified and physicians concentrated on clinical manifestations. Yet the image of blacks as "a notoriously syphilis-soaked race" did not fade. Public health officials were the only group to challenge the professions's lethargy.

CHAPTER 3

"Disease Germs Are the Most Democratic Creatures in the World"

BY the end of the nineteenth century public health officials had discovered that they could not afford to ignore the health of black Americans. To protect whites they also had to help blacks. Scientific medicine had taught health officials that the same germs caused essentially the same illnesses in both races, thus placing the potential for controlling most communicable diseases squarely within mankind's reach. But that knowledge would have been all but useless had public health officials not acted to clean up the environment—on both sides of the tracks. Through bitter experience, measured in lives lost from epidemic diseases such as cholera, they learned that filthy homes and squalid streets anywhere in a particular area formed a threat to everyone's health. Public sanitation, clearing away the filth and rubble, and keeping things clean, provided the only antidote that worked.

Public health officials had also learned to work effectively within state and local governments to enact laws to protect the public's health. In the absence of mandatory national planning and control, however, progress varied from state to state and from community to community. During the second half of the nineteenth century health departments in most local areas were strengthened by the acceptance of the germ theory of disease. A new emphasis upon preventive medicine and sanitation was added to the old role of maintaining vital statistics registration and combating epidemics. Such measures could not be left to the individual, for personal irresponsibility could jeopardize the entire community. Most states created boards of health in the 1880s and 1890s, recognizing the need for uniform measures to control disease. By 1914 all the states but Wyoming and New Mexico had established these boards.

To a large extent national health programs mirrored activity at the state and local levels. Before the twentieth century, the federal government had played little role in protecting the nation's health. During the nineteenth century marine hospitals were constructed at various port cities under the Marine Hospital Service Act of 1798. These hospitals primarily served seamen, but medical personnel increasingly supplied diagnostic services and medical care for epidemic diseases such as yellow fever, smallpox, and cholera. In 1902 the Marine Hospital Service changed its name to the Public Health and Marine Hospital Service to better reflect the full scope of its work. In the same year, Congress established a national hygienic laboratory to regulate the interstate sale of drugs. Finally in 1912, the federal government's health-related activities were united under the Public Health Service, organized to provide four basic services: improvement of public health administration, distribution of federal aid to state and local health departments, interstate control of communicable diseases and sanitation, and basic and applied research.

Not all segments of society profited equally from the public health movement. Poor people, both urban and rural, continued to suffer a disproportionate number of illnesses and deaths (especially during the first few years of life) from diseases associated with overcrowded housing and poor sanitation. The challenge confronting health officials at the close of the nineteenth century was to promote cooperation and coordination among local, state, and federal agencies to bring the benefits of modern medicine to all Americans.

During the first few decades of the twentieth century, despite continuing black poverty and lack of education, the prospects for improving the health of minority groups increased dramatically. Application of the germ theory of disease, the

public health programs, and the efforts of philanthropists produced a shift in attitudes toward black health problems. Most
physicians in private practice continued to echo racial explanations for the high mortality rate among blacks. Increasingly,
however, their views were countered by public health officials
and physicians who practiced in public hospitals and univer-
sity-affiliated teaching hospitals. Perhaps because these groups
had more day-to-day contact with blacks than most of their
colleagues in private practice, they were less likely to blame
black health problems on race.

Public health officials believed more in the power of science
than the weakness of any race. Whatever else might be said of
blacks, they were incontestably human, and science enabled
physicians to help diseased humans. Public health officials
were not willing to admit to any blindspot in their expertise;
the canons of science had to apply equally to all races. If a specific germ caused a specific disease in one race, then the same
germ had to produce the same disease in another race. Moreover, identical treatments had to be effective for every race.
These principles had to prevail for public health officials
to support their claims that they could diagnose correctly
and treat effectively human ailments. Racial inferiority and
moral depravity as catchall explanations had become incongruous with the scientific laws upon which modern medicine
rested.

The medical profession itself underwent important changes
during the first few decades of the twentieth century, changes
that exerted subtle influences on the attitudes of white physicians toward black patients. Many marginal and substandard
medical schools were closed, not only eliminating numerous
centers of inferior training but also vastly reducing the number
of new physicians. The Flexner Report of 1910 merely accelerated this trend. And as a result of the introduction of more
standardized curricula and higher admission standards, the
glaring disparities that had marked the training and competence of physicians were diminished if not totally removed.[1]

The introduction of state licensing boards also contributed
to the creation of a more homogeneous profession. Medicine
during the nineteenth century was so hopelessly divided into
sects that otherwise responsible medical societies could not
agree on causes and cures for diseases, let alone define and uti-
lize a common body of knowledge and training for physicians.

Concentrating control of certification in the hands of special-ists trained in scientific medicine was a major step toward pro-fessionalization.

A better educated and more carefully self-regulated profes-sion had reason to feel confident. Physicians commanded an esoteric body of knowledge that enabled them to monopolize services society prized dearly, and their prestige rose in direct proportion to their ability to diagnose accurately and treat properly life-threatening diseases. Indeed, medical scientists, working in conjunction with nonclinical scientists, presided over a veritable explosion of medical knowledge after World War I. Medical research and medical practices became more specialized; improved surgical techniques and safer anes-thetics were developed, and numerous effective drugs were dis-covered. Within the life span of a single generation, the sum total of medical knowledge attained in the twentieth century exceeded the collective achievement of all the generations that had preceded it.

Many of these reforms in the medical profession occurred during the period historians have called the Progressive Era, roughly 1890 to 1920. Activists in these decades developed ap-proaches to problem-solving that became essential to physi-cians who sought to improve the health of black Americans. Many reformers attempted to adopt the methods of "disinter-ested" scientific inquiry to set things right. The United States had evolved an industrial, urban, material culture, and the "experts" were quickly pressed into service to govern it. Steeped in scientific methodologies and values, the "experts" stood ready to apply their knowledge and techniques to the intelligent, orderly, and efficient resolution of problems. Physi-cians, lawyers, professors, government bureaucrats, scientists, engineers, and journalists made up the bulk of the "experts" who formed America's new secular priesthood.[2]

Reformers believed that the "experts" would prevail. As en-vironmentalists, they were confident that improving people's living conditions would ameliorate most social problems. Moreover, they had faith in the power of education to uplift people. And if problems were especially large or complicated, they did not hesitate to engage the power of the state.

Most public health officials who began agitating early in the twentieth century to improve black health shared in this reform ethos. As practitioners of scientific medicine, they recognized no limitations on their expertise. They were confident that they could apply the principles of public health to blacks. To be sure, finding solutions to the health problems confronting blacks would not be easy. Progress would be slow and costly. The Negro's environment would have to be improved and massive educational programs would have to be developed to prepare blacks to maintain healthy life-styles. For these reasons, physicians argued that the problems associated with improving black health demanded government intervention.

Physicians in private practice, of course, were aware of the problems in black health. Indeed, many private physicians worked long hours administering to the health needs of black people in their communities. Because private physicians worked on a fee-for-service basis, however, the poverty of most blacks made them unprofitable patients. Racial prejudice also excluded many blacks from medical care, closing the doors of many private offices and hospitals alike. Thus, those blacks fortunate enough to receive care usually wound up as patients in publicly or privately supported clinics where health care was either free or inexpensive.

Beginning at the turn of the twentieth century, public health officials moved to fill the vacuum created by the failures of the private medical sector. Quite apart from the humanitarian duty to help diseased people, the self-interest of white Americans required improved health care and more sanitary living conditions for blacks. Moreover, public health officials never tired of reciting figures documenting the economic cost to the nation of neglecting black health. Black illnesses threatened not only whites' health, but also white pocketbooks.

Philanthropic foundations became staunch allies of public health officials in the struggle to safeguard the nation's health. The South, as the most needy section of the country, was a prime target area for organized charity. Before World War II, the Rockefeller Foundation, in particular, worked with federal, state, and local health officials first to combat hookworm and then to stamp out pellagra. Because blacks made up a large portion of the South's population, they benefited mightily from these programs.

Blacks themselves joined in the efforts to improve their health. In 1913, the Negro Organization Society of Virginia launched the first statewide campaign to encourage blacks to clean up their homes, their yards, and their entire communities. The state department of health, along with local health departments and various voluntary organizations, helped to publicize the objectives of the movement, and the "cleanup week" that followed in many black communities in Virginia earned such favorable public acclaim that the news spread beyond the state.

Booker T. Washington, the leading black proponent of self-help and founder of the Tuskegee Institute, immediately sensed the potential of the program. The idea of a national Negro health week fitted nicely into his practical philosophy of "head, heart, hand, and health." He made certain that one day of the 1914 Annual Tuskegee Negro Conference was devoted to a discussion of black health. In addition, Washington followed up this conference by arranging for the National Business League to issue a proclamation in 1915 announcing a National Health Improved Week, which later was renamed the National Negro Health Week. Modeled after the Virginia program, the movement sought to enlist the support of national and state organizations that touched all phases of black life—medical, educational, religious, business, fraternal, civic, urban, and rural. Local health week committees were established to stimulate cooperative and individual efforts in a variety of public health and self-help measures.[3]

Booker T. Washington did not live to see the development of the movement that he began. He died in 1915, and it fell to the man who succeeded him as principal of the Tuskegee Institute, Robert R. Moton, to guide National Negro Health Week into a truly national concern. During the 1920s, the Public Health Service became the movement's working arm, and financial backing came from the Julius Rosenwald Fund, a private philanthropic foundation with a special interest in programs to help blacks. Together these three groups orchestrated a movement that by the 1930s had become multifaceted and truly national in scope. Surviving into the 1950s, National Negro Health Week helped to spread the gospel of health among the black people of the United States, and increased awareness of their problems among white Americans who were concerned with the public's health.[4]

It was a frustrating struggle. To dramatize the gravity of the black health problem, the American Public Health Association devoted an entire issue of its journal in 1915 to a far-ranging discussion of the issues. Local and state health officers from the South contributed the six articles that composed the issue. Together with a piece by a federal health official on the same subject that appeared in the same journal the following year, the articles provide an excellent example of how reform-minded physicians viewed black health problems.[5]

Environment, not race, emerged as the chief determinant of health. Dr. L. C. Allen, a local health official in Hoschton, Georgia, flatly denied that a racial proclivity to tuberculosis had anything to do with the high incidence of the disease among blacks. "I contend, then," wrote Allen, "that it is not a peculiar racial susceptibility to tuberculosis that is causing this disease to destroy so many people among the negro race, but his environment—his bad habits and his unsanitary conditions of living." Unhealthy environments affected whites the same as blacks. "After all," Allen explained, "the problem does not differ greatly from the same problem regarding certain portions of our white population. Ignorance and poverty are everywhere associated with disease and vice. Filth and contagion, coupled with ignorance and indifference, always bring about disease and death."[6]

Dr. William F. Brunner, the chief health officer of Savannah, Georgia, found the environment in which blacks had to live appalling. Year after year he begged city officials to appoint a special commission to investigate the living conditions of Savannah's black population. He knew what they would find: grossly overcrowded housing and dreadful conditions of public sanitation. Knowledge of these conditions could not fail to drive home the hopelessness of the situation. "Investigate them," Brunner pleaded, "and you will soon learn that if he desired to improve his sanitary conditions, he could not do it. Observe the house he must live in; the food he must eat and learn of all his environment." He stated that blacks were too ignorant to look after their own health, but denied that they were to blame. "These people have no fair fight for health," wrote Brunner. "While they are ignorant, their environments are such that they will always be ignorant."[7]

Most of all, Dr. Brunner sought to emphasize the cost in lives and suffering that black people paid for their environment, making clear that the price would be just as high for whites under the same conditions: "Note how many of his children are born dead and then follow the high infantile mortality up to the fifth year, and then go and observe carefully the reason for it. It would be the same result with the white race if they lived in the same environments." The same conditions plagued adults as well as children: "After he is grown, he gets no better chance, he is in the same bad sanitary environments and loses his resisting power to disease, the same as any other human being would under the same conditions."[8]

The argument that social class had a direct bearing on health attacked the very foundations of the racist belief that the high black mortality rate was due to physical inferiority. While this theme was implicit in much of what other authors wrote, Dr. John W. Trask, an assistant surgeon general in the United States Public Health Service, proved the point statistically. He began by acknowledging that the Census of 1910 had shown a higher mortality rate among blacks than whites (just as late-nineteenth-century census reports had). The task he had set for himself, Trask explained, was to ascertain why the disparity existed, specifically, "whether the cause is an essential one, inherent in one element of the population and not in the other," and what, if anything, could be done to lower the Negro's death rate "until it approximates that of the white element of the population."[9]

Dr. Trask established a relationship between environment and health by comparing the mortality figures for urban and rural dwellers. The death rate for whites who lived in cities having more than ten thousand inhabitants in 1910 was 14.6 per thousand, while the corresponding figure for blacks was 24.3 per thousand. In rural areas, however, the death rate for whites fell to 12.5 and the death rate for blacks dropped to 17.7. Dr. Trask emphasized that only a few deaths per thousand separated the mortality rates of the races if urban whites were compared with rural blacks. Here was dramatic proof that where people lived directly influenced their health.

Dr. Trask also contrasted death rates from city to city. While admitting that age distributions probably accounted for much of the wide spread, he noted that the black mortality rate in Charleston, South Carolina, stood at 37.2 per thousand compared with 15.2 per thousand for Coffeyville, Kansas. Less dramatic differences existed among cities better suited for comparisons. The death rate for blacks in Washington, D.C., was 24.4, while Roanoke, Virginia, boasted a rate of 22.5. The difference was slight, but it helped disprove the idea that nature had endowed all blacks with identical biological time clocks. Trask discovered even more heartening evidence when he examined the black death rates for cities such as Mobile, Alabama, and Washington, D.C., and learned that the rates had dropped steadily for more than a decade. To his mind, the facts clearly demonstrated "that the colored death-rate is subject to influences which produce variations and that the rate is by no means fixed."[10]

For Dr. Trask the most decisive influence was wealth. "In considering the separation of deaths into those of white and colored," he cautioned, "one must bear in mind the possibility that in many communities such a separation may amount to a classification according to industrial or economic status, the colored deaths being those in households having the smaller income." He reminded his colleagues that numerous studies had linked income to the rate of infant mortality and the relative prevalence of certain diseases, such as tuberculosis. It was clear that "if in the average community deaths could be classified according to economic status, that is according to the family or household income, a difference in the mortality rates would be obtained approximately as great as that resulting from a white and colored classification." To illustrate his point, Dr. Trask cited a 1908 study in New York City that classified death rates according to ethnicity. This study indicated that the Irish and Italians suffered death rates exceeding that of blacks. There was no mistaking the message: Income, not race, was the index that mattered most for health.[11]

Ignorance compounded the problems related to low income. The issue was not just income but class. By focusing on class, health officials opened the way for education to mediate the problem. They saw education as a vehicle of moral uplift and individual socialization; a thorough tutoring in the responsibilities of citizenship and a means of social control. Education could enable people to improve conditions within each class. Moreover, if blacks could be taught to eschew bad habits and adopt life-styles conducive to health, the work of the public health officials would be made easier. While remaining silent on the issue of segregation, they recommended that black schools be improved and agitated for courses on individual and community hygiene. They also urged the creation of community education programs to "preach the gospel of health" at public expense.

Dr. Allen embraced education as "the remedy of greatest importance" for the amelioration of black health. By education, he stressed, he did not mean what had been taught during the fifty years since emancipation. Greek and Latin were a waste of time. He had warm praise for the black leaders who advised "giving the Negro an industrial education" and added, "Proper ideas of cleanliness, sobriety, chastity, honor, and self-reliance should be instilled into his mind." Dr. Allen stated that the "physician should be consulted, and his expert knowledge made use of, in the education of the negro race" because "an education that does not teach cleanliness and the proper care of the body is a defective education." Another health officer recommended that health education begin early in life and predicted a handsome return in years to come from educating black youths: "Teach the simple laws of hygiene and sanitation in the schools and begin this subject early, say the second grade. This will, in due time, make it easy for the health officer in his work."[12]

Dr. Lawrence Lee, who had worked for several years as a health official in Savannah, Georgia, thought that educating blacks would benefit both races. "By the education of the Negro he may be made a better citizen," Dr. Lee wrote, "and come to live in better homes and more healthy surroundings. Instead of being a burden he may come in time to look after himself." Dr. Lee dismissed as sheer madness an editorial in the *Columbia State* recommending that no public funds be spent on black education until every white child in the state was enrolled in school. The entire community would suffer if blacks remained uneducated.[13]

Health officers were aware that whites would have to be educated to the need for helping blacks. No one understood this better than Dr. A. G. Fort, the director of Field Sanitation of the Georgia State Board of Health in Atlanta. "Ignorance and poverty on the part of the negro and indifference caused by ignorance on the part of landlords and voters," wrote Dr. Fort, "are the prime factors in the 'Negro Health Problem in Rural Communities.'" White landlords and voters, as well as blacks themselves, would have to be brought to a new awareness of black health problems before progress could be made. Once educated, Dr. Fort predicted, "the landlord will begin to understand that health for his employees pays. The voter will instruct his representatives to support health laws and appropriations."[14]

Medical reformers stopped short of advocating improved education for blacks as a step toward first-class citizenship. Like most other white Americans, they did not believe in racial equality. For health officers the belief that blacks were inferior to whites created a tension between social prejudices and professional duties. They resolved the conflict by keeping their social and professional views separate. On the one hand, they believed that the present status of blacks did not entitle them to all the benefits of American citizenship. On the other hand, they denied that there was anything about the physical makeup of blacks that prevented their benefiting from modern medicine.

Health officials persisted in the belief that racial differences existed in susceptibility, severity, and complications of diseases. Blacks were thought to be particularly immune to scarlet fever, for example, and peculiarly prone to tuberculosis. Yet health officials continued to emphasize environment in their thinking: if blacks were especially susceptible to certain diseases, then all the more reason to improve their environment and medical care.

Dr. Lee charged that the poor quality of health care in black hospitals was responsible for the reluctance of many blacks to seek medical help. "It is no surprise to me that the negro is afraid of a hospital," wrote Dr. Lee. "The negro hospitals I have seen are warranted to repel and even terrify people less superstitious than the negro." Because Savannah had no black poorhouse, he explained, the hospitals were forced "to take care of the aged, infirm, paralyzed, and blind." Terrible overcrowding resulted. In Savannah's largest black hospital there were often ten or fifteen more patients than beds. According to Dr. Lee, "no matter how hot the weather, two patients have to sleep in a single bed, and some on the floor or in chairs." During the nineteenth century, lower-class white Americans had regarded hospitals as little better than pesthouses—places to which the poor were sent to die. Blacks, well into the twentieth century, apparently looked at segregated hospitals and reached the same conclusion.[15]

Health officials discounted the prospects for improvement without intervention, agreeing that the white man would have to save the black man. "The negro health problem is one of the 'white man's burdens,'" wrote Dr. Allen, and he went on to characterize the black population as "the most difficult health problem with which the people of the South are confronted." Dr. Brunner put the matter bluntly: "The negro is here for all time. He depends upon the white man for everything that makes up a civilization. These two statements being true, he is what the white man makes him." Dr. Lee thought that uplifting the race would prove difficult. "By themselves the negroes will not better themselves," he wrote, and added that help would have to be "almost forced on them."[16]

Health officials did not discard racial prejudice; they simply did not let their racism blind them to their professional duties. Compared with the real black-baiters of the day, however, the racism of these health officers was mild. Their prejudice took the form of paternalism. They believed that there were differences in temperament and ability between the races, but they did not define these differences in absolute terms or as conditions that could not be altered. "While he is not a white man painted black, with all the mentality and morality of that race," wrote Dr. Brunner, "neither is he incapable of improvement over his present position." For Dr. Brunner, the issue was whether white people would give black people the help they needed. "Unless you legislate for him so that his sanitary position will improve," he warned the white rulers of Savannah, "he will continue to furnish a high mortality."[17]

The need for legislation focused attention on the power of the state. Health officials argued that it was the duty of the state to solve such a large and complicated problem, and they demanded public support for a concerted effort to bring the benefits of modern sanitation to rural and urban blacks alike. According to Fort, the health menaces with which rural blacks had to live were shocking. Diseases such as hookworm and typhoid fever flourished among blacks, he explained, because less than half of their homes had privies. The sanitation situation in rural churches and schools was no better. These conditions posed a frightful threat to health because the springs and wells that supplied drinking water became contaminated. Moreover, the absence of screens over doors and windows invited epidemics of infectious diseases transmitted by flies. "Ignorance," declared Dr. Fort, "lack of knowledge of practically all of the sanitary laws, is responsible for many diseases among this race." The public had no choice, he contended, but to give "rural districts modern standards of cleanliness and modern local and state machinery for applying sanitary methods everywhere, supported by local and state taxation."[18]

Similar arguments were made about cleaning up the black sections of the South's cities. Dr. Brunner rejected the idea that physical growth was the measure of a city's greatness, and denied that a swelling population offered convincing testimony that a particular city was desirable. "Your health officer has always held," wrote Brunner, "that the prevailing American idea that the city which shows the greatest increase in its population is the city which attracts the best class of citizens is an erroneous one." In place of crude organic growth, he advocated increased attention to the conditions under which people lived: "the city which provides best for its citizens is the city which will attract the best people to it." Dr. Brunner pleaded for legislation to improve the sanitary conditions in black neighborhoods.[19]

One public health official even advocated federal intervention. Dr. M. L. Graves, a health officer in Galveston, Texas, was prepared to break with his heritage in order to bring adequate health care to the South. "For myself, born and raised in the South, and impregnated with the idea of States Rights, I am convinced that when it comes to sufficient and efficient protection of the public health it will require the powers of the National Government to do it," wrote Dr. Graves. "Political myths and party shibboleths," he added, "should no longer be permitted to retard our progress and cause such enormous waste of valuable lives and the economic loss from preventable illness and deaths." Dr. Graves had, he freely admitted, been seduced by the accomplishments of government during the Progressive Era. "When we contemplate the efficiency of the National banks and their regulation by the Federal Government," asserted Dr. Graves, "when we consider the respect and fear in which our Federal courts are held by wrong-doers everywhere, it is no wonder our minds turn to the National Government for protection of the health and economic efficiency of our people."[20]

To create the ultimate instrument for rationalizing control over the public's health, Dr. Graves recommended the organization of a "National Department of Public Health in the United States Government" to preside over "all the operations for public health anywhere within its borders." He also recommended that funds from private philanthropy be secured "to finance a Commission of Research among the negroes of the South to improve health conditions." Nothing good would be accomplished unless the commission was well paid and thoroughly organized. "The great work already done by the Hookworm and Pellagra Commissions, both made possible by generous donations of citizens interested in public health," explained Dr. Graves, "should inspire some other wealthy man or woman to go and do likewise and organize a Research Commission to study health problems among the negroes of the South."[21]

To create support for health programs for blacks, health officers appealed to the self-interest of whites. Quoting from his own annual reports over the last decade, Dr. Brunner issued declarations on the inseparability of white and black health that fell like hammer blows. His 1904 report pleaded for action on behalf of blacks for "in doing this we protect ourselves." His 1906 report included the blunt warning to whites: "If he is tainted with disease you will suffer." Year after year, he begged the city to appoint a special commission to study the health problems of blacks. In 1908 he predicted that if such a commission were formed "it would demonstrate beyond doubt that there is a contamination of the white race by the negro race and this contamination is both physical and moral."[22]

Dr. Allen turned to the Bible for an inspired illustration of why the white man had to become the black man's keeper. In his Epistle to the Romans, the Apostle Paul had written: "None of us liveth to himself, and no man dieth to himself." The germ theory of disease would permit no other conclusion. "Disease germs are the most democratic creatures in the world," he reminded his readers, "they know no distinction of 'race, color, or previous condition of servitude' "[23]

Segregation afforded no protection. Communicable diseases might be bred on the wrong side of the tracks, but blacks

spread them into the white communities daily. "We meet them
in our homes, offices, stores, in street cars, and almost everywhere we go," wrote Dr. Allen. While it was "not pleasant to
contemplate," he wanted the public to realize that "colored
persons afflicted with gonorrhea, syphilis, and tuberculosis"
were employed as servants "in many of the best homes in the
South today." As long as this remained true, every effort had to
be made to improve black health.[24]

Thus, a new perspective on black health gained ground during the Progressive Era. By rejecting racial and moral explanations of mortality and illness, public health officials shifted the
debate over black health to an environmental analysis and insisted that scientific medicine and modern public health management could benefit blacks. The years between World War I
and World War II represented a transitional period when
health officials working with black leaders and white philanthropists instituted a variety of programs designed to improve
the health of black Americans. The public health movement
did not reach many parts of the South until the 1920s and
1930s, when health officials, philanthropists, and black leaders
combined forces in the campaigns against hookworm and pellagra. And in the late 1920s, these same allies launched an attack on syphilis.[25]

CHAPTER 4

"Holding High Wassermann in the Marketplace"

EARLY in the twentieth century, scientific medicine gave health officials the tools to combat syphilis. In 1905 came the long awaited announcement that two German scientists, Eric Hoffman and Fritz Schaudinn, had isolated the specific microbe that causes syphilis. They named it *Spirochaeta pallida* (pale spirochete). Next came the Wassermann test, a pigment fixation test developed in 1907. As a generic term, it refers to several blood tests that enable physicians to diagnose syphilis and assess the progress of treatment. Then, in 1910, the medical world rejoiced at the news that the first specific therapy for a germ-caused disease had been discovered. Still another German scientist, Paul Ehrlich, had created the "magic bullet"—salvarsan, a preparation of organic arsenic that was reported to cure syphilis in a week by a single injection.

Joy soon gave way to skepticism. A miracle cure had not been found. Some patients had severe reactions to the drug. Within a year, other patients thought to be well began to relapse. But what had been discovered was chemotherapy in modern medicine. Because the drugs were highly toxic, the rate and amount of treatment had to be carefully calculated to destroy the disease without killing the patient. It was eventu-

ally established that twenty to forty doses of the drug, administered over more than a year, were necessary to arrest the infection and prevent relapses. Treatments were administered
through intramuscular injections and were often quite painful.
Moreover, physicians learned that arsphenamine and
neoarsphenamine (the two arsenic derivatives most commonly
used) had to be supplemented by applications of mercury or
bismuth ointments. Discredited as wonder drugs, the arsenicals nevertheless became the standard therapy for syphilis. By
the 1920s, physicians had resigned themselves to the fact that
curing syphilis was an arduous task, requiring careful attention to detail and close observation of the patient. Through additional experience working with the drugs, they gradually re-
gained their faith in chemotherapy. Many came to believe that
syphilis could be controlled, and perhaps eliminated in their
lifetimes.[1]

Their optimism extended even to blacks. While many private physicians continued to insist that black patients could
not benefit from the new treatments, health officials and physicians in large hospitals and clinics began reporting good
results. Dr. Henry H. Hazen, who taught at Georgetown University and ran a large syphilis clinic at the Freedman's Bureau
Hospital in Washington, D.C., a charitable and pre-
dominanatly black institution, noted: "They attend just as
faithfully as do white patients, and the magic words 'blood-
test' have much influence over them. . . . Usually they are very
docile patients: while they complain of the pain of intramuscular injections, they will come back for more." The secret to
treating blacks, he added, "is to show them that you are taking
an interest in them, and also that you mean just what you say."
If physicians would follow these instructions, good results
could be obtained. Hazen revealed that "a number of cases
have been coming in regularly for two or three years."[2]

The failure to remain under treatment until cured, argued a
Birmingham, Alabama, doctor, was common to syphilitic patients of both races. In his experience working with public
health officials in syphilis control programs, he found the key
was to develop a mechanism to keep patients under care. "No
clinic or private practice is complete without a follow-up system," the doctor wrote. Hounding patients with reminders was
one way of dealing with their tendency to discontinue treat-

ment prematurely. Yet even the best follow-up service could prove ineffective unless heroic actions were taken. The doctor explained: "My nurses rather frequently tell me, 'I must go for them in the car or they will not come.' " In fact, he considered blacks ideal subjects for an epidemiological program. "The negro race is oftentimes more readily herded in than whites. This is not so much through interest in cure but simply due to the fact that they are more readily driven."[3]

When blacks did stay away, Dr. Hazen blamed inadequate health care. "The way that syphilis is treated in the average ward of outpatient department is a disgrace," Dr. Hazen charged. The source of the problem was that many physicians "do not care to bother with the treatment of this infection, and so leave the work to the intern, and many other physicians are profoundly ignorant of the immense amount of detail work required for the proper treatment of syphilis." Physicians had to master new treatments in order to bring the benefits of scientific medicine to their patients. "The old method of prescribing a few pills is, and should be, a thing of the past. We must now work with our serum reactions and injections of salvarsan and mercury, avoiding the injury that may come from overdosage, while taking care to give a sufficiency." Like other Americans on the eve of World War I, Dr. Hazen admired the efficiency of the business community, and chided his colleagues: "If a factory turned out goods in the slipshod way that the average hospital hands out syphilitic medication, it would soon go to the wall."[4]

Ironically, health officials received little help from the social hygienists—the most outspoken opponents of venereal diseases of the day. The social hygiene movement was organized in the late nineteenth century to combat prostitution, venereal diseases, and the double standard of sexual morality. Members of the movement were white, urban, well-educated, middle-class Americans who saw prostitution and venereal diseases as threats to the nuclear family.[5]

Concerned citizens first attempted to raise these issues before the public in the late 1870s and early 1880s but were opposed by the purity crusaders—people of similar backgrounds to the social hygienists who did not think such topics suitable for public discussion. Social hygienists persevered because they believed that the need for public awareness far outweighed the case for preserving society's devotion to Victorian reticence. Prostitution, they argued, indulged men's basest instincts and corrupted women who were supposed to serve as the moral guardians of the nation. It also endangered "decent women," for sooner or later the philanderer was bound to contract syphilis or gonorrhea and then the real tragedy began. Social hygienists coined the term "syphilis of the innocent" to describe the inequity and the horror of faithful wives who were infected by wayward husbands. Infants who in turn were infected by their diseased mothers became the sainted martyrs of the movement.[6]

Blacks did not figure prominently in the early plans of social hygienists. These reformers directed their movement toward white middle-class Americans like themselves. Apart from emphasizing the need to set a good example for the lower classes, they gave little thought to the poor of any race. In the case of blacks, however, this neglect was especially baffling because physicians for years had been warning that syphilis threatened to exterminate the black population of the United States.

By the turn of the century social hygienists had built a formidable coalition of physicians, public health officials, clergymen, educators, lawyers, social workers, businessmen, and philanthropists. The American Social Hygiene Association, organized in 1913–1914, emerged as the leading exponent of a single sexual code for men and women. The double standard was to be destroyed by elevating men to the women's standard. The underlying assumption of social hygienists was that human sexual behavior could be controlled by reeducating the public to demand a single code of moral behavior from both sexes. Few assumptions reveal more fully the optimism of the age.

The white image of black sexuality was responsible, at least in part, for the neglect of blacks by social hygienists. Blacks suffered from venereal diseases because they would not, or could not, refrain from sexual promiscuity. Social hygiene for whites rested on the assumption that attitudinal changes could produce behavioral changes. A single standard of high moral behavior could be produced by molding sexual attitudes through moral education. For blacks, however, a change in their very nature seemed to be required. Thus, the neglect of blacks by social hygienists stemmed only in part from their

Editorial cartoon by "Roberts," *Rocky Mountain News,* Denver, Colorado, July 1972. (*Library of Congress*)

Editorial cartoon by Lou Erikson, *Atlanta Constitution*, July 1972. (*Courtesy Lou Erikson*)

'NOW can we give him penicillin?'

Editorial cartoon by Tony Auth, *Philadelphia Inquirer*, July 1972. (*Courtesy Tony Auth*)

Editorial cartoon by Clifford H. Baldowski, *Atlanta Constitution*. (*Courtesy* Atlanta Constitution)

Cabins in the cotton. (*From Charles Johnson*, Shadow of the Plantation, *1934, by permission of The University of Chicago Press*)

"Ain't make nothin', don' speck nothin' til' I die." (*Johnson*, Shadow of the Plantation)

"Dis ole fence need fixin' too." (*Johnson*, Shadow of the Plantation)

"Dis ole mule lak' me—he ain't much good no more." (*Johnson*, Shadow of the Plantation)

"Seem lak' I ain't never break even." (*Johnson*, Shadow of the Plantation)

Taliaferro Clark. (*National Library of Medicine*)

Oliver Clarence Wenger. (*National Library of Medicine*)

Raymond A. Vonderlehr wearing Public Health Service dress uniform. (*National Library of Medicine*)

Raymond A. Vonderlehr (left) and Thomas Parran. (*National Library of Medicine*)

John R. Heller. (*National Library of Medicine*)

William J. Brown. (*National Library of Medicine*)

general disinterest in the lower classes; racial prejudice unquestionably underpinned the slight.

After World War I, social hygienists began to shift the emphasis from race to class, paralleling the discussion in medical and scientific literature. To serve the small but growing black middle class, the American Social Hygiene Association hired a black professional, Franklin O. Nichols, as a field representative. Originally, the plan was for him to divide his time between familiarizing black leaders with the objectives of the social hygiene movement and promoting venereal disease control work among blacks. He gave the latter assignment little attention, despite the crying need of lower-class blacks for medical care. Instead, during the 1920s, Nichols spent most of his time lecturing at black colleges and working with black educators to develop college courses in sex education. His audience offered a good example of the "saved preaching to the saved" and revealed the constraints that class consciousness placed on the reforming zeal of social hygienists. The people who really needed to learn about social hygiene, the lower classes, were not being reached.[7]

And yet poor people of all races benefited from the social hygiene movement because of the emphasis these reformers placed on treatment. When physical examinations of recruits during World War I revealed a high incidence of venereal infections, social hygienists had warned that venereal disease threatened to disable America's fighting men. Congress responded in 1918 by establishing an interdepartmental social hygiene board composed of the secretaries of war, navy, and treasury. More important, the 1918 law created a Division of Venereal Diseases in the United States Public Health Service. Congress provided the PHS with a generous administrative budget for this division and appropriated an additional one million dollars to help states organize social hygiene work, both for prophylaxis and treatment.

Federal support produced movement. Within a year forty-four states had organized separate bureaus for venereal disease control work in their health departments. Much of the attention of these new agencies centered on treating the poor. By 1919 no less than 202 clinics had been organized in thirty states, with more than 64,000 patients under care who otherwise could not have afforded treatment.[8]

The construction of this national superstructure of federal, state, and local agencies for syphilis control work had hardly gotten under way before politics dealt it a severe blow. The early successes of social hygienists had depended, in large measure, on the "Win the War" psychology. After the war, the public's sense of urgency declined. Social hygiene became an easy target for economy-minded Congresses looking for progams to cut in the 1920s. By 1926 the federal government had withdrawn all aid to the states for venereal disease work. The PHS Division of Venereal Diseases managed to survive drastic reductions in its budget, but functioned as little more than an appendage of the American Social Hygiene Association. Sex education, with a heavy dose of moral preaching, became its principal activity, while its earlier efforts at providing federal leadership in the development of treatment facilities across the country were all but abandoned.

Alabama illustrates the consequences of waxing and waning federal support. The Alabama State Board of Health first began its campaign against venereal disease in 1918 in direct response to the war-related efforts of federal authorities. Health officials in the state had no reliable data on the size of the problem or any idea how to attack it. They decided at the outset, however, that treatment had to form a major component of any social hygiene program. The task became more difficult when federal support declined and then stopped. In response, Alabama's health officials divided syphilitic patients into three groups: (1) private patients who could afford medical care on a fee-for-service basis; (2) the medically indigent; and (3) those who could afford partial treatment.

Apart from their need for sex education, the first group was not regarded as a public health problem. The second group, however, was a source of grave concern. To reach them, public health officials organized free clinics in the large centers of population and appealed to private physicians to treat indigent patients in smaller towns and rural areas. By 1930, the Alabama State Board of Health operated (solely or in conjunction with municipalities) fourteen free clinics. It also donated the necessary drugs to private physicians who were willing to accept indigent cases.[9]

To meet the needs of those who could pay for part of their care, the state board of health developed a network of cooperative clinics, each staffed by private physicians appointed by the county medical societies. By 1930, approximately 175 clinicians had agreed to devote a few hours each week to clinic patients. The state furnished the necessary drugs, syringes, needles, and other equipment, requiring in return that physicians charge no more than two dollars per treatment from patients. Supervision of these cooperative clinics rested not with the Alabama State Board of Health but with county health departments. Full-time health departments were maintained in fifty-two of the state's sixty-seven counties in 1930, in theory reaching 85 percent of the population. In the fifteen counties that did not have health departments, the clinicians dealt directly with the state board of health.

The clinics began operating in 1919 and within two years had over six thousand patients under treatment. By 1929, their patients numbered more than ten thousand. Yet Alabama's social hygiene program provided treatment for only a small fraction of those who needed it. The free clinics operated in urban areas in a state that was predominately rural, and it was naïve of state officials to think that private physicians in the rural areas would treat more than a few indigent patients without compensation. Moreover, giving physicians the power to decide which patients could pay for treatment guaranteed that few would be designated as indigents. Doctors in poor areas often adjusted their charges to the patient's ability to pay, but they usually demanded something for their services.

Health officials also overestimated the amount doctors should be permitted to charge patients who could share the cost of treatment. Two dollars probably represented the least amount that health officials thought would give private physicians an incentive for cooperating with the program. This fee was 40 percent of the standard rate. Yet even this reduced amount was financially prohibitive for many. Most people, including the desperately poor, could probably have managed to come up with two dollars for a few visits, but effective syphilis therapy required upwards of twenty treatments in a single year. The cost to the patient of Alabama's treatment program could easily exceed forty dollars in a single year for the clinician's fee alone. Syphilis therapy was thus beyond the means of many people in Alabama, a state with a high concentration of sharecroppers who were chronically short of cash.

Alabama's treatment program all but ignored rural blacks.

Although they made up a significant percentage of the patients who received free treatments from public clinics in urban areas and low-cost treatment from private clinicians in the small towns, the rural hinterland, where more than 72 percent of the state's population lived, remained the *terra incognita* of public health work. Speaking before the Southern States Conference of the American Social Hygiene Association in 1930, Dr. D. G. Gill, the director of the Bureau of Preventable Disease of the Alabama State Board of Health, expressed satisfaction with the gains that had been made during the previous twelve years in the state's social hygiene programs, but he readily admitted that "the solution of the problem of syphilis amongst the rural Negro population still awaits fulfillment."[10]

Funding for new treatment clinics would not become available until the late 1930s, but even as Dr. Gill spoke an important trial program was being tested in Alabama. The pilot treatment program was a joint venture by the Julius Rosenwald Fund and the Public Health Service. In 1929 the Fund asked the PHS for assistance in developing health programs for southern blacks. Endowed by a Jewish immigrant who helped build the Sears and Roebuck Company into a giant mail order business, the Fund was a philanthropic organization that played a key role in promoting the welfare of black Americans. Booker T. Washington drew Julius Rosenwald into the struggle, and the Fund became famous for building schools for blacks in the South. In 1928 the Fund was reorganized and modeled after the Rockefeller Foundation and management was turned over to a professional staff. The Fund continued to work on behalf of blacks, developing programs in medical economics, fellowships for the professions, library service, social studies, general education, and race relations.

As part of the reorganization, Michael M. Davis was appointed director of medical services. Before joining the Fund, Davis had served as director of the Boston Dispensary, one of the nation's oldest and most prestigious charitable health care institutions. He was an aggressive innovator in what would later be called community medicine and had done pioneering work in the field of medical economics. A medical reformer with a national reputation, Davis sought to make the medical system more efficient by defraying costs. His primary goal was to bring adequate health care to Americans who otherwise could not afford it.[11]

Throughout his career, Davis raised incisive questions about the assumptions behind medical philanthropy in the United States. For example, in sharp contrast to the traditional view that charitable institutions should limit their services to the indigent, he established evening clinics at the Boston Dispensary for working men who suffered from venereal diseases. Salaried physicians, instead of the usual volunteers, staffed these clinics. Operating expenses came from the nominal fee of fifty cents per visit paid by the patients who used the clinics. The clinics were highly successful, and by the time Davis came to the Rosenwald Fund late in 1928, he had established himself as one of the nation's leading authorities on developing alternatives to private medicine on a fee-for-service basis.

Since the Fund had never had a medical division, Davis enjoyed wide latitude within the broad boundaries of preserving the Fund's special interest in improving race relations and securing wider opportunities for blacks. Within a few months, he had fashioned plans for new programs, including enlisting the aid of the PHS. Davis regarded an alliance with the PHS as vital because he lacked experience dealing with the health problems of rural blacks. In April 1929, Davis met with Dr. Hugh S. Cumming, the surgeon general of the United States Public Health Service.

The ideas that Davis laid before Cumming were indeed ambitious. Henceforth, the Fund planned to encourage the employment of Negro nurses as community health workers; to experiment on a limited scale with the use of black sanitary inspectors; to train black public health personnel; to promote the adequate training of black physicians by arranging internships; to increase black hospital facilities through building endowments; to aid in construction and assistance in their support and maintenance (with an eye to developing black institutions that would serve as good teaching hospitals); to aid in the establishment and maintenance of racially mixed hospitals; to support studies designed to provide answers on how to secure medical care for blacks; and to provide scholarships for black nurses in public health training.

The need for a PHS adviser was obvious. News that the

Fund had created a medical division, Davis revealed, had already generated numerous inquiries and proposals from state health officials. The adviser's primary responsibility, therefore, would be to review these (and future) proposals and recommend policies that would govern the Fund's responses.

The surgeon general selected Dr. Taliaferro Clark for the appointment, a southerner whose pedigree reached back to colonial Virginia. Dr. Clark had entered the Public Health Service in 1895 at the age of twenty-eight, filling numerous responsible posts until he retired in 1933. His previous assignments included work in mental testing, public sanitation, tropical medicine, and immigration quarantine. The appointment of such a senior officer meant that the surgeon general was serious about cooperating with the Fund.

In addition to supplying an adviser, Dr. Cumming tried to interest the Fund in an important new health project. In July 1929, he wrote Davis about a Wassermann survey that the PHS had recently completed on more than two thousand blacks employed by the Delta and Pine Land Company in Bolivar County, Mississippi. Nearly one-fourth of those tested had syphilis. The surgeon general stressed that, as one of the few reasonably accurate studies on the prevalence of syphilis in rural blacks, the survey offered the PHS the chance to demonstrate how effective a treatment program could be. "If adequate methods of treatment can be applied among this group," predicted Dr. Cumming, "it should furnish a demonstration which will be of value in connection with similar programs in other localities and industries in which there is a high prevalence of syphilis."[12]

Dr. Cumming estimated that $10,000 would be required over a one-year period "to give adequate treatment for syphilis to this group." The plantation officials, he reported, had agreed to bear one-half of the cost of treatment for employees. Since state health officials could not supply the shortfall, Dr. Cumming asked the Fund for support.

Davis was interested, but insisted that the program be modified to fit the Fund's operating policies and social goals. He told Dr. Cumming that support could not be used for salaries for personnel; that a grant would have to be regarded as "seed money," and, as such, not necessarily renewable; and that the addition of a black nurse to the project's staff would definitely increase the likelihood of approval. In other words, Davis seized the opportunity to push for one of the Fund's major goals—encouraging their grantees to use black personnel whenever possible as a means of promoting integration in the professions. Yet Davis was so impressed by the project that he obtained the personal approval of Julius Rosenwald even before Dr. Cumming replied.[13]

The man in charge of the Mississippi Wassermann survey was Dr. Oliver Clarence Wenger, director of the PHS's Venereal Disease Clinic in Hot Springs, Arkansas. Dr. Wenger's attitudes toward blacks mirrored the changes that were occurring within the medical profession. In unguarded moments he was capable of making racial slurs, but he deplored his profession's widespread neglect of the health needs of blacks. He had no sympathy for the misplaced sense of professionalism that prompted many private physicians to oppose public health programs for the poor, and he developed considerable skill at circumventing their opposition. Paternalistic in his dealings with the poor and uneducated, he seemed to enjoy excellent rapport with the lower-class patients with whom he worked in the South. Indeed, among his fellow officers in the Public Health Service, Dr. Wenger was widely regarded as an expert in dealing with rural southern blacks. And his fellow health officers were not alone in this assessment. When Dr. E. L. Keyes of New York City, a former president of the American Social Hygiene Association, observed Wenger taking blood samples from blacks on a Saturday afternoon in a crossroad country store, he likened it to "holding high Wassermann in the marketplace."[14]

Upon learning that the Fund had agreed to support the program in Mississippi, Dr. Wenger filled Davis in on the demonstration's background. "The situation in Mississippi," explained Dr. Wenger, "is perhaps no different from that of any other southern state where the public health problems of the colored population have heretofore been ignored." Only recently, he continued, had a few white planters begun to realize "that the negroes' health is one of the most important factors in the economic life of the community and in the production of cotton," a fact that was "brought home to the cotton planters when they realized that the negro exodus to the industrial centers of the north has caused a scarcity of labor in the cotton country."[15]

Concern about syphilis, Dr. Wenger revealed, had developed accidentally. It all began when the county health officer noted "that many of the local physicians in the Delta were claiming good results from the use of neoarsphenamine in the treatment of pellagra." The confusion was cleared up, however, when physicians discovered "that much of this improvement was due to the fact that many of these patients had syphilis in addition to their pellagra." The PHS had been brought in, Dr. Wenger observed, to ascertain "just how much syphilis existed among the colored race in the Delta."[16]

The planters had turned to the PHS and philanthropic foundations because their own private physicians were charging more than blacks could afford, thus denying them treatment. Shortly after World War I, when enthusiasm was at a pitch, Mississippi, like the rest of the nation, joined the venereal disease campaign and organized a venereal disease division within the State Board of Health. "Several clinics were established but existed only a comparatively short time," Dr. Wenger charged, "due to the antagonism of the medical profession who saw in this movement another step toward state medicine." After abandoning these clinics, the state launched an education campaign consisting mainly of lectures and pamphlets, but this program "did not reach the plantation negro" because many of them could "neither read nor write."[17]

What followed was predictable. "Since the physicians of Mississippi are something of a political factor in state affairs the free clinics were not reestablished," wrote Dr. Wenger, "and what little treatment is given to this group, which must be considered indigent, is given by private physicians at a price far beyond the patient's ability to pay." Translating the matter into figures, Dr. Wenger stated that "the physician usually charges five or ten dollars for a dose of neoarsphenamine and considers two or three doses sufficient, because that is all the treatment the plantation owner will advance for his employees." The result, of course, was that "the patient does not receive adequate treatment, becomes infectious again in a short while, and having no conception of the ravages of the disease, continues to infect others."[18]

Dr. Wenger argued that the only way to break the cycle of inadequate treatment and reinfection was to test "large groups of negroes in different communities and devise some means of treatment; not in the hope of effecting a cure but to make as many of these patients who present a four-plus Wassermann noninfectious." Like most physicians of his day, Dr. Wenger belived that it was possible to cure syphilis. With medically indigent patients, however, he had to distinguish between what was medically possible and what was economically feasible. Going for "the cure" was simply too costly. The best he could hope to accomplish was to render infectious patients noninfectious.[19]

Aided by the Rosenwald funding, Dr. Wenger had the opportunity to test his theories by turning the Mississippi syphilis survey into a treatment demonstration. The arduous task began late in the summer of 1929. The work taxed Dr. Wenger's energy and resourcefulness, for his goals were ambitious. He planned to give "each patient twenty-five doses of neo [neoarsphenamine] and two hundred inunctions [mercury rubs] for the year's treatment." Conditions in his makeshift clinics were extremely primitive and he felt constantly thwarted by having to accommodate the examinations and treatments to the work schedules of his patients. He also felt frustrated over not being able to do more for them. In September he reported to Dr. Thomas Parran, the director of the Division of Venereal Diseases: "We are finding a great many physical defects among these patients, none of whom have ever received proper medical attention. They are illiterate and it is very hard to overcome their suspicions."[20]

But all was not bleak, for Dr. Wenger retained a lively sense of humor, albeit at the expense of his patients. Both his search for comic relief in the midst of misery and his paternalistic attitudes were evident when he related an incident involving one of the physicians under his supervision:

> We have had some funny experiences showing the childlike reaction to this work among the Negroes. After taking some blood at Tunica, two Negroes returned to Dr. Brevard and complained that they felt very weak after having this blood drawn out of their veins and their sexual powers were impaired. Dr. Brevard listened to their story very patiently and said that if they wanted their blood back he would give it to them. He fixed up a one-ounce

placebo colored red and advised them to take this mixture in tea-spoonful doses. Both Negroes were perfectly satisfied and reported immediate improvement.[21]

As the Mississippi treatment demonstration neared completion, Dr. Wenger told Dr. Parran that a meeting of southern health officers should be called to discuss the possibility of starting new testing and treatment programs. Dr. Parran was receptive to the idea for he was determined to make the PHS the leader of a national campaign against syphilis. Ever since taking charge of the Division in 1926, he had worked to move it in new directions. Instead of concentrating on sex education and the prophylaxis of syphilis, Dr. Parran shifted the Division's orientation to health surveys, scientific research, and treatment demonstrations. He welcomed the chance to conduct syphilis control demonstrations among the South's blacks. In addition to addressing a serious health problem, the demonstrations could serve as a springboard for establishing federal leadership and control over a national campaign to eradicate syphilis.[22]

Dr. Parran had helped plan and organize the syphilis control demonstration in Mississippi, and he had followed the work there very closely. By early fall he had seen enough to become convinced that the program was sound and that similar demonstrations should be conducted in other states. Drawing heavily on Dr. Wenger's reports and recommendations from the field, Drs. Parran and Clark drafted a proposal to expand the program. Early in October 1929, Dr. Clark sent it to Davis.

In their proposal to the Rosenwald Fund, Drs. Clark and Parran candidly admitted that private physicians and public health officials had not demonstrated that they could effect "the practical control of syphilis in this country." But with obvious reference to Davis's early work with syphilis clinics in Boston, they observed: "Methods of furnishing treatment to infected persons in urban populations through organized clinics have been adequately demonstrated." The trick to controlling syphilis was to catch it early and treat it rigorously, and the best way to accomplish this, they contended, was to work "through established health agencies because of lessened expense and the assurance of permanency," for, as they stated, "health departments will continue to exist as long as there are governments."[23]

In selecting the study sites, Drs. Parran and Clark proposed that "preference be given to control activities in rural districts with a large negro population." And as a matter of routine operating procedure, Parran and Clark recommended that "the methods to be followed in any State be agreed upon with the State health authorities and the Public Health Service; and that the major interest be the development of more effective medical service to infected individuals as a means of preventing the spread of these diseases and of promoting their cure."[24]

The program's medical services were designed to meet the Fund's long-range goals. The demonstrations would provide training for "private physicians, white and colored, in the elements of venereal disease treatments" and the "more extensive distribution of antisyphilitic drugs and the promotion of wider use of State diagnostic laboratory facilities." In addition, the demonstrations promised to promote the "utilization of negro clinicians and nurses to supplement existing personnel in county health departments," not to mention "cooperation with industrial corporations in providing more effective treatment service for employees." The final medical goal of the program, the "extension of existing clinical service or the establishment of additional clinical service," must have been especially appealing to Davis.[25]

In short, the proposal offered the Fund the chance to join the PHS in a pioneering program. As Dr. Clark later explained: "The field had not been preempted by any other foundation." Earlier health campaigns in the South had ignored syphilis, and despite decades of speculation in the nation's best medical journals, reliable data did not exist on the incidence of syphilis in the South's black communities. Private physicians had long agreed that the problem was serious, but most despaired of being able to do anything about it, preferring instead to exchange stories on the difficulties of treating black patients. Thus, the Public Health Service's dramatic statement of the problem did not seem excessive, nor its urgent cries for action inappropriate.[26]

The Fund approved the proposal. The trustees voted in November 1929 to spend up to $50,000 during the 1930 calendar year "for demonstrations of the control of venereal disease in the rural South, in cooperation with the United States Public Health Service and with the state and local authorities."[27]

The surgeon general promptly informed the health officers of the southern states of the Fund's action and invited them to submit proposals. The response was gratifying. Drs. Parran, Clark, and Wenger reviewed the proposals and selected sites on the basis of geographical setting, the population density and vocational diversity of blacks, the caliber of the local health department, the likelihood of cooperation from local physicians and other influential leaders, the budget, and the number of professional personnel that state and local health departments were willing to supply. But when Dr. Parran reflected a few years later on their deliberations, he suggested that the selection process came down to choosing areas that were basically dissimilar so that they could learn how to deal with the problem under a variety of circumstances. All the proposals had in common was a concern about syphilis control and a strong desire to carry out the study.[28]

The Public Health Service recommended five new programs to the Fund. Joining the Scott County, Mississippi, syphilis control demonstration were programs in Tipton County, Tennessee; Glynn County, Georgia; Macon County, Alabama; Pitt County, North Carolina; and Albemarle County, Virginia. As a group the six sites represented a broad cross-section of the conditions under which blacks lived in the rural South. And while each demonstration has its own fascinating story, the program in Macon County represented by far the greatest challenge.

CHAPTER 5

"The Dr. Ain't Taking Sticks"

MACON County has been economically depressed throughout the twentieth century. Located in east central Alabama (approximately thirty miles east of the state capitol in Montgomery), its 650 square miles lie within a region of rich dark soil called the "black belt." While some progress has been made in recent years toward reducing the county's dependence on agriculture, its economy has always been tied to cotton. Sharecroppers grow most of it, eking out a bare existence on small plots of land. The Census of 1930 listed Macon County's population at just over twenty-seven thousand residents, 82 percent of whom were blacks.

Forty years did little to change these figures. By 1970, the county's population had dipped below twenty-five thousand, but the racial composition had stayed almost exactly the same. Macon County remained a predominantly rural community in which blacks still outnumbered whites by about four to one. Moreover, nearly half of its residents were listed in 1970 as living below the poverty level; a third lived in houses with no indoor plumbing.

Macon County faced conditions in the 1930s that were worse. The Great Depression exacerbated the region's long-standing economic woes, creating a level of rural poverty that was appalling. In the hinterland around Tuskegee, the county seat, housing conditions were terrible. The typical dwelling was a tumble-down shack with a dirt floor, no screens, little furniture, a few rags for bedding, and a privy only when underbrush was not nearby. Drinking water came from an uncovered, shallow well, often totally unprotected from direct surface drainage.

The people who lived in this rural slum ate a pellagrous diet. "The only well-fed Negroes I saw in Macon County were the students in Tuskegee Institute and the patients in the nearby Veterans Hospital," wrote Dr. Parran after a visit there during the early 1930s. Salt pork, hominy grits, cornbread, and molasses formed the standard fare of the majority of Macon County's black residents, while red meat, fresh vegetables and fruit, or milk (even for families with infants) seldom appeared on their tables. As a result, chronic malnutrition and a host of diet-related illnesses were serious health problems.[1]

Even a seasoned veteran like Dr. Wenger was shocked. After working in Macon County early in 1931, he wrote Dr. Clark a vivid description of cruel rural poverty. The county's young black nurse, Sarah Freeman, had organized a school program to feed the children at least one hot meal a day. The plan called for each child to bring something to be cooked in a large pot on the heating stove every morning. Out of seventy-seven children, however, only nineteen were able to furnish something for the common stew. And while fifteen youngsters brought their own tin lunch baskets to school, only two contained so much as a scrap of meat. The remaining buckets held "nothing but a soppy piece of cornbread or a few biscuits." Conversations with the children revealed that several had not had breakfast and two did not expect anything more to eat that day than they received in school. Those who were lucky enough to have eaten that morning "said the breakfast consisted of bread and molasses, bread and milk in 5 cases only, bread and meat in two cases, greens and biscuits in at least a dozen cases, and so on."[2]

The adults suffered, too. Dr. Wenger stated that the county health officer informed him "of an old man who died after eating a large number of raw sweet potatoes he found in a field." Dr. Wenger himself reported seeing "four white women with breast babies who are living on corn bread and sweet potatoes." All the incidents moved him to confess: "I've seen what happens when the rice crop fails in the Philippines and am somewhat familiar with reports from China, but this is the first time I realized what is going on in the South at the present time."[3]

In Macon County, as in most parts of the country, local relief institutions were no match for the Great Depression. Dr. Parran described with irony the inadequacy of public relief measures:

> When I was there in 1932 a devoted social worker who combined the positions of county truant officer, welfare commissioner, and children's aid official in this county of 30,000, said: "I think they have done very well in this county in taking care of the poor. The county appropriated $300 for me to use this year. Then, too, I can get some clothes and things from the church groups, which helps out."[4]

Inferior school facilities for children and widespread illiteracy among adults went hand in hand with poverty in Macon County, despite the presence of the Tuskegee Institute. Year in and year out Alabama ranked at or near the bottom nationally in the amount of money spent per pupil on education, and Macon County was not a leader in black education within the state. Only seven of Alabama's sixty-seven counties had a lower percentage of black children in school. To Horace Mann Bond, a black educator, it was obvious "that the claims . . . for the influence of Tuskegee upon the schools, and, through the schools, upon the life of the Negroes of Macon County, are hardly justified by facts pertinent to their present status."[5]

In retrospect, Bond's judgment may have been accurate but unduly harsh, for the Tuskegee Institute did not command the financial resources to educate single-handedly the county's blacks. Moreover, the Institute had made contributions in many areas—the construction of scores of elementary schools for Negroes, for example. The real responsibility for the blacks' educational plight lay with Alabama's poverty, which kept state appropriations for education well below the national average, and racial discrimination, which kept blacks segregated in inferior schools that received far less support per student than white schools. Separate and unequal aptly described Alabama's two-track educational system. And as might be predicted, different systems manufactured different products. The illiteracy rate for every 1,000 adults in Macon County in 1932 was 23 for whites and 227 for blacks.[6]

Macon County's medical facilities for rural blacks were meager. The United States Veterans Hospital, located at the edge of the Tuskegee Institute's campus, was a segregated, but well-equipped, institution with an all black staff that included twenty-two physicians. Unfortunately, it did not maintain an outpatient clinic. In fact, according to a trained medical observer, Dr. Clyde D. Frost, who made a study of medical facilities and personnel in Macon County in 1931, the staff of the Veterans Hospital had very little to do with the community at large and displayed "an attitude of intellectual aloofness and professional isolation."[7]

The John A. Andrew Memorial Hospital, founded on the campus of the Tuskegee Institute just before World War I, was more involved with the community. The primary duty of the four black physicians employed there was serving the students, faculty, and staff of the Institute, but Andrew Hospital also maintained an outpatient service for local residents. Dr. Frost thought that the administrators of the Institute and Andrew Hospital were "very sympathetic to the local or community needs," but charged that the hospital had "not to date participated substantially in the larger project of serving as a community health center." Thus, in his judgment, neither the Veterans Hospital nor Andrew Hospital had made a significant contribution to community health.[8]

Sixteen private physicians, all but one white, practiced medicine in Macon County during the early 1930s. Tuskegee Institute had five physicians, and the area in which the Fund's syphilis control work was conducted had five more—two in the little community of Shorter and three in and around Notusulga. Their services did not have much impact on the health of blacks in the rural areas, the vast majority of whom went from cradle to grave deprived of proper medical care. "I ain't had a Dr. but once in my life and that was 'bout 15 yrs. ago," an elderly black resident confessed in 1932. The man simply could not afford medical care. "The Dr. ain't taking sticks, you know; if you go to him, you better have money and if he comes to you, you better have it. So you see that makes a po' man do without a Dr. when he really needs him."[9]

Other black residents told similar stories. What determined whether a person saw a physician was not race but money, for white physicians routinely treated blacks who could afford to pay. A man who had become ill with what he thought was yellow jaundice stated: "I was really sick enough for a doctor, but I didn't call one. They say they won't come less you have money." The cost of medical care included a mileage charge for home visits as well as the examination fee. "The doctor charges $1.00 a mile to come out here and that is about twelve miles," recalled another resident of the county, adding, "You just have to do without the doctor sometimes cause they sho won't come lessen you got the ready cash."[10]

The man was right. People whose incomes often averaged less than a dollar a day could not afford to pay for proper health care. Many were reduced to treating themselves with home remedies or patent medicines. As one venerable woman confided: "Ain't spent nothing for medicine more than a little black draught. If I had money I would go to the doctor. I'm old enough to cross over and it worries me I ain't been to no doctor." Cost had placed modern medicine beyond her reach and that of her neighbors', forcing them to rely upon traditional self-prescribed medicines such as castor oil, salts, calomel, and quinine—in addition to the much valued "Black Draught."[11]

For tenant farmers there was always the hope that their landlords would engage physicians to look after them. Some planters did, but many could not afford to pay the medical bills for their tenants. Moreover, some landlords would call physicians in to attend valued tenants, while refusing to do so for others. Discussing his employer, a sharecropper in Macon County recalled, "Mr. Segrist will send you a Dr. though or send you to a Dr. either when you get sick if you're a good worker. 'Course if you don't work, he'll let you die. I'll give him credit, the old man'll do that."[12]

Since blacks consulted physicians only in emergencies, they had to endure chronic diseases like syphilis. The protracted treatment schedule ensured that the few patients who were diagnosed would not be cured. State health authorities admitted that the syphilis programs did not reach rural blacks, and Macon County did not even have a health department until 1928. A local health unit was organized then only because one influential planter wanted to know the incidence of syphilis among the seven hundred blacks employed on his plantation. He had noticed a decline in live births among his tenants and attributed it to syphilis. A health department was organized to undertake the survey and administer treatment. But its efforts were limited to a few hundred people, while the menace to public health involved thousands.[13]

Thankful for allies, health officials in Macon County responded enthusiastically when Surgeon General Cumming announced the syphilis control program. State authorities agreed to sponsor Macon County as a demonstration site in January 1930, and an application to the Public Health Service followed. Dr. Clark met with Dr. Stuart Graves, the acting state health officer of the Alabama State Board of Health, in Montgomery to work out changes in the proposal. Late in January, Dr. Graves submitted an application to the surgeon general "to conduct in Macon County, Alabama, a syphilis control demonstration in a group of from 7000 to 10,000 negroes located in a section of the county where the percentage of negro population is highest, approximately eight negroes to one white."[14]

State health officials had selected Macon County for several reasons. Dr. Graves revealed that the Tuskegee Institute had endorsed the program, promising "such assistance as it may be able to give in carrying out the work." He also stressed that "local physicians, including all members of the Macon County Board of Health and the Macon County Health Officer, together with several of the leading employers of negro labor, have approved the project and offered their active cooperation in the work." Finally, Dr. Graves assured the surgeon general that the program would benefit from "an active, well organized health department and an exceptionally well qualified county health officer under whose immediate supervision the project will be carried out." The Alabama State Board of Health, of course, would be directly responsible for the demonstration.[15]

The plan called for an initial Wassermann survey, followed by a one-year treatment program. Dr. Graves requested $7,750, pledging to spend $3,000 of that sum to employ a black physician and nurse. Hiring black professionals to conduct the field work met one of the Rosenwald Fund's objectives, but the state failed to guarantee the salary of a state venereal disease control officer. This omission was a clear violation of the Fund's policy of requiring states to pay at least part of the salaries of key personnel. Thus, from the beginning, Alabama's financial commitment to the program was in doubt.

Nevertheless, Dr. Clark strongly supported the proposal. Davis hesitated momentarily, but finally decided to gamble that Alabama would be able to pay its share. On February 12, 1930, the Fund's executive committee approved separate grants of $7,750 and $2,250 to the Alabama State Board of Health, the second grant to be "conditional upon the state's appropriating an equal amount toward the salary and expenses of the state v.d. control officer."[16]

A few weeks later a team of medical workers was busy taking blood samples in Macon County. The field work was supervised by the county health officer, and in keeping with the Fund's racial policy, a black physician, assisted by the black county nurse, performed the blood tests. Before long, the division of labor between the black and white clinicians broke down and both men took blood samples and dispensed treatment. They were often joined for extended periods by Dr. Wenger, who seemed to have a special affinity for Macon County among the several demonstration sites.

The cooperation and support of influential whites were crucial. To win them over, the health officer reminded the planters of the great success that earlier public health campaigns in the South had enjoyed against diseases such as typhoid fever, yellow fever, and pellagra. Syphilis, too, could be conquered, they stressed, provided that permission was granted for them to come and do the work.

The planters also had to be convinced that it was to their advantage to stamp out syphilis among their tenants. Drs. Parran and Wenger agreed that appealing to the economic interests of the planters was their best bet. As Dr. Parran later explained:

> I knew that the majority of these plantation owners, fine fellows that they were, would give us their sympathetic good wishes in whatever we ourselves chose to do to improve the welfare and promote the happiness of the Negroes on their plantations. But if we expected them to do anything about it, I knew we had to use the argument that it would be more profitable to work a healthy field hand than a sick one.[17]

The argument worked well. Permission for the demonstration was usually granted on the spot, and it was not uncommon for a planter to order his tenants to participate. One commanded his foreman:

> Tell those niggers the health doctor will be at the Possom Hollow school tonight. He's got some government medicine to cure the blood disease. A lot of these niggers have got blood trouble, sickly, no count, lazy; but maybe it's not their fault. This doctor will find out.

Nor was it unusual for a planter to grant permission to test his workers without so much as word of explanation to them, never mind obtaining their prior consent. After listening to the pitch made by health officials, a planter replied: "Yes, Doc, go ahead, I've got about forty of them here pickin' cotton. Can you test them here? How long does it take?"[18]

Macon County's black people not only obeyed orders, but also cooperated willingly with the program. Charles Johnson, the famous black sociologist and president of Fisk University, explored the reasons for their eager participation in his classic study of blacks in the Deep South, *Shadow of the Plantation*, published in 1934. The book was commissioned by the Rosenwald Fund because Davis wanted a sociological analysis of the blacks who participated in the syphilis control demonstrations. Johnson and his assistants interviewed more than six hundred families in Macon County in 1932. Inquiries about health care in general and the syphilis control demonstration in particular formed an entire section of his questionnaire, and he specifically asked his subjects why they had cooperated. Their responses led Johnson to assert: "The tradition of dependence and obedience to the orders of authority, whether these were mandatory or not, helps to explain the questionless response to the invitation to examination and treatment."[19]

Dr. Frost, the black physician sent by the Fund to observe the syphilis control demonstration in Macon County, made much the same point. "As a group they were susceptible to kindness," wrote Dr. Frost of the program's patients, "and there may have been an inducement of implied official authority, although there was no volitional effort to create this impression." But as he correctly perceived, there was no need to invoke official authority in a community in which generations of white rule had made black people accustomed to following orders. Their deeply ingrained deference to authority figures, coupled with their eagerness to receive medical attention, made them willing subjects. "Local government dictation is followed quite freely," explained Frost, "and with the county health officer and state departments of health proposing to give treatment, the rural and native favor of medication of any sort have required minimum stimulation."[20]

Where Dr. Frost saw deference to authority figures, Dr. Parran saw trust in benevolent friends. Blacks had cooperated with the program, he explained, because they trusted everyone associated with it. He did not hesitate to assert that

> it is true in the South, by and large that the Negro instinctively trusts the white man, except where he has suffered from sharp dealings and has good reasons to be suspicious. He trusts the doctor—thanks to the fine character of many of our rural southern physicians. He trusts the Government, because . . . he has believed that the Government is a friend of his and tries to help him. The "government health doctor" therefore has an entree. If he deals fairly and is considerate, it is not too difficult to get cooperation.[21]

Dr. Frost also commented on the use of authority figures within the black community. First the health officials won over local leaders. Then, they used schoolhouses and churches as makeshift clinics, with local schoolteachers and ministers serving as "advance people" who spread the word about where and when the "government doctors" would be in the area. As Dr. Frost observed: "There may . . . have been an implied sanction in the use of schools and churches for treatment centers." Offering treatment in the neighborhood encouraged participation for yet another reason. No doubt many cooperated, Dr. Frost concluded, because they enjoyed "social gatherings and a half day [away] from the field."[22]

Old people were an especially important resource. Ordinarily, health officials preferred not to treat them, for the elderly were rarely infectious and had difficulty tolerating the toxic treatment. In private practice therapy schedules could be prescribed on a case-by-case basis, but in public health work patients had to be dealt with by age groups. The PHS therefore warned clinicians in the field:

> DO NOT FORGET: It is not a four-plus Wassermann being treated in these old cases, but a man or woman whose kidneys,

liver, and cardio-vascular system are 50 or more years of age. The
four-plus Wassermann is just an incident in their lives. To treat
them as one does a younger patient only means grief for the clinician and the patient's family.

Despite the attendant difficulties, Dr. Wenger argued in favor
of therapy. "Treat the old syphilitic with 'rheumatism,' give
him the painless mercury rubs. He will feel better and will
bring in the whole family for the treatment they need. Don't
forget, they listen to their grandaddies."[23]

The form of treatment also influenced cooperation. Arsphenamine had to be administered by intraveneous injection,
but mercury could be given by intramuscular injection or inunction—absorption through the skin. "It was early decided
... ," wrote Dr. Parran, "that intramuscular injections of bismuth or mercury in the buttocks could not be used. Except
with very careful management, they may cause painful lumps
which, it has been observed in clinics, the Negro particularly
dislikes."[24]

That left inunction, but the health officers did not have the
time to administer it. Dr. Parran recalled tales of sailors in the
olden days congregating on deck, sitting on stools formed into
a circle, and rubbing each other's bare backs with mercury.
With their example in mind, he wrote:

> Could the same plan be used here? Get them together in the
> church, sitting in a circle, have the pastor lead them in a spiritual,
> keeping time to the up-and-down and round-and-round rubbing
> of mercury into the backs. This was tried, but with indifferent
> success; partly, someone said, because the pastor thought he
> didn't get rubbed hard enough.[25]

The method ultimately adopted was a rubber and canvas
belt, "endowed by the doctor, it is true," chuckled Dr. Parran,
"with all the white magic of health and strength-giving quali-
ties his tongue could contrive." Each patient was ordered to
apply a prescribed amount of mercury ointment on his abdomen every morning immediately upon rising and to wear the
specially devised belts over the treated area all day. As the day
progressed, the muscular expansion and contraction of the
body's movements rubbed the mercury in. The exact instructions given to the patients, Dr. Parran recalled, went something like this:

Take this package of salve, cut it into six pieces. Every morning, smear one piece on the belt; like this. Tie the belt tightly around your waist; on the seventh day, wash yourself thoroughly and meet me here. Don't forget, one week from today, and you'll feel strong as a mule.[26]

From the outset of the program, Dr. Parran and the others had fretted over the problems posed by working with people who "had never in their lives been treated by a doctor." The clinicians were not even sure how to "start the job among folk who did not even know the word syphilis." They decided to forgo efforts to teach their patients the correct medical term for the disease, adopting instead a phrase that black people in the rural South already knew.[27]

Public health officials announced that they had come to test people for "bad blood." No doubt they had the best of intentions in using this language. By referring to "bad blood," health officers must have thought that they were speaking the rural black argot. But certain phrases have a generic quality. "Bad blood" meant different things to different people among rural blacks, and usually more than one thing to all of them. It was a catchall phrase that referred to many different ailments.

Dr. H. L. Harris, Jr., a black physician employed by the Rosenwald Fund to evaluate the syphilis control demonstrations, reported after a visit to Macon County that

the people were entirely ignorant of the character of the disease for which they were being treated, the reports submitted stating that one's blood was bad, in which case he should report to treatment at the designated center, or that the test showed that one's blood was all right, in which case no treatment was necessary.

Considerable confusion had resulted from this practice, Dr. Harris contended, because "a number of cases which had received reports that their blood was all right insisted that they were not all right." As an example, he cited the case of a man who kept insisting that he was not well. Upon closer examination, the man was found to be suffering from "phagendenic ulcers and multiple fistulae of a most distressing character," not to mention "a cyst of about 30 years' standing" and "a case of moderately advanced t.b."[28]

Professor Johnson's interviewers heard similar complaints again and again, for the failure of health officials to explain the program to the participants left a trail of confused and frustrated people in Macon County. An old woman was quite upset because her grandson had not been given "shots" by the "government doctors." When the interviewer asked why she thought that he needed them, she replied: "He look so puny." Another elderly gentleman could not reconcile being told that his wife's blood was good with her ill health: "Now 'bout those shots at the clinic. I never did understand how come they turned Ellen [the wife] down. Sick as she was they come telling her she got good blood and I know better. She's been sick as a dog many a day." A third participant complained: "Me and my wife went over to the schoolhouse and they drawed our blood and say it was good, but I can't understand why we are always so painful." Apparently convinced that "bad blood" referred to many diseases, still another participant observed: "Look like mine ought to be bad 'cause I was bothered with pellagacy [pellagra] sometime ago."[29]

Health officials ignored this confusion. Drs. Parran, Wenger, and Clark all used the terms syphilis and "bad blood" interchangeably, never concerning themselves with the multiple meanings that the latter term had for their black patients. Indeed, the practice was widespread throughout the medical profession. One of the Fund's black physicians fell into the same trap. Dr. Frost wrote: "The Negro, as found in this rural area, associates no moral or social stigmata with syphilis. 'Bad blood,' to him, was to be expected."[30]

Professor Johnson analyzed the meanings of the expression in *Shadow of the Plantation*. "In the entire 612 families interviewed there was not a single expression which seemed to connect syphilis with the sexual act," wrote Johnson. "The fact of 'bad blood' carried little social stigma and was spoken of in about the same manner as one speaks of having a 'bad heart' or 'bad teeth.'" He recalled only one interviewee who thought that "bad blood" was congenital: "I knowed I had bad blood 'cause my mamma had scrofula when I was born." And he mentioned the only participant who had "bad blood" and was aware that it might be contagious—a woman with enormous sores on her breast and arm who, trying to nurse her baby, complained: "Dese boils hurt so bad" that "dey's sore from de kernel." After treating her sores with sulfur and Vaseline, she spoke of the need to wean the infant "so de boils won't turn on it."[31]

Professor Johnson discovered that "bad blood" referred to many ailments. "Accordingly," he wrote, "treatments for bad blood were expected to cure headaches, indigestion, pellagra, sterility, sores of various sorts and general run down condition." Perhaps the best example of the total confusion that surrounded this aspect of the program was the woman who thought that the treatment caused women to have babies. "I never knowed women to have babies like they do this year," she exclaimed. "Them shots is making them babies." She knew women who had been married "a long time and this year they are all poking out." She simply could not understand why this was happening. "You reckon them shots make you have babies?" she asked the interviewer. "I sho' don't want no more and if they do I rather have bad blood."[32]

All that can be said for the use of the term "bad blood" is that it cast a broad net within the black community. Because "bad blood" subsumed a multitude of ailments under a single label, it was ideal from the standpoint of getting people to come in and be tested. The health of black people in Macon County was so poor that practically everyone suffered from some illness. They attritubed most ailments to "bad blood."

No wonder people turned out in droves for the tests and treatments. Based on what they had been told, Macon County's blacks thought they were being tested and treated for whatever ailed them. They had no reason to feel ashamed of participating in the program. But Dr. Harris, the young black physician who worked for the Fund, raised a penetrating question when he wrote Davis:

> It would be interesting to discover the effect upon clinic attendance were the terminology of bad blood replaced by a term which would identify this disease with the bad disease which the patients know under a variety of local names. The large Negro attendance is due in part to the fact that in the minds of these people there is nothing to suggest that syphilis is not entirely respectable.[33]

Dr. Harris could have been a great deal more critical in questioning the use of euphemisms by physicians. In addition to the patient's right to know as a matter of principle, the issue involved the withholding of information that was vital to the program's ultimate objective of controlling syphilis in Macon County. How was syphilis to be controlled among a people who

were not informed that they suffered from a specific, definable
disease; who were not informed that the disease was contagious; who were not told that the disease was transmitted
through sexual intercourse; and who were not informed that in
congenital syphilis the germ passes from the mother through
the placenta to the fetus?

These questions were not raised because the health officials
set very limited goals for the program. They all saw it as a
pioneering piece of public health work whose overriding objective was to prove to state and local health officers, as well as
private physicians, that rural blacks could be tested and
treated for syphilis. The Public Health Service's officers and
the Fund's officials apparently decided that there was no room
in their one-step-at-a-time approach to conduct social hygiene
work among poorly educated blacks, or to lecture them on the
prophylaxis of syphilis. The doctors wanted to get on with the
work at hand.

The results of the syphilis control survey in Macon County
were dramatic; indeed, far higher than anyone had expected.
According to figures based on a continuing survey (begun in
1926) of some twenty-five communities across the United
States, the Public Health Service placed the incidence of syphilis among patients "under observation or treatment" at "4.05
cases of syphilis per 1,000 population, the rate for whites being
4 per 1,000 and that for Negroes 7.2 per 1,000." These figures
put the infection rate for blacks at nearly twice that of whites,
but the statistics uncovered by the syphilis control demonstrations were truly alarming. The average incidence of syphilis
discovered among the six counties was 195 cases per 1,000. Macon County had by far the highest rate, a shocking 36 percent,
while Albemarle County, Virginia, boasted the lowest prevalence figure, slightly more than 7 percent.[34]

Macon County's infection rate threatened to reinforce the
image of syphilis as a black disease. Davis was concerned that
limiting syphilis control work to blacks might add to the racial
connotations of the disease. Late in March he confided to Dr.
Clark that he had been "thinking a good deal about our V.D.
demonstrations . . ." and emphasized that he wished to raise "a
general question regarding the material, particularly in its racial bearings." Expressing the Fund's concern with race relations, Davis warned: "There is bound to be danger that the im-

pression will be given that syphilis in the South is a Negro problem rather than one of both races." He was especially troubled by the possible backlash that this "really unfortunate emphasis" could have in "rousing resentment among Negro groups" in "either northern or southern communities having any large proportion of Negroes."[35]

Dr. Clark responded with caution and soothing reassurances, for he knew that the Fund would not long support a program that might damage the image of black Americans. While admitting that he could not guarantee how blacks in the North would respond, Dr. Clark ventured the opinion that "the vast majority of them will not give the matter a second thought." He was sure, however, that southern blacks supported the program. Indeed, his only regret was that whites did not participate as well. "It is a matter of cooperation and not of discrimination that the work is limited to the negroes," he explained.[36]

The tone of Dr. Clark's response to Davis was polite and proper, but when he described the whole affair to a friend, Dr. Clark charged that Davis's concern "must have been inspired by someone having an exaggerated race consciousness." Yet at least one of the patients in the treatment program shared Davis's feelings, asking a Johnson interviewer: "Why you all ain't going to everybody if you wants to find the sick ones. White folks is sick just like us."[37]

Dr. Clark denied that the high prevalence rates among blacks were due to "inherent racial susceptibility," arguing that the variations could be explained by "differences in their respective social and economic status." He made the same point about the glaring disparities among the six demonstration sites, stating that it was "difficult to explain these varying rates other than on social and economic grounds."[38]

The contrast between Albemarle County, Virginia, and Macon County, Alabama, illustrated his point perfectly. In Albemarle County public health officials found the most prosperous, healthy, and well-educated blacks whom they met anywhere in the South. The demonstration centered around Charlottesville, and because the University of Virginia was the biggest employer in the area, the town's inhabitants were shielded from the worst effects of the Great Depression. The University's medical school there had long maintained a venereal disease clinic where treatment was available day and night for both races. For those who could afford to pay, a small fee was charged for treatment; for those who could not, the treatment was free.[39]

In contrast, Macon County's blacks lived in constant poverty exacerbated by the depression. Their access to treatment facilities was extremely limited, for "there was no public hospital or treatment center open to them in the whole county." In practical terms, this meant that syphilitic patients rarely received treatment, and when they did, it was seldom continued long enough to be effective. Dr. Clark revealed that "of the total of 1,400 cases admitted to treatment but 33 of them had ever had any previous treatment and that averaged only 4.5 doses of neoarsphenamine to the individual." Moreover, the disease had become endemic and had lost its venereal quality: 62 percent of the patients admitted to the program in Macon County had congenital syphilis. Dr. Wenger told Dr. Clark in confidence that he knew "of places in the Philippines and in China where better medical services are rendered to the heathens than we find right here in Alabama under the shadow of the 'Negro Harvard'—the Tuskegee Institute."[40]

The PHS officers feared that the syphilis rate in Macon County might embarrass the Tuskegee Institute by casting doubts on its claims to being a salutary influence in the area. Early in May 1930, Dr. Wenger, accompanied by Dr. Miller (the county health officer in charge of the demonstration) paid a visit to Robert R. Moton, the principal of the Tuskegee Institute, to explain how the work was progressing, calling attention, in particular, to the alarming incidence of syphilis that was being discovered. In a letter to Dr. Clark, Dr. Wenger described what happened next: "I asked Dr. Moton what his own impression of our work was, after we told him of our findings and he calmly stated he was surprised to find it did not run 50 percent instead of 36."[41]

Dr. Moton's only request was that reports on the findings be limited to medical journals so as not to prejudice black chances for securing employment. Far from opposing the program, he suggested that it be expanded, expressing the hope that "the information if properly used might aid us in getting more funds from the States to carry on a state wide program." Dr. Wenger assured Dr. Moton that the Public Health Service would never permit such information to be publicized and that great caution would be exercised with medical groups. Dr. Wenger was confident the issue of race had been defused, explaining: "As we left I requested him to be frank with us if he heard any rumblings and that we would expect him to advise us so we would not embarrass his group in any way. This he heartily promised to do and insisted we could count on his cooperation and support."[42]

The understanding was never violated. When Dr. Clark later published an article on the Rosenwald Fund's syphilis control demonstrations, its circulation was limited to persons directly involved with medicine. There was no way that he could disguise the fact that the Public Health Service found black people living in ignorance, poverty, and disease in Macon County, but Dr. Clark made it a point to praise the Tuskegee Institute as "one of the leading examples of Negro culture in this country." Similarly, when Dr. Thomas Parran returned to the Public Health Service in 1934 as surgeon general and published *Shadow on the Land: Syphilis* a few years later, he devoted an entire chapter to the Fund's demonstrations containing no hint of criticism against black people in general or the Tuskegee Institute in particular. He blamed social and economic factors for the high incidence of syphilis uncovered among rural Negroes and went out of his way to stress that Macon County's "primitive conditions" existed "in spite of the wholesome influence of the Tuskegee Institute."[43]

Thus, PHS officers succeeded in reassuring the Rosenwald Fund and the Tuskegee Institute that the syphilis control demonstrations would not be used to attack the image of black Americans. During the final months of the demonstrations, however, they failed to persuade the Fund that further work could break the cycle of poverty and disease in Macon County.

CHAPTER **6**

"Buying Ear Muffs
for the Hottentots"

THE Rosenwald Fund monitored the Macon County
syphilis control demonstration very closely. As a pioneering health experiment, the program came under especially close scrutiny from several medical observers
whom the Fund employed to make site visits and report on
medical conditions in the field. The first inspector was Dr. H.
L. Harris, Jr., a black physician who made several trips to Macon County and whose reports to the Fund raised troubling
questions.

Accompanied by Drs. Wenger and Gill, Dr. Harris first
spent a few days in Macon County early in May 1930. Much of
what he reported to Davis had a certain tone of wide-eyed dis-
belief, for Dr. Harris had not been reared in the South, and the
conditions under which blacks there lived came as a shock. Yet
his comments proved insightful.

Inadequate planning, Dr. Harris reported, had created
problems. Valuable time had been lost during the first few
weeks by attempting to secure blood samples on a house-to-
house basis before this method was abandoned in favor of announcing a meeting place and inviting local residents to con-
gregate there for testing. Despite the change, doubts existed
about whether the program was reaching everyone who

needed it, "because . . . the efforts of the physicians have been confined to areas near the paved highways." Dr. Harris was concerned that the geographic distribution of their sample might be skewing their findings. He admitted, however, Dr. Wenger was probably right in asserting that any area in which 36 percent of those tested have syphilis "presents a problem regardless of the question of the extent to which it is representative of the population as a whole." Describing Dr. Wenger's attitude as a practical one, Dr. Harris wrote, "He still believes that any sort of approach to the problem is better than inaction."[1]

Though able to sympathize with this view, Dr. Harris was troubled by the demanding work schedule and the primitive clinical conditions. He reported that work began promptly at nine o'clock each morning and lasted until five in the afternoon with no time out for lunch. The physicians and their assistants "worked steadily and under great pressure" for months on end, creating the danger that they would not "hold up very much longer under the strain." The clinic he had observed was a Negro school building where a gasoline camp stove was used to sterilize medical equipment. "With a milling crowd of between 200 and 300 men, women and children gathered in the small building," he asserted, "satisfactory physical examinations were of course out of the question."[2]

The combination of an overworked medical staff, primitive working conditions, and the absence of thorough physical examinations raised the possibility that treatment would not be administered properly. Dr. Wenger had admitted that there had been some reactions to salvarsan that he thought were due to manufacturing defects, but Dr. Harris wondered whether "the exposure to air and the possibilities of contamination of distilled water" were at fault. "The conditions under which the salvarsan is given would also make it easy to have air emboli, arm infections, tissue extravasaction [effusion from the vein into surrounding tissue], or in fact almost any of the commoner accidents," he added. Dr. Harris also questioned the use of mercury and rubber belts under the conditions that existed in Macon County. The heat melted the mercury, making it extremely doubtful "whether as much as 5 or 10 percent of the mercury distributed ever reaches home."[3]

Patients interviewed by Johnson's team corroborated Dr.

Harris's observations. One of the older patients who witnessed the distribution of some pills at a clinic recalled a scene that bordered on chaos: "They was just throwing 'em out in the crowd, not telling 'em how to take 'em and nothing and somebody asked how to take 'em and he yelled out, 'Three times a day with a little water,' and that's all he said." Another patient sharply criticized the bedside manner, not to say competence, of the "government doctor" who treated him. "He lay our arm down like he guttin' a hog," the man complained. "I told him he hurt me. . . . He told me 'I'm the doctor.' I told him all right but this my arm."[4]

On the whole Dr. Harris's criticisms were balanced. "To the extent that the demonstration has caused county, state and federal authorities to take an interest in the health problem of a very backward Negro community," he wrote, "the effort is very much worth while." But when it came to the "possibility of obtaining cures under the existing conditions," Harris described the program's chances for success as "problematical." While impressed by "the interest and zeal of persons participating in the experiment," Dr. Harris left Macon County haunted by "the complete disproportion between the forces at hand and the extent of the problem."[5]

Dr. Wenger was disturbed by Dr. Harris's evaluation. He attempted to dismiss it as "an honest report made by a good observer on a subject he knew nothing about, after a bird's eye view of a few hours, on a group of his own people who are as foreign to him as so many Chinese." He accepted Dr. Harris's description of conditions in Macon County and agreed that black people there needed "more medical service not only for venereal diseases but for other ailments as well." Still, the tone of the report led Dr. Wenger to declare "that these people are entirely as foreign to Doctor Harris as if they came from Mars."[6]

Dr. Wenger was especially perturbed by the suggestion that the program was not reaching the right people in Macon County. People who lived in inaccessible places were coming for treatment "in wagons and on mules," giving the clinics a "good cross section of the people" who lived in the back country. "If we are not getting the infected group, as Doctor Harris intimates," bristled Dr. Wenger, "we might as well quit right now and advise Mr. Rosenwald to spend his money buying ear muffs for the Hottentots, because the money would be doing more good."[7]

Dr. Wenger had little sympathy for the criticisms about working hours and patient management. "Regarding our working hours," he thundered condescendingly, "one can't do field work among negroes who are as ignorant and stupid as these groups are and worry about lunch." Moreover, Dr. Harris's assessment of the clinics was premature if not totally misguided, for the patients he observed had never seen a doctor before. "Of course the crowd milled around like so many sheep," wrote Dr. Wenger. "The old Uncles and Aunties asked a million unnecessary questions and all that, but—a week later—at the same place, with the same patients," he boasted, "our records show we gave 157 doses of Neo, examined 28 new cases, took 66 new Wassermanns, gave 68 other medicine . . . a total of 316 patients actually given treatment in one day and were all through by 2:00 P.M." Scoffing at the idea of "any one of the personnel dying in harness," Dr. Wenger explained that "as soon as a little extra help is provided and the clinic shakes down, which means we can discourage the old Daddies and Mammies to either stay at home or go off under the trees and chew snuff, we will have more time for those who need our attention."[8]

Dr. Wenger flatly rejected Dr. Harris's suggestion that the clinicians had botched the job of administering neoarsphenamine, stating that "the air embolism myth was exposed long ago" and that infections were so rare that he had neither seen nor read of one. He admitted that tissue extravasaction had occurred in nine cases and that he personally was responsible for most of them, but insisted that this was not a bad record considering that more than two thousand injections had been given. Moreover, he denied that any of these cases was serious enough to prevent the patient from using his arm, adding, "The only reactions we have had so far were minor ones and in each instance due to patients disregarding rules about eating a heavy breakfast. We have *not* had any reaction due to drug or any other causes."[9]

Dr. Harris's comment on the distribution of mercury could not be dismissed as easily. The heat melted the mercury, Dr. Wenger explained, "because the negroes wrapped it up in their handkerchiefs or put it in their pockets and then sat around gossiping." It was a gross exaggeration to say that "only 5 or 10 percent ever reached home," he continued, "because when I discovered what was going on I went quietly among the crowd and instructed them to apply the Hg. [mercury] at once on their skins." Without commenting on whether this was an especially desirable method of administering the treatment, Dr. Wenger concluded that "very little was wasted—the patient merely got all of his weekly ration at one sitting."[10]

Final judgment of the demonstration should be suspended until the results were in, Dr. Wenger insisted. Provided they were given sufficient time and money, he told Dr. Clark, "we can convince any reasonable person who knows the present situation and the people we are handling, that our plans are practicable for the control of syphilis."[11]

Dr. Harris made a second inspection in the fall of 1930. In the first of two separate reports that he filed on this trip, he was strangely optimistic, stating that there appeared to be "no great difficulties in the way of instituting mass treatment for Negroes in the rural sections of Alabama." As long as state and local health authorities remained committed to the program, he predicted the cooperation of blacks could be secured. To date, some 1,271 cases of syphilis had been brought under treatment in the six clinics that were operating in Macon County. However, Dr. Harris expressed grave concern about "a record of untoward reactions occurring in the group," which included "three cases of Jaundice, twenty-five cases of Dermatitis, five of Oedema, nine of abdominal pain, five of vomiting, two of fainting, two of Diarrhea, nine of Infiltration, forty-three of Ptyalism, and four deaths."[12]

Of the four deaths, asserted Dr. Harris, "two ... seem entirely attributable to effects of treatment." The first case involved a patient who suffered from "arrested tuberculosis" that was "aggravated by the administration of potassium iodide, and resulted in a very rapid miliary tuberculosis from which the patient promptly died." The second patient, he explained, died of "acute nephritis." The subject "had previously shown an idiosyncracy to arsenicals and had been told never to take this form of treatment," Dr. Harris explained, adding, "This patient was unfortunately given several injections of neo-arsphenamine—an acute nephritis and death ensued."[13]

Dr. Harris offered several recommendations for reducing the risks to future patients, including thorough physical examinations, careful matching of blood tests to physical findings, and hospitalization for serious cases. He also suggested consultations with leading syphilologists to evaluate the demonstration as well as calling in experts in sociology and economics to fashion an interdisciplinary approach to community health.

By the time Dr. Harris filed his second report at the end of a week's visit in Macon County, he had grown decidedly more pessimistic. Firsthand observations had convinced him that

> it is useless to attempt to cure syphilis in the rural Negro population in Macon County, Alabama, until and unless some way is found to treat the large number of cases of tuberculosis, malnutrition and pellagra, and also to give some fundamental training in living habits, with the necessary attention provided to enable one to earn a living.

In short, the community desperately needed a comprehensive health and social welfare program. Dr. Harris therefore concluded that the syphilis control demonstration in Macon County had "accomplished practically all that can be hoped from it," and should not be extended.[14]

Davis accepted Dr. Harris's suggestions. Late in October, Davis laid the groundwork with Dr. Clark for an outside review of the syphilis control demonstrations by a team of syphilologists and a sociologist. Dr. Clark was amenable to the idea, expressing confidence that a review would be "welcomed by the State and local officials." Instead of having the sociologist visit all the demonstrations, however, Dr. Clark recommended "an intensive sociologic study in Macon County, Alabama, as a preliminary to, or at least concurrent with, our present program and its integration with the general scheme of county health promotions to include the whole county."[15]

The suggestion was adopted. After a lengthy search for the right scholar, Davis suggested Dr. Charles Johnson, chairman of the Department of Social Science at Fisk University, a sociologist whose talents were widely acclaimed and who had worked closely with the Rosenwald Fund on earlier projects. Dr. Johnson and his graduate student assistants began the study in June, concentrating on a group of families who had participated in the demonstration during the previous year.

Shadow of the Plantation was the direct result. The book included a chapter on the syphilis control demonstration that was by and large favorable to the manner in which health officials had conducted the program.[16]

The outside review by syphilologists, however, proved more difficult. The PHS resented the criticism implicit in a review by outside clinicians. Only when they, as well as state and local officials, approved the choice of the Committee on Administrative Health Practice of the American Public Health Association as the review agency did the PHS grant its approval. Sensing their hesitation, Davis stressed the essentially nonthreatening nature of the review, saying: "The point of view of the whole inquiry would be only incidentally to appraise what has been done; primarily it would suggest methods of extending this kind of work or of introducing it elsewhere."[17]

In April 1931, Davis convened a blue-ribbon panel at the Hotel Pennsylvania in New York City to confer on the sociological and medical aspects of the demonstrations. Joining Davis at the meeting were Dr. William F. Snow of the American Social Hygiene Association; Dr. Thomas Parran, Jr., who had resigned as director of the PHS's Division of Venereal Diseases to become commissioner of health of the New York State Department of Health; two members of the Committee on Administrative Health Practice of the American Public Health Association (whose full names were not recorded); and Professor Johnson and Dr. Clark as principal speakers. Following a brief report by Dr. Johnson of his findings, the participants focused on the proposed clinical review. They agreed that the evaluation should not be conducted until the demonstrations were completed.[18]

Davis surprised everyone by suggesting that Dr. Parran conduct the review. While acknowledging that Dr. Parran was "eminently qualified to make such an investigation," Dr. Clark was placed in the curious role of having to point out that "such action by him [Dr. Parran] would most likely be considered as tantamount to the Public Health Service investigating and appraising its own activity." In deference to Dr. Clark's objection, Davis recruited Dr. E. L. Keyes, the noted syphilologist and former president of the American Social Hygiene Association, to collaborate with Dr. Parran on the review. More than a year after the New York meeting, Davis informed Dr. Clark that "the reports which have been rendered to us by Drs. Parran and Keyes ... commended the projects strongly both for the important information which they had secured regarding the prevalence of syphilis and for the results in controlling it which they seemed to promise."[19]

Thus, the reviews ended in praise for the syphilis control demonstrations from a leading black sociologist and two distinguished experts on syphilis. But Dr. Harris's broader concern over the futility of extending the program beyond its original expiration date confronted Davis with a difficult decision. How much could the Fund hope to accomplish unless it was prepared to expand the program to include not only other diseases but the entire county as well? And even if the Fund financed a comprehensive health program for the county's more than twenty thousand Negroes, how long could its results be expected to last in the face of such appalling ignorance and poverty?

Referring to the widespread hunger among the patients in the field clinics, Dr. Wenger wrote Dr. Clark: "When I questioned them about an increase in weight which we should expect as their syphilis infection is brought under control they usually replied that it wasn't a question of 'bad blood' but of no blood at all, due to lack of food." One woman cut to the very heart of the issue in her parting comment to a Johnson interviewer: "I hope you all will be successful and help those that is sick. They give you shots, but I think they ought to give you something to eat."[20]

The problems confronting Macon County would have taxed the resources of an agency with a purse far deeper than the Public Health Service's. Nor was the Rosenwald Fund equipped to tackle a project of this magnitude and complexity. Even if Davis had wanted to try (and he did), the Fund's firm policy of requiring state and local agencies to share expenses precluded any large-scale expansion of the Macon County program. Neither the local nor the state officials could muster enough money for health work (especially among blacks) to meet this requirement, for public services in the state were in a period of retrenchment due to the Great Depression. But the fact that they were destitute did not prevent Alabama's health officials from besieging the Fund with numerous requests for private philanthropy to do what the state could not. Though

sympathetic to their requests, Davis was unable to remake the
Fund's policies. He could do little more than probe the rules for
any sign of flexibility.

During the next few months, state officials encouraged by
Dr. Clark floated several plans for converting the syphilis control demonstrations into a comprehensive health care program
for Macon County and eventually for the state. Each overture
failed because the state could not contribute its share of the
expenses and the Fund was reluctant to develop new programs
in the midst of the depression. Yet Davis continued to hope
that the Fund's trustees might grant an extenion of syphilis
control work in Macon County.

The syphilis control program was on the agenda of the
meeting of the Rosenwald Fund's trustees in November 1931.
In preparation for the review, Davis wrote a personal letter to
Julius Rosenwald, strongly supporting the six syphilis control
demonstrations in the South. He had, he explained, seen Surgeon General Cumming the preceding week in Montreal at the
annual meeting of the American Public Health Association.
"After one of the main conferences," Davis continued, "I went
off with the Surgeon-General for a private talk and he said, 'I
think that in getting at syphilis in this way, we have probably
hit upon the most important piece of public health work that
has ever been undertaken in the South since the campaign
against hookworm.'" Nor was the enthusiasm for the program
limited to Dr. Cumming, for Davis stated that he had talked
with several state health officers from the South and had discovered "an immense amount of interest expressed in what
had been accomplished so far."[21]

Davis stated that forty thousand people had been examined
in the six counties, approximately 25 percent of whom had
syphilis. The question before the Fund was whether to follow
up this experimental stage with a large-scale effort, or whether
the problem should be turned over to state authorities. "I don't
yet know what *we* can do about the future, until we have studied out with the Public Health Service the results in the six
counties," wrote Davis. "The baby threatens to grow so big
that he will mash us if he sits in our lap. But I don't want to
turn him loose till I'm sure he can live alone in a cold world."[22]

Davis was equally vigorous in commending the program to

the Fund's trustees. The brief that he distributed to the trustees declared that the syphilis control demonstrations had "turned out to be much more important than was anticipated." He knew, however, that the Fund would never support a comprehensive treatment program. That was clearly the responsibility of federal and state agencies. Therefore, Davis stopped short of recommending that the program be expanded until the results of the pilot program could be evaulated. He proposed an interim grant of $15,000 to carry on the work until the evaluations were completed and the program could be discussed again at the spring meeting of the trustees.[23]

The trustees gave Davis precisely what he had asked for— authorization to conduct a limited program while awaiting the results of the reviews by Professor Johnson and Drs. Parran and Keyes. As described by Davis to Dr. Clark, the trustees had been made aware of the "immense importance of the problem of syphilis . . . in a dramatic way by these studies" and were not aware that the disease ranked "as a problem of the first magnitude affecting not only public health, but the vitality of a large proportion of the population and their efficiency as workers." Moreover, Davis declared: "The work had made clear that in rural areas, it has been practicable to find cases, and a procedure seems to have been evolved which is effective in getting and keeping a substantial proportion of them under treatment."[24]

"What is the next step?" Davis asked rhetorically. The answer he proposed was an intermediary stage "between the six initial experiments and a final stage of large-scale application." During this phase, explained Davis, administrative methods would have to be standardized, the program would have to be integrated into the general health work of each community, costs would have to be determined, and a method for payment acceptable both to the public and the medical profession agreed upon. So that there would be no mistaking the Fund's desire to lift the financial burden from the shoulders of those who could least afford to pay, he added: "It is apparent in many of these rural areas that only a very small proportion of the population can afford to pay on the usual private-rate basis for the complete treatment of so expensive a disease as syphilis." Yet the solution would have to be reached by the states, for the Fund's resources would "not permit its participating in contributions to general state-wide programs of large-scale application of syphilis control."[25]

The possibility of an interim grant did not affect Macon County because the work there had lapsed at the end of August due to Alabama's chronic inability to assume its share of the cost for continuing the demonstration. But even if Alabama had been able to help defray expenses, the program would not have been extended for long. When they convened for their spring meeting, the Rosenwald Fund's trustees voted against continuing the syphilis control program. The crushing effects of the depression on public revenue in the South precluded state participation in syphilis control work at a meaningful level, and the Fund could not assume the lion's share of such an enormous burden. It, too, was experiencing financial difficulties as the market value of its stock declined. The trustees therefore decided against further support of syphilis control work in particular and new long-term commitments in general.

Dr. Clark was bitterly disappointed by the Fund's decision. "Personally I have sensed this decision for a long time," he confided to his friend Dr. Parran. "I have realized that the Trustees, and particularly the President, are more concerned with the education of the Negro than the preservation of his health." In fact, Dr. Clark revealed that he had tried to persuade Davis to cut back education grants to make more funds available for health work. "While I did not say so," he continued,

> I am inclined to question the logic of over-educating the Negro and raising up generations of what we might call white-collared Negroes, with nothing to do but get into mischief. There certainly is no great opportunity for this class of Negroes to make a living wage under existing conditions. As I look over the field where the Fund and the local communities have expended $26,000,000 for the building of schools for Negroes I cannot see any returns commensurate with this expenditure, though I am hopeful in generations to come the results thereof may be in evidence.[26]

Perhaps sensing that Dr. Clark was profoundly disturbed by the Fund's withdrawal of support, Davis tried to console him with assurances that no criticism of the Public Health Service was implied by the board's action. The decision was purely financial, reflecting the board's "blanket resolution to the effect that no new commitments will be made by us for the present." Davis concluded an important chapter in the history of public health work in the United States with these words of thanks: "The Fund has regarded it as a privilege to be able to assist during this preliminary period of study and attack upon this great problem in southern rural areas."[27]

What had the demonstrations accomplished? According to Surgeon General Cumming, everything that the Public Health Service officers responsible for the program had planned. After reviewing individual case records, monthly statistical reports, and numerous special field reports from his own officers, he proclaimed in a letter to Davis that "the primary objectives of this pioneer health work have been attained." Specifically, Dr. Cumming asserted that the demonstrations had proven

> that it is possible to make a Wassermann survey among the Negroes on a community basis, establish a true prevalence base line for future comparison, administer treatment in infectious cases in reasonably adequate amount to render them no longer infectious, and utilize Negro personnel as an integrated part of both State and local health departments in this particular field of public health endeavor.

Success on this scale deserved praise, and the surgeon general was equal to the occasion. "I am tempted to say . . . that these demonstrations will be considered epochal in the history of syphilis control in this country," Dr. Cumming declared, "and have done much to bring the health agencies of the country, both official and volunteer, to a clearer realization of the gravity and immensity of the problem."[28]

Dr. Cumming's words proved prophetic. Under the dynamic leadership of Dr. Thomas Parran, who succeeded Dr. Cumming as surgeon general in 1934, the United States launched a vigorous nationwide syphilis campaign in the late 1930s. Building upon what had been learned during the Rosenwald Fund demonstrations, the PHS covered the nation with a Wassermann dragnet. The campaign reached whites and blacks alike, as mass testing and mobile treatment clinics introduced a bold new program of public health work in the United States. Writing to an officer of the Rosenwald Fund in

1940, Dr. Wenger identified the antecedent of Dr. Parran's campaign, declaring: "I repeat and reiterate that the present national venereal disease control program is nothing but an expansion of the Rosenwald demonstrations," and added: "Personally, I shall always feel grateful to the Rosenwald Fund for initiating these programs."[29]

Yet Dr. Parran's national campaign never reached a select group of black men in Macon County, Alabama. Years before the program began, the PHS had sealed them within a scientific experiment that systematically cut them off from all treatment programs for syphilis—whether conducted by local, state, or federal health officials. Shortly after Dr. Cumming issued his glowing assessment of the Rosenwald Fund's demonstrations in 1932, PHS officers returned to Tuskegee and converted the treatment program into a nontherapeutic human experiment.

CHAPTER 7

"It Will Either Cover Us with Mud or Glory"

AFTER the Rosenwald Fund withdrew its support from the syphilis control demonstrations, Dr. Clark wrote a final report. Instead of ending the story, however, work on the report provoked an idea for a new study, one which evolved into the Tuskegee Study of Untreated Syphilis in the Negro Male—the longest nontherapeutic experiment on human beings in medical history.

The idea for the study originated with Dr. Taliaferro Clark. As Dr. Clark later explained to a colleague, he was busy analyzing data for the final report when "the thought came to me that the Alabama community offered an unparalleled opportunity for the study of the effect of untreated syphilis." Macon County had by far the highest incidence of syphilis that the Public Health Service had uncovered anywhere in the South during the syphilis control demonstrations. Dr. Clark called it "an incredibly high prevalence rate . . . 35 percent." Assuming this figure held true for black people in the remainder of the county, investigators could expect to find an ample supply of subjects for study.[1]

And precisely the right kind of subjects at that—not just syphilitic blacks, but syphilitic blacks who had not received any medical treatment. Indeed, from the standpoint of medical neglect, it would be difficult to imagine an infected population that was more pristine. Drawing upon figures compiled during the Fund's syphilis control demonstration, Dr. Clark estimated that "of the 1,400 Negroes admitted to treatment but 33 had ever had any previous treatment for syphilis." Not one of these patients had received the full course of medication that was prescribed by the Public Health Service in 1932 as standard therapy for syphilis.[2]

Macon County also offered unique medical facilities. Dr. Clark was delighted to recommend "near the center of the county, a very complete John A. Andrew Memorial Hospital at Tuskegee Institute where practically all of the necessary examinations may be made." In short, Macon County offered thousands of infected Negroes who lived outside the world of modern medicine yet close to a well-equipped teaching hospital that could easily double as a scientific laboratory.[3]

There can be no doubt that Dr. Clark would have preferred to return to Macon County to treat rather than study syphilitic blacks. The leadership and hard work that he had devoted to the syphilis control demonstrations made that clear. But new treatment programs were not possible—at least not in the foreseeable future. The Fund's withdrawal of support had seen to that. Therefore, the question that confronted the PHS in 1932 was whether it would be able to salvage anything of value from the defunct treatment program.

To Dr. Clark's mind, the best chance lay in following the treatment program with a scientific experiment. While it is true that medical scientists already knew a great deal about the natural history of syphilis, he saw merit in learning more—especially about the effects of the disease on blacks. Despite the profession's long-standing fascination with the subject, medical scientists of his day had not produced a single empirical study proving that syphilis affected blacks any differently than whites. The medical literature was full of articles positing numerous differences, to be sure, but they were all based on clinical observations, totally unsubstantiated by a rigorous application of the scientific method.

Any appropriate comparison would have to draw upon a study of untreated syphilis in whites. Medical science had already produced one. Dr. E. Bruusgaard, chief of the Venereal Disease Clinic in Oslo, Norway, published a report in a leading

German medical journal in 1929 on the fate of several hundred patients with primary or secondary syphilis who were examined but not treated at the Oslo Clinic between 1891 and 1910. Dr. Clark cited the article by name and discussed it at some length in a letter to Michael M. Davis of the Rosenwald Fund in which he outlined his plans to study untreated syphilis in blacks.[4]

The Oslo Study had yielded fascinating data on the incidence of cardiovascular compared to neurologic involvement in patients suffering from latent syphilis. Dr. Bruusgaard's findings were unequivocal: Cardiovascular damage was common, while neurologic complications were rare. The importance of these findings for Dr. Clark's proposed study of syphilis in the Negro can hardly be overstated. The most significant difference that physicians of his day posited between the effects of latent syphilis on whites and blacks was that the disease was more likely to attack the neural system in whites and the cardiovascular system in blacks. While it is true that the Oslo Study had offered no data on Negroes upon which to base a comparison, it did supply evidence that neural involvement as a complication of latent syphilis in whites was rare in comparison to cardiovascular damage. That was precisely what physicians believed to be true of blacks. Anyone who was not predisposed to find differences might have looked at these facts and concluded that the disease was affecting both races in the same way.

Dr. Clark also cited the work of Dr. Joseph Earl Moore as a precursor to the proposed study. A distinguished syphilologist and member of the famed Cooperative Clinical Group, Dr. Moore was a leading member of the faculty at Johns Hopkins University School of Medicine, where he conducted numerous studies on syphilis at the outpatient clinic. Indigent patients, many of whom had suffered years of medical neglect for their ailments, often appeared in Dr. Moore's office. He was especially interested in patients with latent syphilis who had not received any previous treatment because these individuals revealed the spontaneous evolution of the disease. Dr. Moore's investigations on latent syphilis, Dr. Clark explained to Davis, "indicate that the chances of a latent syphilitic to go through life without development of any active lesions are approximately 2 in 10." While Dr. Clark did not specify the race of Dr.

Moore's subjects, it was well known that blacks constituted a majority of the patients at Johns Hopkins's outpatient clinic.[5]

The Oslo Study and Dr. Moore's investigations were both retrospective studies—work based on case histories instead of ongoing examinations. Dr. Clark was certain that he could improve on them by conducting a prospective study, one that would be based on current examinations of living patients. "The results of these studies of case records," he explained to Davis, "suggest the desirability of making a further study of the effect of untreated syphilis on the human economy among people now living and engaged in daily pursuits." After recapitulating the unique advantages of Macon County for such a study. Dr. Clark assured Davis that it was nothing less than a "ready-made situation, if I may be permitted to use this expression . . . for carrying on the proposed study" of untreated syphilis in Negroes.[6]

There was something utterly confident, not to say casual, about Dr. Clark's use of phrases like "unparalleled opportunity" and "ready-made opportunity" in referring to the study. The phrases seemed to equate the absence of obstacles with a mandate. They were not the words of a man who entertained any ethical or moral qualms about what he was proposing. The fate of syphilitic blacks in Macon County was sealed (at least for the immediate future) regardless of whether an experiment went forward. Increasing the store of knowledge seemed the only way to profit from the human suffering there. Indeed, the PHS had only to place a de facto situation under a microscope to convert the region into a scientific laboratory.

Such a study would be an expression of concern for Negro health problems, keeping the PHS involved as a vital force in promoting medical attention to blacks. The more damaging the disease was shown to be, the more pressure would build on southern legislatures to fund treatment programs. The study would also permit the PHS to maintain the momentum of public health work in Alabama by continuing the close working relationships with state and local health officials, not to mention black leaders at the Tuskegee Institute.

Dr. Clark knew that the experiment entailed risks to the subjects. While most of the procedures were harmless, the physical examination called for lumbar punctures to diagnose neural syphilis. To obtain a sample of fluid, a rather large needle had to be inserted directly into the spinal cord. The procedure itself was painful, and patients often suffered severe headaches as aftereffects. In rare cases, lumbar punctures resulted in paralysis or even death. Dr. Clark obviously concluded that the benefits to be derived to science from the experiment outweighted the risks to the men.

In the beginning, Dr. Clark did not intend that anyone be denied treatment on a long-term basis; the experiment was supposed to last only six months to a year. Whatever thought he may have given to defining "acceptable risks" did not have to be weighed against the ethical propriety of withholding treatment from people if it became generally available in the future. He was not contemplating a longitudinal study, merely a short-term affair.

Dr. Clark's freedom to pursue his scientific curiosity revealed much about the insular position physicians had fashioned for themselves within American society. By the 1930s, medicine had emerged as an autonomous, self-regulating profession whose members were in firm control of the terms, conditions, content, and goals of their work. Indeed, from a sociological standpoint, medicine had emerged as the quintessential profession.[7]

Resistance to lay control was the cornerstone of medicine. If professional status meant anything to American physicians, it was the right to set the standards and define the terms of medical education, licensing, and practice—in short, they had constructed a monopoly that left them as the sole arbiters of medical affairs. And while the profession was hardly monolithic, it was remarkably homogeneous. There was little danger that the values and attitudes of physicians would be tested against those of the larger society.

Critics charged that doctors had a self-serving sense of professionalism, one which did not pay enough attention to the end product of the medical system—the quality and accessibility of health care. Of special concern was the profession's failure to regulate or even monitor the work of licensed practitioners. When pressed on these issues, physicians invariably pointed to the regulatory role of local medical societies. Defenders of the profession also pointed to state licensing boards, reinforced by several layers of professional associations ranging from local medical societies to national organizations such

as the American Medical Association. But the truth remained
that physicians of the 1930s had managed to free themselves of
most vestiges of lay control, and there was no gainsaying the
fact that the medical system that they had constructed was far
more concerned with controlling who was permitted to practice medicine than with reviewing the work of licensed practitioners.[8]

Peer review was supposed to regulate medicine. While
critics charged that this left the fox to guard the henhouse, physicians argued that they (and they alone) possessed the specialized knowledge necessary to evaluate medical questions. For
matters that were not the exclusive domain of medicine, physicians were quick to point out that they were moral people
whose judgment on nontechnical issues could be trusted.

It was simply assumed that individual practitioners would
divine correctly the ethical code of their colleagues and act accordingly. But what if they did not? "Good medicine" during
the 1930s was what physicians in any particular locale said it
was, not that anything approaching a definition had to be
spelled out. On the contrary, physicians stoutly resisted putting anything on paper resembling a statement of what constituted acceptable standards of professional competence for licensed practitioners. The question of ethical standards was, for
all intents and purposes, *terra incognita*. This reluctance to define sound medical practice or to articulate a code of ethical
behavior was entirely consonant with their overriding concern
with preserving professional autonomy. Definitions would
have imposed limits and invited review, but silence nurtured a
universe of tacit approval. Perhaps, too, the problem of defining with any degree of exactitude what constituted "sound
medical practice" simply staggered a profession largely composed of technicians and almost wholly comprised of people
uninterested in theorizing. Thus, an unwritten law evolved
that one physician's professional competence and standards of
ethical propriety were about as good as another's.[9]

Not surprisingly, licensed physicians seldom passed judg-
ments on each other. Rarely did they question and hardly ever
did they censor the professional conduct of colleagues. Abuses
had to be blatant, arousing a public that was characteristically
docile, before medical societies would investigate, let alone
take action against, one of their own. Apparently, physicians

reasoned that they could not censure a colleague without undermining the public's confidence in the profession.

Medical scientists of the 1930s enjoyed as much autonomy as physicians in private practice—perhaps more. For if lay people did not possess enough knowledge to review intelligently the professional competence of the average practitioner, how much more inscrutable were the activities of scientists who were involved in highly specialized research? Medical scientists were seldom asked to justify projects or investigative methods. Spokesmen for the lay public had neither the knowledge nor the opportunity to review the research projects of medical scientists.[10]

Moreover, the public's attitude toward medical research was anything but antagonistic—respect tinged with awe would be closer to the mark. Medical science had revolutionized the ability of Dr. Clark's generation of physicians to diagnose accurately and treat effectively a host of illnesses. A pro-science bias informed the reception that medical researchers could reasonably expect to encounter in their limited and infrequent contacts with the public.

Scientific investigators formed an elite group within the medical community, one whose distinctions rested squarely on the unique nature of their work. Research required a special turn of mind and highly developed expertise in specific bodies of knowledge, attributes that set scientists apart from practitioners. Researchers alone decided which projects needed to be undertaken. Thus, medical scientists enjoyed considerable autonomy and deference within the profession.[11]

In medical research, as with medical practice, work was evaluated by peer review. The scientific method provided the yardstick for measuring the validity of investigations, and the assessments of fellow workers determined which researchers received kudos. Results were what counted. Many investigators whose work involved nontherapeutic research on human beings no doubt were enlightened souls who viewed their patients as people and thought in terms of "informed consent" decades before the term was coined, but there was no system of normative ethics on human experimentation during the 1930s that compelled medical researchers to temper their scientific curiosity with respect for the patients' rights. Here, as in private practice, a formless relativism had settled over the profession, holding that one investigator's methods of conducting an experiment were about as ethical as another's.

Peer review was a total travesty when private practitioners scrutinized public health programs. Private physicians and their associations routinely monitored the activities of public health officials with keen interest, not so much out of concern whether the health programs were offering sound, ethical medicine as whether these programs threatened private medicine's economic interests. As long as public health officers limited their work to the poor, they had little to fear from private physicians, provided, of course, that certain precautions were followed. Standard operating procedure of the Public Health Service dictated that federal officers first consult with all concerned medical authorities, both public and private, before entering their jurisdictions to initiate new programs.[12]

Dr. Clark understood that he lived in a goldfish bowl within the medical profession and had grown accustomed to proceeding prudently. He recognized at the outset that Macon County's private physicians would have to be won over before the experiment could begin. In addition, Dr. Clark knew he had to have the support and cooperation of officials from the Alabama State Board of Health, the Macon County Health Department, and the Tuskegee Institute, the home of the John A. Andrew Memorial Hospital.

After discussing the idea with several colleagues within the Public Health Service, Dr. Clark, accompanied by his trusted lieutenant, Dr. O. C. Wenger, traveled to Alabama in September 1932 to lay the groundwork for the proposed study. The first stop was Montgomery, where they met with two colleagues from the syphilis control demonstrations, Dr. J. N. Baker, the state health officer, and Dr. D. C. Gill, the director of the Bureau of Preventable Diseases. Dr. Clark's remarks could not have been detailed, for he had yet to work out the study's protocol. No doubt he was explicit in stating that the purpose of the experiment was to learn how untreated syphilis affects Negroes (he had said that much in his letters arranging the meeting), but his comments about the exact procedures to be employed must have been vague.

Neither Dr. Baker nor Dr. Gill objected to the study in principle, but Dr. Baker extracted an important concession from Dr. Clark in exchange for his approval and cooperation: Everyone examined and found to be syphilitic would have to be treated. How much treatment was the problem. Since Dr. Clark planned to finish the study within six to eight months, it would have been pointless for Dr. Baker to have insisted upon the full program of treatment necessary to cure syphilis. That required more than a year to complete.[13]

No doubt the state officials were most concerned with patients who were infectious. Realistically, the best Dr. Baker could hope to extract from the situation was a short program of treatment, not nearly enough to induce a radical cure in patients but perhaps enough to render some at least temporarily noninfectious. Such a compromise would have been consonant with the average health official's overriding concern with contagion. Judging from the amount of treatment actually administered after the study got under way, Dr. Baker apparently decided to settle for a minimal program of therapy. Every patient who was examined and found to have syphilis, including those who were selected for the study, was supposed to receive eight doses of neoarsphenamine and some additional treatment with mercury pills, unless treatment with either drug was contraindicated on medical grounds.

The record does not reveal why Dr. Baker insisted on treatment. He probably thought that physicians should treat patients who were diseased and wanted to take advantage of the services of the medical personnel who wished to conduct the experiment. Chronically short staffed, he needed all the help he could get, especially in the state's rural areas where the public health movement had made relatively little progress. Another motive may have been a desire to conceal the true purpose of the study from Macon County's white population. Studying syphilis instead of treating it might not make sense to them. The Rosenwald Fund's syphilis control demonstration had increased public awareness of what a menace the disease posed in the area. Dr. Baker may have reasoned that white employers would not cooperate unless the physicians offered some relief.

Dr. Baker was adamant that the experiment not be administered by the officers of the Public Health Service working alone. He did not wish to antagonize the private physicians of Macon County who might feel threatened if public health officers started providing free treatment for black patients. Therefore, Dr. Clark would have to find local sponsors for the study, physicians who would appear to be in charge of treatment and whose affiliation with the study would help reassure the local medical establishment.

The Tuskegee Institute was the obvious solution. The white physicians of Macon County had grown accustomed to watching the staff at Andrew Hospital, all of whom were black, conduct various programs for Negroes in conjunction with local and state health officials. The Institute's cooperation would permit the study to go forward without arousing the fears and suspicions of private physicians. The participation of black physicians would also help secure the cooperation of subjects for the experiment, for the Tuskegee Institute commanded trust and respect among the black population of Macon County.

Dr. Baker's demands unquestionably worked to the advantage of the study. If the Public Health Service succeeded in persuading the physicians at Andrew Hospital to cooperate, the old syphilis control demonstration team of clinicians would be reunited and the study would have the appearance of a revival of syphilis control work. The true purpose of the experiment would be totally obscured, leaving the investigators free to trade upon the good will and trust that the Rosenwald Fund's syphilis control demonstration had generated among the black people of the county and their white employers. Dr. Clark quickly saw the potential of presenting the study to the lay community of Macon County in these terms and apparently was not the least bit embarrassed by the deceit. After the study had actually gotten under way, he confided to Davis of the Rosenwald Fund: "In order to secure the cooperation of the planters in this section it was necessary to carry on this study under the guise of a demonstration and provide treatment for those cases uncovered found to be in need of treatment."[14]

Drs. Clark and Wenger emerged from the meeting in Montgomery convinced that the Tuskegee Institute was the key to the study's success. Dr. Gill drove them the forty miles or so down to Tuskegee where they met with Dr. Eugene H. Dibble, medical director of the Tuskegee Institute and head of Andrew Hospital.

Dr. Clark did most of the talking. Supported at every turn by Drs. Wenger and Gill, he made a forceful and apparently persuasive case for Dr. Dibble to join them. Dr. Clark then returned to Washington, D.C., but Dr. Wenger remained in Alabama for another day. He used the additional time well. He and Dr. Gill met again with Dr. Dibble to learn whether Dr. Dibble had decided to cooperate with Dr. Raymond Vonderlehr, the Public Health Service officer whom Drs. Clark and Wenger had selected to be in charge of the study.[15]

The second meeting ended with a pledge of cooperation from Dr. Dibble. Dr. Dibble volunteered the services of his interns and nurses to administer syphilis treatments under Dr. Vonderlehr's supervision; the loan of an office and examination room for conducting the clinical examinations and lumbar punctures; and the use of the hospital's X-ray equipment and technicians, provided the PHS supplied the plates. He also promised to meet with officials of the Macon County Board of Health and private physicians in the region to explain the study and avoid any possible misunderstanding.[16]

All that remained was for Dr. Robert R. Moton to approve the Tuskegee Institute's cooperation. Dr. Dibble worked hard to win him over. He told the principal that the experiment would not cost the Institute anything, and stressed that the surgeon general had personally requested their cooperation. Dr. Dibble also predicted the study would have "world wide significance" and would offer valuable training to their interns and nurses. For years the Tuskegee Institute had offered a program in nurses' training and Dr. Dibble had been intimately involved with that program. Negro nurses, however, often had a hard time securing employment even in good times because of racial prejudice. With the retrenchments in public health work that accompanied the depression, these difficulties had increased. Dr. Dibble was therefore understandably elated that Dr. Clark had authorized him "if the thing goes thru' to appoint one of our own nurses to assist . . . in carrying on this work."[17]

The advantages to his teaching hospital were foremost in his mind when Dr. Dibble added that their nurses and interns would benefit greatly from the training they would receive through working in the study. Summarizing his position in a letter to Dr. Moton, Dr. Dibble wrote:

> While this would not bring any additional compensation to our hospital, it would certainly not cost us any more and would offer

very valuable training for our students as well as for the Interns.
As Dr. Clark said, our own hospital and the Tuskegee Institute
would get credit for this piece of research work. He also predicts
that the results of this study will be sought after the world over.
Personally, I think we ought to do it.[18]

Dr. Dibble's arguments no doubt prepared Dr. Moton for
the personal appeal that arrived a few days later from the surgeon general, Dr. H. S. Cumming. Like Dr. Clark, the surgeon
general emphasized the relationship between the PHS's interest in studying untreated syphilis and the previous syphilis
treatment program. Dr. Cumming asserted that the high concentration of untreated syphilis victims, coupled with the anticipated cooperation of Andrew Hospital, "offers an unparalleled opportunity for carrying on this piece of scientific
research which probably cannot be duplicated anywhere else
in the world." Stressing the importance of Andrew Hospital to
the experiment, Dr. Cumming told Dr. Moton: "You can readily see, therefore, that the success of this 'important study' really hinges on your cooperation."[19]

Dr. Clark must have been confident of the Tuskegee Institute's support because he started making arrangements for the
study before Dr. Moton replied to Dr. Cumming's formal request. First he ordered Dr. Wenger at the Venereal Disease
Clinic in Hot Springs, Arkansas, to send Dr. Dibble all the supplies he could spare. Then he sent Dr. Dibble appointment
forms to be completed by the nurse whom Dr. Dibble had selected. So that there would be no misunderstanding concerning the nature of her work, Dr. Clark informed Dr. Dibble:
"You will note that she has been designated as scientific assistant because her duties will be essentially those of an assistant
in an important piece of scientific research." Her salary was to
be computed at the rate of $1,800 a year, $600 of which was to
reimburse her for transporting patients to and from the clinic
in her automobile. One hundred dollars a month, plus expenses, was a handsome salary for a nurse to command in Alabama in 1932, especially a black nurse.[20]

Yet Dr. Clark was still anxious about Dr. Moton's decision.
"I would feel much more comfortable and be in position to take
more definite action if I can be assured that you will be in position to make the necessary facilities for examination availa-

ble," he wrote Dr. Dibble, "and will be able to have one of your men carry out the relatively small amount of treatment at designated points in the county required by Doctor Baker of the State Board of Health as a prerequisite to his approval of the project." A few days later Dr. Clark received a telegram from Dr. Dibble stating that Dr. Moton had approved all plans for the study. Dr. Moton's consent virtually guaranteed the study would go forward.[21]

With arrangements in Alabama concluded, Dr. Clark turned his attention to formulating a protocol for the study. Previously, he really had not given the matter much thought. Apart from the vague notion of studying the effects of untreated syphilis in Negroes, Dr. Clark did not have a clear idea of what he wanted to accomplish or how to go about it. Talks with fellow officers in the PHS had centered on the need for and feasibility of the proposed study, not on specifics. Now he needed to decide a number of questions. How many people were necessary to constitute a statistically reliable sample? Should the study be limited to men or women, or should both sexes be included? What age groups should be singled out for study? How long should the subjects have had syphilis? What procedures would be employed to determine the scientific basis for diagnosing the disease and its effects on the subjects? How long were the subjects to be followed, or, put another way, how long was the experiment to last? What, if anything, was to be done for the subjects when it ended?

Dr. Clark did not try to frame a protocol alone. In keeping with the best scientific tradition of consultation with peers, he solicited advice and criticisms on the general plans he and Dr. Wenger had worked out together. The experts he consulted were members of the Cooperative Clinical Group, an association of medical researchers composed of the most distinguished syphilologists in the United States. That Dr. Clark should seek help from these men was not surprising. He had worked closely with them on various research projects ever since the association was organized.

Late in September Dr. Clark journeyed to Baltimore and met with Dr. Joseph Earle Moore and Dr. Albert Keidel of the Venereal Disease Clinic of The Johns Hopkins University School of Medicine. The plan Dr. Clark presented to them was little more than a skeleton, badly in need of critical review.

According to his notes on the meeting, Dr. Clark told them about his desire "to assemble as many adult Negroes as possible at one place in the selected communities or plantations and do a preliminary Wassermann." The blood samples would then be sent for evaulation to the state laboratory in Montgomery. The positive cases would be brought to Andrew Hospital for thorough examinations consisting "of a complete history, particularly with regard to the date of infection, the presence or absence of clinical indications of syphilitic activity, a Wassermann re-check, X-ray of the chest and of the bones when indicated, and finally a routine spinal puncture on as many cases as will consent to submit to this operation."[22]

Dr. Keidel apparently said little, but Dr. Moore made several useful suggestions. Instead of including both men and women, he recommended limiting the study to males. Neither chivalry nor devotion to the double standard lay behind this restriction. He wanted women excluded, Dr. Clark's notes explained, "because it is next to impossible to get reliable information as to the date of infection of syphilis in the female." Here, Dr. Moore had merely reminded Dr. Clark of what every good clinician knows: women often fail to recognize the early symptoms of the disease because their genitals are largely internal and because the early symptoms are frequently mild and can easily be mistaken for unrelated problems involving vaginal itching and burning. By the time more severe symptoms develop and force them to seek medical care, women often learn to their dismay that the disease is well advanced. They also find it hard to pinpoint for their physicians when the early symptoms of the disease appeared, making it difficult to determine when the disease was contracted.[23]

Dr. Moore further recommended restricting the study to males who were thirty years of age or older. Admitting younger men, he feared, would reduce the chances for observing the late clinical manifestations of the disease, specifically the neurologic and cardiovascular complications that often appear in patients whose infections are of long duration. According to Dr. Clark's notes, Dr. Moore argued for the exclusion of younger men "because any data collected on cases of but few years duration may not be considered as showing the effect of untreated syphilis."[24]

The most important suggestion made by Dr. Moore concerned the need for securing accurate clinical histories. Dr. Moore suggested that the men be brought "in batches" to the clinic where a careful history would be taken from each individual in order to exclude all who could not give a clear history of the date of their infections. By way of explanation, Dr. Clark added: "He considers this information of prime importance because the conclusions based on individuals with an indefinite history of the date of infection will subject our findings to very adverse criticism." To save time and avoid unnecessary risks to the men, Dr. Moore advised against routine spinal punctures, suggesting that the procedure be limited to subjects in whom neurologic involvement was suspected.[25]

A few days after their meeting in Baltimore, Dr. Moore sent a detailed blueprint of what needed to be done. The Wassermann negative cases had to be examined as well as the positive (syphilitic) cases. "This inclusion of all males is essential," Dr. Moore explained, "because of the fact that the spontaneous evolution of untreated syphilis may lead to the spontaneous production of negative Wassermann reaction in a considerable proportion, perhaps twenty-five percent, of cases. If you rely on a Wassermann survey only," he cautioned, "you will miss this group entirely when, as a matter of fact, they may prove to be the most important group of the lot." In other words, Wassermann tests alone could not be trusted; they had to be supplemented by thorough clinical histories.[26]

Dr. Moore's follow-up letter dwelled at length on the selection of what he called "clinical material." When dealing with blacks the "mere history of a penile sore only would not be adequate [in making a diagnosis of syphilis], inasmuch as the average negro has had as many penile sores as rabbits have offspring." A case history from this population should "be accepted as positive only if it includes a story of the lesions of secondary syphilis following at an appropriate interval after a genital sore."[27]

Dr. Moore specifically warned against contaminating the experiment by admitting subjects who had received treatment. He stressed that "patients who have been previously treated should be excluded from the detailed survey." Provided that the clinicians who conducted the study canvassed the county thoroughly, Dr. Moore predicted there would be no difficulty finding "perhaps two or three hundred males" who fulfilled his selection criteria completely.[28]

Following selection of the subjects, Dr. Moore recommended a complete medical history that would "lay particular stress on the possible occurrence of bone or cardiovascular symptoms," complications he thought were "especially common in the negro." The fifteen-step physical examination he then outlined was incredibly thorough, dictating a medical evaluation of patients from the pupils of their eyes to the soles of their feet. He also recommended laboratory tests including urine analysis, blood Wassermanns, spinal fluid examinations, and X-ray and fluoroscopic examinations of the chest.[29]

Aware that his suggestions would require a huge amount of work, Dr. Moore expressed confidence that the study "would be of immense value." The race of the subjects virtually guaranteed it. "Syphilis in the negro is in many respects almost a different disease from syphilis in the white," declared Dr. Moore.[30]

No statement from Dr. Moore could have had greater significance for the future of the study. By the 1930s science had settled the question of whether there were any racial differences in the disease's etiology with a resounding "No!" Similarly, clinicians agreed that treatment was the same for both races. But belief in the notion that syphilis developed differently in blacks and whites ran through every echelon of the medical profession. To have a syphilologist of Dr. Moore's stature make that statement lent scientific respectability to more than half a century of clinical speculation. The meaning was not lost on Dr. Wenger, who wrote Dr. Clark: "I am glad to see in print for the first time by a clinician of Doctor Moore's experience and reputation the statement 'Syphilis in the negro is in many respects almost a different disease from syphilis in the white.' " Dr. Wenger added pointedly, "This study will emphasize these differences."[31]

As plans for the study neared completion, Dr. Clark had to decide which of Dr. Moore's suggestions should, or could, be incorporated. He and Dr. Wenger immediately agreed to limit the study to men over a specified age. Dr. Wenger argued that the minimum age should be twenty instead of Dr. Moore's recommended thirty. Based upon figures from the Rosenwald Fund's treatment program, the highest incidence of syphilis in men was between the ages of twenty-five and thirty. Failure to include men who were in their twenties, Dr. Wenger argued, would deprive the study of its largest pool of potential subjects. Dr. Wenger also wanted "to see included cases who have had their infection 5 years or longer because between 5 and 10 years we might conceivably find definite early pathology, especially in a group who have had no treatment." In the end, Dr. Clark decided on a compromise of twenty-five as the minimum age, stipulating that men who had not had their infections for at least five years be excluded from the study.[32]

More difficult to accommodate was Dr. Moore's suggestion that the study include negative as well as positive Wassermann cases. Dr. Wenger was adamantly opposed to the idea. He emphatically denied that any one or two physicians, regardless of their training or experience, could carry out under field conditions the detailed and accurate examinations that Dr. Moore's plan demanded. Dr. Clark agreed. Despite Dr. Moore's warning that failure to include Wassermann negative cases might cost the study up to 25 percent of the potential population pool suffering from untreated latent syphilis, Dr. Clark decided to restrict the study to patients with positive Wassermann tests.[33]

Dr. Wenger also rejected Dr. Moore's advice on the use of clinical histories to fix the date of infection, especially his insistence that the appearance of a secondary rash had to be used to confirm the syphilitic origin of penile sores. While conceding that it might be feasible "to get the year and perhaps the month of the primary lesion in these cases," Dr. Wenger argued that it would not always be possible to document the appearance of secondary rashes because

> so many of these cotton-patch negroes have had scabies and other skin infections. . . . Filthy mouths, infected tonsils, Vincent's angina, and bad teeth cause mucous membrane lesions of the mouth which might be confused by the patient with secondary manifestations. Last, but not least, is the fact that skin manifestations in the negro skin are often hard to discern because the important distinction of colors is absent. We must remember that these patients rarely take a bath, sleep in their filthy underwear, and the rash may be so transient as to escape the patient's notice.

Again, Dr. Wenger proved persuasive. Men who could not re-call the appearance of a secondary rash were included in the study and the primary lesion was used to date the onset of in-fection.[34]

While refusing to accept suggestions from Dr. Moore that were either impossible or impracticable, Dr. Clark was not simply looking for shortcuts. He disagreed on purely clinical grounds with Dr. Moore's recommendation that spinal punc-tures be restricted to cases suspected of neural involvement. He argued, as did Dr. Wenger, that routine spinal punctures were necessary to prevent asymptomatic cases of neurosyphilis from going undiagnosed. Dr. Clark therefore decided to per-form spinal punctures on as many of the men as possible. Dr. Wenger justified their departures from Dr. Moore's advice by pleading extenuating circumstances. "We are attempting, with limited personnel, under field conditions a study which ordi-narily should be made in a medical center," he wrote Dr. Clark, "but since in such centers it would be hard to find the same group of untreated cases we are justified in taking Mahomet to the mountain, since there is no way of bringing the mountain to Mahomet."[35]

With the protocol completed, only one task remained before the study could begin—securing the consent of Macon County's private physicians. In response to Dr. Wenger's nudgings, Dr. Gill met with the Macon County Board of Health. "They agreed to sponsor it under the condition that some treatment was ad-ministered to these people," wrote Dr. Gill. How much treat-ment was not specified, but with the consent of the local physi-cians, expressed through their representative body, the Macon County Board of Health, the last obstacle in the path of the study was removed.[36]

The same attention to detail with which Dr. Clark com-pleted arrangements in Alabama marked the care with which he selected the clinical team. Dr. Raymond A. Vonderlehr was to be in charge of the field work. Dr. Clark knew his abilities well, having served as the chairman of the Public Health Serv-ice committee that examined Dr. Vonderlehr for admission as a career officer a few years earlier. In fact, he had once de-scribed Dr. Vonderlehr to a European colleague as "one of our most promising younger officers."[37]

At the time of his appointment to head the Alabama study, Dr. Vonderlehr was thirty-five years old and a seven-year veteran of the PHS. His background in syphilology was impressive. He had served for two years as an instructor of dermatology and syphilology at the Medical College of Virginia in Richmond, and, in addition, he had completed extensive postgraduate work in several of the finest clinics in Europe where he concentrated on cardiovascular syphilis, the complication of tertiary syphilis that Dr. Clark was most eager to explore in the Negro. And like Dr. Clark, he was a southerner, a native Virginian who had attended the University of Virginia School of Medicine.

Joining Dr. Vonderlehr was Eunice Rivers, the young black nurse whom Dr. Dibble had selected to serve as special scientific assistant. She worked as the supervisor of night nurses on Dr. Dibble's staff, but her roots in the Tuskegee Institute ran much deeper.

Nurse Rivers was born in 1899 in Jakin, Georgia, the first of three daughters of Albert and Henrietta Rivers. Her mother died of pneumonia when Eunice was a child, and her father exerted the dominant influence in her early life. Although he could barely write his name, Nurse Rivers remembered him as "a very progressive man" who did not want his daughters "to have to scuffle as he did."[38]

Albert Rivers's belief in education was pervasive. Because the local schools for blacks were notoriously poor, he sent his daughters to stay with an aunt in another Georgia community where the schools were better. But maintaining them there was expensive. To raise the necessary money, Albert was forced to till their small family farm in the evenings after working full days in a sawmill. He took extraordinary pride in his daughters' education, and at the end of every school year when they returned home for the summer, he demanded a full account of their progress. Those sessions formed vivid memories for Nurse Rivers, who later recalled with love and gratitude how her father "would sit down and give us examinations!"[39]

As the oldest child Eunice was expected to lead the way for her sisters. Along with hundreds of other black parents of his generation who wanted their children to have opportunities that they had been denied, Albert Rivers enrolled his daughter in the Tuskegee Institute in 1918. She took handicrafts during her first year at Tuskegee, but switched, at her father's insistence, to nursing in her second year.

There were few formal courses in nursing. The heart of the program was on the job training at Andrew Hospital, where the student nurses worked under the strict supervision of the hospital's professional staff. In addition to imbibing a large dose of the "up by our bootstraps" philosophy that permeated the campus, Eunice learned two things that formed the core of her sense of professionalism: a nurse must treat all her patients equally, providing the best care possible to every patient without regard to the patient's social status or ability to pay for the services rendered; and a nurse must follow the doctor's orders—completely, unequivocally, and to the letter. Theoretically, no conflicts would arise between the tenets, but her instructors at Tuskegee, especially Dr. Dibble, left no doubt in her mind what to do if a clash did occur: obey the doctor's orders![40]

Following graduation in 1922, Nurse Rivers left the cloistered setting of Tuskegee and entered the larger medical world where she encountered a profession dominated by white males. Compared with many black nurses who were prevented by racial prejudice from pursuing a career in public health, she was extremely fortunate. She immediately went to work for the state of Alabama, which, in conjunction with the federal government, was developing a program of social services for the state's rural black population. Accompanied by a home economics teacher and a farm agent, Nurse Rivers spent the next few years driving all over the state in a specially equipped truck called a "movable school." They concentrated on the rural areas, living for about a week at a time with individual families in whose homes they taught classes. Nurse Rivers recalled emphasizing "just plain home nursing and cleanliness and hygiene because . . .[the people were] very, very poor."[41]

After a few years Nurse Rivers was transferred from the movable-schools project to a challenging new position in the state health department's Bureau of Vital Statistics. Alabama was not included in the registration area for the federal census as of the mid-1920s, and the state's health officials were eager to collect accurate data on births and deaths in the black population. Since most black births were attended by midwives instead of physicians, there were few records of black births. Nurse Rivers's job was to bring the largely unregulated profession of midwifery under supervision, or, as she put it, "to see each midwife, help her get her records straight, show her how to make out a birth certificate, and also some hygiene to use in deliveries." It was a big job that required visits to all of the counties in the Black Belt of Alabama, and she had not completed it when financial retrenchment in the state's budget, precipitated by the Great Depression, forced state officials to discontinue her position in 1931.[42]

That was not a good year for anyone to be looking for work. It was an especially bad time for a black woman trained as a public health nurse. All across the South state budgets for public health work plummeted in the face of ever worsening conditions. Given the acute shortage of positions that were open in her field, Nurse Rivers was indeed lucky when Dr. Dibble offered to return her to Tuskegee as the supervisor of night nurses at Andrew Hospital. She had held that position for eight months when Dr. Dibble asked her to accept Dr. Clark's position as a special scientific assistant to the Public Health Service on detail in Macon County for a study of untreated syphilis in the Negro male. Dr. Dibble selected her for the assignment, he later explained to Dr. Moton, because she "has personally done more effective Public Health work . . . than any of our group."[43]

Nurse Rivers was not certain she could handle the assignment. While she had assisted with the Rosenwald Fund's syphilis control demonstration in Macon County, she was concerned that she did not know enough syphilology to serve as a "special scientific assistant" in a study of this sort and openly expressed her self-doubts to Dr. Dibble. Nearly a half century later his reply still rang in her ears: " 'Oh, Nurse Rivers, you can do whatever they want done. I don't have to worry about that.' " That was all the encouragement she needed, for as Nurse Rivers later admitted, "I was so glad to go off night duty that I would have done anything." She accepted the appointment. And with Nurse Rivers safely on board, the planning stage was completed and the study was ready to begin.[44]

It had taken less than a month to conclude the necessary arrangements. The staff had been selected, and one by one, the Alabama State Board of Health, the Tuskegee Institute, and the

Macon County Board of Health had agreed to cooperate. Dr. Clark's plan called for a six- to eight-month study which included (at the insistence of Alabama's state health officials backed up by demands from Macon County's private physicians) at least a partial program of treatment for everyone examined. Thus, what had begun as a strictly nontherapeutic study of the effects of untreated syphilis on blacks had been transformed into a program with some provision for treatment.

Dr. Clark had gone to extraordinary lengths to invite criticism of the experiment. With the exception of Dr. Moton, the principal of the Tuskegee Institute, each of the men with whom Dr. Clark had discussed the study was a physician, and their willingness to see it go forward stemmed, at least in part, from the proscience bias of the medical community. No one had argued that the proposed study was morally wrong. Indeed, it is doubtful whether many physicians in 1932 would have objected to the study. The consensus was that the experiment was worth doing, and in a profession whose members did not have a well-developed system of normative ethics, consensus formed the functional equivalent of moral sanction.

Dr. Clark was delighted that the work was about to begin, boasting to a friend: "I am confident the results of this study, if anywhere near our expectation, will attract world wide attention." Dr. Wenger's hopes ran equally high. With more foresight than he could have possibly realized, he predicted: "It will either cover us with mud or glory when completed."[45]

CHAPTER 8

"Last Chance for Special Free Treatment"

DR. Vonderlehr arrived in Montgomery on October 19, 1932, following a miserable drive from the nation's capital. He had left Washington, D.C., a few days earlier hoping to vacation briefly in the Smoky Mountains on the way down. But it rained the entire trip, giving him a taste of the foul weather that was to hamper the study over the months ahead.

Waiting for him in Montgomery was Dr. Wenger, whom Dr. Clark had temporarily detailed to Alabama. Together they called on Drs. Baker and Gill to arrange last-minute details so the study could get under way within a day or two. Reassured that the experiment still enjoyed the approval of the state's ranking health officials, they drove the forty miles or so down to Tuskegee and checked into the Carr Hotel, where they took their meals and lodged throughout their stay. They really had no choice; there was no other hotel for whites in town.

After talking with Dr. Dibble and Nurse Rivers, they decided to meet with several prominent white planters. Their help was needed to spread the word to Macon County's black people that a new syphilis control demonstration was about to begin. Following these conferences, Dr. Vonderlehr reported to Dr. Clark that "the planters are quite anxious that the study, and especially the treatment, progress, and we are planning to make the usual talks to colored audiences." Once again, the PHS clinicians proposed to use the black schools and churches of Macon County to assemble audiences and announce that the "government doctors" were returning to give free blood tests.[1]

The plan worked. From little communities with names like Haraway, Notasulga, and Shorter, the black people of Macon County turned out in droves. In some areas they assembled in little white frame schoolhouses, many of which had been built with the aid of the Rosenwald Fund. In other places they gathered in churches; or, if there was no suitable meeting place nearby, they simply congregated beneath a big tree by the side of the road to await the arrival of the "government doctors."

According to Nurse Rivers, they were "overflooded with people coming in to get their blood drawn." Most had never had a blood test and had no idea what one was. They cooperated, she explained, because "it was something new and was some medical attention that they had never had," adding that most of them "had never been to a doctor—never seen one." Naturally, they took full advantage of this opportunity and tried to get help for a host of medical problems. Often their descriptions of sundry ailments and miseries ran on at great length, for, as Nurse Rivers recalled, "they had all kinds of complaints." Drs. Vonderlehr and Wenger listened attentively, comforting patients who were sure to return to their friends and neighbors with glowing reports about the "government doctors."[2]

The division of labor was carefully orchestrated. Dr. Wenger, assisted by one or two black interns from Andrew Hospital, performed the diagnostic and treatment work, while Dr. Vonderlehr, aided by Nurse Rivers, conducted the extensive physical examinations on patients who had been screened for the study by Dr. Wenger. For about a week, Dr. Vonderlehr helped Dr. Wenger with the field work until a backlog of subjects had been selected from the general population. Together they canvassed the county, drawing blood in as many as six or seven hamlets daily. As arranged with Dr. Gill, the blood samples were shipped every day or two to the state health laboratory in Montgomery for analysis. When the results came back, the patients were notified by mail. Positive cases were asked to report for treatment at the portable clinics that were set up at several convenient locations in churches and schools across the county.

By the end of the first week, Drs. Vonderlehr and Wenger had collected blood samples from approximately three hundred patients. Yet Dr. Vonderlehr sounded anything but confident when he wrote Dr. Clark, "We are now wondering what will happen next week when we try to get the negroes in for study at the Institute Hospital." The success of the study depended upon persuading the men to consent to physical examinations. Dr. Clark admitted that he, too, felt "somewhat disturbed" about the men's cooperation.[3]

There was no cause for alarm—the first examinations went like clockwork. Buoyed by this success, Dr. Vonderlehr predicted that they would be able "to sell our physical examinations to the rural negroes after we once find them." He reported that the first two had been "very enthusiastic." A few weeks later he boasted to Dr. Clark: "If a negro can be induced to have a serological examination he can practically always be persuaded to submit to the physical examination."[4]

Dr. Vonderlehr selected subjects in strict compliance with the study's protocol. The men came from Dr. Wenger's diagnostic and treatment centers. Those who had a positive Wassermann test and were at least twenty-five years old became prime candidates for the study. Unlike the general population, they received a second blood test to confirm the diagnosis. After taking case histories from each of the men, Dr. Wenger reduced the remaining pool even further. He excluded anyone who had been treated for "bad blood" or whose infection was less than five years old.

Nurse Rivers was in charge of transporting the men to and from the hospital. Upon learning that her automobile was a coupe without a rumble seat, Dr. Clark calmly observed to Dr. Vonderlehr: "It seems that she will have to make several trips each day." In fact, she had to make two round trips a day (one in the morning and one in the afternoon) to supply Dr. Vonderlehr with the four patients that he quickly established as his daily quota.[5]

In addition to chauffeuring the men, Nurse Rivers often helped Dr. Vonderlehr with the physicals. She performed other duties as well. Most evenings found her washing and boiling syringes and preparing other supplies that were needed for Dr.

Wenger's field clinics. Five days a week, fourteen or fifteen hours a day, month after month she maintained this schedule. Small wonder that she looked back on the early days of the experiment and sighed, "The day had no end when we first started." Dedication of this magnitude did not go unnoticed. A few months after they started working together, Dr. Vonderlehr praised Nurse Rivers as "untiring in her efforts" and freely acknowledged that "it is really due to her that the number of defaulters has been kept down."[6]

Bad weather made the work more difficult. Dirt roads were the rule in Macon County, and they quickly dissolved into impassable quagmires when it rained. And it rained constantly that winter. Christmas Day found Dr. Vonderlehr bleating back to Washington that the weather was "TERRIBLE" and had definitely hindered the experiment because "the patients refused to walk the several miles to the treatment centers under these conditions." That complaint was to become a familiar refrain among the PHS officers over the next four decades.[7]

A flu epidemic that struck Alabama during the winter of 1932–33 also hindered the study. Attendance at the field clinics fell sharply as people were laid up. More important, the epidemic forced a curtailment of treatment. Dr. Wenger feared that some of the patients might catch the flu after visiting the clinics and blame it on treatment for the "bad blood" sickness. "We are going very slow in giving intravenous injections because of this flu situation," he explained, because "it would be extremely unwise to give one of these ignorant patients a dose of Neo and then have him develop a flu or possibly a pneumonia." To the relief of Drs. Wenger and Vonderlehr, the epidemic ended in a few weeks. They knew that unless they continued to provide treatment it would not be possible to keep Macon County's black people cooperating with the study.[8]

Finding men with syphilis proved more difficult than anyone had anticipated. As luck would have it, the first three hundred men tested yielded an infection rate of only 17 percent, less than half the whopping 35 percent uncovered during the Rosenwald Fund demonstration. "Of course, the next 300 may considerably change the picture," wrote Dr. Vonderlehr, "but if it does not we will be forced to survey a much larger group than we originally intended." Treatment, not testing, was the real problem. They were obligated by their agreement with the state health officials to provide a minimum program of therapy for every syphilitic case they diagnosed, provided, of course, that treatment was not medically contraindicated. And while state authorities were willing to supply some of the necessary drugs and medical supplies, most had to be furnished by the PHS at a time when its own budget had been reduced.[9]

The treatment agreement imposed a heavy burden. Toward the end of November Dr. Vonderlehr warned Dr. Clark: "If we continue as we are going at present we must survey at least 5,000 to 6,000 negroes and shall probably be giving 200 to 300 doses of neosalvarsan per week within the next two months." The actual figure far outstripped this estimate. By the first of the year six treatment clinics had to be opened at various locations in the county to accommodate the hundreds of people who were begging for treatment, and, by the end of January, Dr. Vonderlehr reported that they were treating five hundred patients a week, a figure he admitted was not likely to be reduced until the study had ended and all treatment had stopped.[10]

Dr. Clark was anything but pleased. As treatment costs continued to rise, he cautioned Dr. Vonderlehr repeatedly to maintain the strictest economy. Late in January he wrote:

> It never once occurred to me that we would be called upon to treat a large part of the county as a return for the privilege of making this study ... but since such is the situation we must make the best of it or else sacrifice the expenditure of time and effort already made.

His concern might have been less if the patients had been receiving enough treatment to cure them, or if there had been any chance that the state would assume the responsibility. "Unfortunately, I can see no permanence to the related activities we are now carrying on as a requisite to enable us to carry out this research," he confided to Dr. Vonderlehr, "and therefore I am inclined, and even consider it desirable, to limit expenditures for this associated work [treatment] as greatly as may be done without prejudice to our study."[11]

The expanded treatment program required more manpower. In the middle of November Dr. Murray Smith, the health officer for Macon County, approached Dr. Vonderlehr for a job, explaining that the local health department would be closed soon due to lack of funds. Dr. Vonderlehr urged Dr. Clark to approve the appointment. "I think we could not get a better man for the field work than Smith," wrote Dr. Vonderlehr. "With him I believe we could select every desirable negro in the county and his prestige among the white people would lend much support."[12]

Dr. Clark agreed. Late in December when Dr. Smith was dismissed by the county, he went to work immediately as the head clinician of the field treatment clinics, replacing Dr. Wenger, who returned to Arkansas. Dr. Smith fit into the program beautifully. After watching him in action a few times Dr. Vonderlehr reported to Dr. Clark: "Dr. Smith seems to be handling the field work well and the number of men in for primary survey is increasing in the field clinics. I do not know how well Smith knows syphilis but he certainly knows the rural negro."[13]

Dr. Clark viewed Dr. Smith's success as a mixed blessing, for a rise in the number of blood tests invariably produced an increase in the caseload of patients under treatment. Dr. Clark became more and more suspicious that Dr. Smith's humanitarian concern might be causing him to lose sight of the study's real purpose. Dr. Vonderlehr flatly denied this accusation. "I feel certain that Doctor Smith's first interest is in seeing our project through and not to establish temporary treatment centers," he wrote Dr. Clark. "He fully appreciates, I believe, the relative inefficiency of these temporary measures."[14]

Dr. Clark and Dr. Vonderlehr kept up a running battle over treatment, despite Dr. Vonderlehr's repeated assurances that the field clinicians were doing everything within their power to hold it to an absolute minimum. Dr. Vonderlehr was adamant that a minimum program of treatment had to be maintained until the complete sample of men had been selected and examined. A peculiar problem of logistics demanded it. Dr. Vonderlehr decided shortly after arriving in Macon County to defer lumbar punctures until sometime in the spring, after he had completed all of the physical examinations. All the men would have to be brought to Andrew Hospital twice—once for the physical examinations and a second time for the spinal taps. This meant a short delay between visits for men who were seen toward the end of the field work but a lapse of several months for those who had been examined at the beginning of the study.

Treatment was the only way to keep the men in the fold during the interlude. "It is desirable and essential if the study is to be a success to maintain the interest of each of the cases examined by me through to the time when the punctures can be completed," explained Dr. Vonderlehr. "Expenditures of several hundred dollars for drugs for those men would be well worth the while if their interest and cooperation could be maintained in so doing." Every time Dr. Clark complained about the expense, Dr. Vonderlehr's reply was always the same: "Our experiment cannot be carried out without treatment."[15]

All the men in the study received treatment. The quantity and the form depended on when the patient was examined, what drugs happened to be on hand at the moment, and whether the patient was too old or too ill to be given both neoarsphenamine and mercury. Moreover, a drug shortage hampered the study throughout the winter and spring. Dr. Gill could not furnish all that was needed; Dr. Clark would not. On at least one occasion the treatment clinics were forced to turn people away without medication, prompting Dr. Vonderlehr to decry "the unfavorable impression made on the negro." But the worst consequence of the drug shortage was treating people with whatever happened to be available rather than the balanced program of neoarsphenamine and mercury that proper therapy demanded.[16]

Priority for treatment went to study subjects. Many received both neoarsphenamine and mercury; others only one drug. The short supply was partly responsible, but in many cases the differences in treatment were medically warranted. Dr. Vonderlehr informed Dr. Clark early in January that due to the advanced ages of the patients "more than half of the cases ... are suitable for heavy metal therapy only."[17]

Early in February Dr. Vonderlehr decided to do a spotcheck on the results of the treatment by giving some of the men second blood tests. "Of 50 patients retested after the first (and only according to our agreement) course of treatment, consisting of eight doses of neoarsphenamine and more or less of heavy metal," he wrote Dr. Clark, "only 3% showed a serological reversal." In other words, practically all the men still gave a positive reading on their blood tests. That was hardly surprising. The treatment given, which constituted the max-

imum received by any man in the study, was less than half
the amount recommended by the Public Health Service to
cure syphilis.[18]

Even ineffective treatment was expensive. Dr. Vonderlehr
made repeated efforts to increase the yield of subjects and hold
down the number of patients who were being added to the
treatment clinics. The obvious solution was to test only men,
reducing by half the number requiring treatment. The problem, however, was that as many women as men showed up at
the field clinics and efforts to segregate the men often aroused
suspicion. Dr. Vonderlehr reported to Dr. Clark: "In trying to
get a larger number of men in the primary surveys during December we were accused in one community of examining prospective recruits for the Army."[19]

Dr. Vonderlehr had better luck when he devised schemes
for capitalizing on federal programs in the area to combat un-
employment. Funds from the Reconstruction Finance Corpora-
tion (RFC) began reaching Macon County shortly after the
study got under way, and Dr. Vonderlehr immediately approached the RFC's local leaders for permission to station two
teams of clinicians at the RFC's registration centers to take
blood samples from the black men who came to sign up for
public employment. "Local workers in the R.F.C. gave us complete cooperation in permitting a simultaneous Wassermann
survey on all negro registrants," wrote Dr. Vonderlehr, adding,
"The result of this fortunate incident was the uncovering of
between 30 and 40 cases for the study."[20]

An identical fate awaited black men who visited the Red
Cross House in Tuskegee. Dr. Vonderlehr arranged for a team
of clinicians to make daily calls there to take blood samples
from men seeking medical care or a hot meal. "We now obtain
blood from some five to ten men in the correct age group from
this source each day with very little trouble," reported Dr.
Vonderlehr. "Great difficulty was experienced in the field getting these men, who are now really quite literally at our front
door."[21]

Though often annoyed by the problems of blood testing and
treatment, Dr. Vonderlehr found the physical examinations ex-
citing. He was especially fascinated by the pathologies he uncovered. "For the last day or two I have seen more pathology
due to syphilis than ever before," he exclaimed to Dr. Clark

early in December. "Four of the last five cases presented profound changes," he continued. "One case had optic atrophy, a second gummata involving the nares & destroying the nasal septum, and the third seriginious ulcerating syphilis of the left leg." Because the fourth case "had syphilitic involvement of the cardiovascular system," Dr. Vonderlehr stated that he had "made a note on this patient's record that an aneurysm . . . existed." Unable to conceal his delight, he exclaimed: "I call this my prize case." Pleased by these findings, Dr. Clark wrote back: "If you continue to find residuals of syphilitic infection in the Negro at the rate you are now, our study should forever dispel the rather general belief that syphilis is a disease of small consequence to the Negro."[22]

As the examinations progressed Dr. Vonderlehr became more and more enthusiastic about the cardiovascular complications he was uncovering in the men. Yet his diagnoses rested on admittedly subjective readings of X-rays of the men's chests, and he was not a specialist in interpreting X-rays. He therefore decided to call upon the services of Dr. Jerome J. Peters, a black physician who served on the staff of the Veterans Hospital in Tuskegee as both a pathologist and expert radiologist. Dr. Peters's interpretations of the X-rays supported Dr. Vonderlehr's view that the incidence of cardiovascular syphilis was running very high in the men.

Dr. Clark was a bit taken aback by the reports and decided to seek another opinion. "I am not altogether satisfied to have simply one interpretation of these films," he confided to the experiment's Baltimore consultant, Dr. Joseph Earle Moore, "and write to ask whether you may not be able to assist us in the matter." Dr. Clark emphasized that he was taking this precaution because Dr. Vonderlehr was "uncovering more pathology than I thought would be the case, particularly [in] the cardiovascular system, which seems to be the Negro's vulnerable point in syphilitic attack."[23]

Over the next few months, Dr. Moore received hundreds of X-rays. He returned the films promptly after every shipment, with interpretive comments on each X-ray. His readings tended to reduce Dr. Peters's figures on the number of cases with syphilitic complications of the cardiovascular system, but Dr. Moore stressed repeatedly that he did not have sufficient data to render definitive diagnoses on many cases. Nevertheless, by the time the physical examinations were nearly completed in the spring, Dr. Moore had no hesitancy in declaring: "Doctor Von der Lehr seems to have uncovered a perfect gold mine of cardiovascular syphilis."[24]

The physical examinations yielded far less evidence of central nervous system syphilis. Because they all believed that neural syphilis was extremely rare in Negroes, the investigators did not expect to find a high incidence of central nervous system complications. But there was some concern that isolated cases might go undiagnosed unless Dr. Vonderlehr was especially alert and perceptive in conducting the physical examinations. In fact, one consultant, an expert on neurosyphilis, warned that the clinical symptoms "usually manifest themselves in a *bizarre and atypical manner in the negro.*"[25]

Dr. Vonderlehr made a special effort not to miss any cases of neurosyphilis. He did not expect to see many advanced cases "because they would be confined in an institution." What troubled Dr. Vonderlehr was the total absence of any clinical evidence of early neural involvement in the men. After more than two months of futile searching, a frustrated Dr. Vonderlehr confided to Dr. Clark: "I am aware of the great difficulty offered in recognizing the early subjective symptoms of paresis in the negro . . . but it seems unusual that I have failed to recognize a single early case of paresis with subjective symptoms in the 200 odd cases examined."[26]

Dr. Clark blamed the behavior of lower-class blacks for obscuring clinical manifestations. He consoled Dr. Vonderlehr: "I quite agree with you as to the hopelessness of recognizing mild paresis among these illiterate people of such circumscribed cultural horizon. I am hopeful that the spinal fluid examinations may throw some light on this question."[27]

Tactical discussions on how best to proceed with the lumbar punctures had actually begun when Dr. Vonderlehr first arrived in Tuskegee. He had decided at the outset to delay the spinal taps until the end of the project. He knew that the men would not enjoy them. Even when performed in a well-equipped hospital by a skilled clinician, spinal taps are risky, for the margin for error in inserting the needle is small. The slightest miscalculation can produce temporary or even permanent paralysis. Moreover, the actual spinal taps may go well, only to have a considerable portion of patients suffer unpleasant aftereffects. Severe headaches that may last for days or even weeks are common, as are numbness or stiffness (partial paralysis) in the neck or limbs.

Dr. Vonderlehr knew what would happen if someone in the experiment became paralyzed or if word of blinding headaches spread throughout the county. The spirit of cooperation and voluntarism upon which the experiment depended would be weakened. Since candor offered little hope of securing the men's cooperation, another approach had to be devised.

Dr. Vonderlehr decided on a policy of bald deceit. He planned to assemble the men at the various field clinics and then transport them by automobile at a rate of twenty a day to Andrew Hospital, where the spinal taps would be performed and the men would be kept overnight for observation in case of adverse reactions. Describing his strategy in detail to Dr. Clark, Dr. Vonderlehr wrote:

> My idea in bringing them in large groups is to get the procedure completed in a given area before the negro population has been able to find out just what is going on. Individual patients would be told that they are coming in for an examination but they would remain all night after we had them here, and the details of the puncture techniques should also be kept from them as far as possible.[28]

Dr. Clark liked the plan, but cautioned that the procedure would "entail considerable expense to the hospital" and warned Dr. Vonderlehr to bear in mind that the PHS had "no funds with which to pay for hospitalization." The Tuskegee Institute would have to absorb the cost of hospitalizing the men overnight. Significantly, Dr. Clark did not object to the lack of truthfulness with the men about the procedure or to the idea of using the treatment centers to camouflage what they were really up to. "I agree with you that the treatment work should continue during the period of spinal fluid testing in order to minimize the amount of attention that will be given to this activity by the people of the community," wrote Dr. Clark. He later justified the ruse to Dr. Moore by explaining: "These negroes are very ignorant and easily influenced by things that would be of minor significance in a more intelligent group."[29]

As preparations for the lumbar punctures went forward, Dr. Vonderlehr gave a great deal of thought to preventing serious injury to any of the men. He argued that "it would be unsafe to carry out routine spinal punctures on men past the age of 65 years" and that it would be similarly "unwise to attempt to do a puncture on the more advanced cardiovascular cases." Omitting these groups had a direct bearing on the total number of men who would have to be examined in order to yield the desired number of subjects for spinal taps. "Should 300 cases be decided upon as the number to complete spinal punctures," reckoned Dr. Vonderlehr, "I believe we shall need about 400 cases to complete the first part of the study."[30]

As the examinations progressed, Dr. Vonderlehr became even more convinced that speed was the key to his plan's success. In April, he told Dr. Clark that they would have to "rush through all the punctures as rapidly as hospitalization will permit because if sufficient time is permitted to elapse for news of reactions to spread before a neighborhood is completed the remaining patients will default." To help expedite the work, he asked that Dr. Wenger be temporarily assigned to Tuskegee, and Dr. Clark agreed.[31]

Dr. Vonderlehr was confident that he and Dr. Wenger could perform twenty spinal taps a day, the maximum number of fluid samples that could be tested by the laboratories of the National Institute of Health and the Naval Hospital in Bethesda, Maryland. In 1930, Congress had created the National Institute of Health (NIH), giving independent funding and structure to the laboratory and research operation that had developed in the Hygienic Laboratory in PHS. (The National Institutes of Health were not organized until 1950.) The laboratory in NIH focused largely on cancer research, but it was among the best in the nation. Having the spinal taps analyzed by laboratories of known excellence was crucial to gaining acceptance for any scholarly publications that might result from the experiment. As Dr. Wenger explained to Dr. Vonderlehr, studying Negroes required that specimens be examined

> by some man of unquestioned ability because when your work is criticized every authority in the country will make every effort to find flaws in your conclusions. We must always keep in mind that the profession still insists that changes in the spinal fluid of negroes is comparatively rare because the clinical evidence of neuro syphilis in that race is not so pronounced.[32]

Perhaps it was this concern over the scientific controversy surrounding syphilis in blacks that made Dr. Vonderlehr at least consider, if not truly confront, the experiment's most obvious scientific shortcoming: namely, what effect the small amounts of treatment the men had been receiving had on the spontaneous evolution of the disease. "In carrying out the spinal puncture," he wrote Dr. Clark, "I plan to use this opportunity of again seeing the patient(s) to check up on the various pathological findings made at the first examination in order to ascertain the changes that have taken place since treatment was started." While a clinical checkup was all that seemed necessary, Dr. Vonderlehr asked Dr. Clark whether he wanted "to extend another X-ray study routinely to all cases." Dr. Clark ruled against it, arguing: "It is hardly conceivable that any important change(s) would have taken place in so short an interval."[33]

Freed from the need to monitor the effects of limited treatment, Dr. Vonderlehr put all his energies into compiling data. The examinations enabled him to see both a greater quantity and variety of gross pathologies associated with syphilis than most clinicians observed in a lifetime. Others might have found the grueling schedule exhausting; he thrived on it. Indeed, he found the work fascinating. Not even the mounds of paper work could dampen his enthusiasm. At the end of a long evening spent updating his files, Dr. Vonderlehr complained a little in a letter to Dr. Clark, but then added: "Please do not think that I am tired or discouraged, however, for I have the feeling that this is about the most interesting detail I have ever had. Had twice the amount of paper work been necessary it would still have been worthwhile."[34]

Indeed, Dr. Vonderlehr did not want the experiment to end. Early in April, he broached the subject ever so gingerly with Dr. Clark. "For some time I have been thinking of an aspect of the study of untreated syphilis being conducted here which may not have occurred to you," began Dr. Vonderlehr. "I do not submit this idea with the desire that it even be considered a suggestion but rather that you keep it [in] mind until I return to my work in Washington." What followed was a bold blueprint for continuing the experiment years into the future.[35]

Dispersing the group simply did not make sense in the light

of how much more science stood to gain from them: "Should these cases be followed over a period of from five to ten years," Dr. Vonderlehr explained, "many interesting facts could be learned regarding the course and complications of untreated syphilis." As an example, he noted that "the longevity of these syphilitics could be ascertained" and expressed confidence "that many necropsies [autopsies] could be arranged through the hospital at the [Tuskegee] Institute with the cooperation of the National Institute of Health." Dr. Vonderlehr argued that the men could still be considered untreated because they had received far less treatment than the standards of modern medicine prescribed. "At the end of this project we shall have a considerable number of cases presenting various complications of syphilis who have received only mercury and may still be considered untreated in the modern sense of therapy."[36]

Inexpensive to operate and easy to administer, the study would not tax the Public Health Service's limited resources. The follow-up work could be done by a "part time social worker . . . and the whole scheme could be supervised by one of our officers occasionally." Dr. Vonderlehr was certain that "other interesting points for study could be worked out should this follow-up work be considered seriously." Undeterred by what he himself described as the Public Health Service's "need for economy," he concluded on a note of urgency, pleading: "it seems a pity to me to lose such an unusual opportunity."[37]

Dr. Clark was sympathetic, though hardly encouraging. He agreed that there were "possibilities for further study of syphilis in the Negro" and promised "to discuss the problem" when Dr. Vonderlehr returned to Washington. Pointing to the "very trying times" and the pervasive "spirit of uncertainty" produced by the current financial retrenchment, Dr. Clark concluded soberly: "I cannot at this juncture express any hope that we shall be able to expand our activities."[38]

Dr. Vonderlehr was too engrossed in the work to be deterred. He attacked the lumbar punctures with the enthusiasm of a man just beginning rather than ending a job. The form letter he used to draw the men to the hospital skillfully exploited their ignorance and need. It was a masterpiece of guileful deceit.

No document could have looked more imposingly official. Clearly designed to invoke the prestige of every organization the men could possibly associate with medical authority, the letterhead read *"Macon County Health Department"* with the subheading "Alabama State Board of Health and U.S. Public Health Service Cooperating with Tuskegee Institute." There was no mention of lumbar punctures. Instead, Dr. Vonderlehr offered enticements.[39]

Following the customary "Dear Sir," the opening paragraph read:

> Some time ago you were given a thorough examination and since that time we hope you have gotten a great deal of treatment for bad blood. You will now be given your last chance to get a second examination. This examination is a very special one and after it is finished you will be given a special treatment if it is believed you are in a condition to stand it.

Men who wanted "the special examination" and "the special treatment" were told that they had to meet the nurse at a certain place, date, and hour (a space was left blank in the letter for each item), and that she, in turn, would transport them "to the Tuskegee Institute Hospital for this free treatment."[40] The letter alerted the men to the possibility that they might have to spend a night in the hospital. "You will remember that you had to wait for some time when you had your last good examination, and we wish to let you know that because we expect to be so busy it may be necessary for you to remain in the hospital over one night," the letter explained, but added reassuringly: "If this is necessary you will be furnished your meals and a bed, as well [as] the examination and treatment without cost." The letter closed with the stirring exhortation: "REMEMBER THIS IS YOUR LAST CHANCE FOR SPECIAL FREE TREATMENT. BE SURE TO MEET THE NURSE." It was signed, "Macon County Health Department."[41]

The letter produced the desired results, and work on the spinal taps got under way in May. The physicians continued to conceal the fact that the procedure was diagnostic rather than therapeutic by telling the men that they were being given "spinal shots." Referring by name to Dr. Dibble, one of the men in the experiment recalled: "He said he was going to put some medicine ... in. That's it! Said he was giving me a spinal shot—that's what he told me—in my back." Since many of the men had received injections with neoarsphenamine as treatment for their bad blood sickness, they naturally associated "spinal shots" with therapy.[42]

Dr. Vonderlehr anticipated unpleasant aftereffects in some of the men, estimating "headaches in 20 percent of the cases." Experience not only bore out this prediction but intensified his concern for speed and secrecy. Within days of beginning the lumbar punctures, he confided to Dr. Clark: "The quicker the spinal punctures are completed the better it will be because we are getting the usual percentage of postspinal headaches and news of this is sure to spread." Dr. Wenger, too, referred to postspinal headaches but thought that they were "nothing serious" and noted that "the vast majority of the patients were able to return to work following a 24 hour rest in the hospital and at home."[43]

Nurse River's memory of the spinal punctures was more sympathetic to the men. From the vantage point of nearly half a century later, she described the procedure as "crude, very crude at that particular time." The principal difficulty she recalled was that "the technique was not smooth" and "a lot of them were stuck two or three times." The actual punctures were "very painful" and many of the men developed "severe headaches." The bumps and jars of the drive home seemed to exacerbate their suffering, for "the roads were rough," she explained, and "by the time I'd get them home they'd have another reaction." Nurse Rivers thought that the lumbar punctures had to be "really dangerous because [there were] very few of the men who didn't have some complaint after."[44]

Nurse Rivers was moved by the terror that filled the men. She had vivid memories of how the men "were scared to death" at the thought of something "going into the spinal column, or cord." Of course her supervisors were accustomed to these reactions from patients and did not share her concern. "Dr. Wenger thought that I was too sympathetic with the patients, and I was," she recalled. "I was concerned about the patients 'cause I had to live here after he was gone."[45]

The men's own accounts of the spinal punctures reveal that she did not exaggerate their reactions. "It knocked me out," one of the men in the study recalled. "I tell you I thought I wasn't going to make it. I fainted, I fainted, you know. Just paralyzed for a day or two. Just couldn't do nothing." Another man's neck was so stiff that he had to remain at home in bed for two weeks. "I thought several times I would ease around and get off the bed but I'd have to hold my neck [back] . . . and just crawl along on my knees," he moaned. Still another man remembered being laid up for a week with a terrible headache. "That's my trouble," the man complained more than forty years after his spinal puncture. "I never have got over that shit."[46]

In a sense, none of the men ever did. The spinal taps left a residue of fear and mistrust toward the "government doctors." Nurse Rivers recalled hearing more than one man exclaim during the drive home from the hospital, "Nurse Rivers, if they gonna stick you in the back every time we come here I don't want to be there."[47]

By the time the work ended late in May, Drs. Vonderlehr and Wenger, joined by Dr. Dibble who helped do the last few cases, had performed spinal punctures on 307 men. Of the 407 men examined before they began the lumbar punctures, Dr. Vonderlehr estimated that approximately 370 showed no contraindications for the procedure. Referring to the men they had missed (roughly 20 percent of the eligible group), Dr. Vonderlehr wrote: "Some of the defaulters are afraid, some cannot get away from their work because their white employers will not permit, and a few have moved out of the county." Still, none of the clinicians regarded the number of defaulters as excessive. Dr. Wenger called their success ratio "a remarkable showing."[48]

Nurse Rivers had less reason to be pleased. She was the first to feel the practical consequences of the damaged relations with the men. Her appointment was extended for a few weeks after Drs. Vonderlehr and Wenger had left the state so that she could contact the men whose chest X-rays were not readable and persuade them to return for a second X-ray. "It has been very difficult to get the patients in for X-rays," she wrote dejectedly. "Three refused to come in at all. Others offered various excuses. I repeat my visits hoping they will change their minds. They are afraid I am trying to get them in for spinal punctures."[49]

Dr. Smith told similar stories. During the summer he was reappointed to his old job as the health officer for Macon County, and his visits to the countryside frequently brought him into contact with men who had been in the study. Obviously amused by their reactions, Dr. Smith reported back to Dr. Vonderlehr: "Wish you could see some of the Old S.P. [spinal puncture] brethren scram to the woods when they see me, as I go over the county now." During the years that followed, the men's fear of the spinal punctures became a favorite subject of jokes and asides by "government doctors." They never seemed to tire of anecdotes about "Dr. Vonderlehr's golden needle treatment." (They had used twenty-gauge golden needles to perform the spinal punctures.)[50]

The last spinal tap was supposed to mark the end of the experiment, at least as far as any further clinical contact with the men was concerned. And for a month or so following May it appeared that the study would conclude as planned. The physicians involved in the experiment returned to their former posts. Nurse Rivers stayed on for a few weeks into June finishing the follow-up work with the men, and then began looking for another job. Of the clinical team, she alone was out of work. Realizing that it was no time to be subtle or proud, Nurse Rivers asked her former employer for help. She wrote Dr. Vonderlehr that she had "not obtained a position" and added: "I certainly enjoyed the work, and ask that you remember me should the occasion present itself that you would be in need of my services again."[51]

It seemed doubtful that the PHS would need her help again—at least not soon. Dr. Vonderlehr's superiors gave every indication that they would end the experiment as planned. Surgeon General Cumming wrote Dr. Moton a personal word of thanks for the "splendid cooperation" extended by him and the staff of John A. Andrew Memorial Hospital. Dr. Clark sent a similar note to Colonel J. H. Ward, the head of the Veterans' Administration Home in Tuskegee.[52]

The experiment might have ended then and there had not important personnel changes occurred. Dr. Clark retired at the end of June, and Dr. Vonderlehr succeeded him as the acting director and then director of the Division of Venereal Diseases. His promotion initiated a clearly discernible bureaucratic pattern over the next four decades, a pattern that unquestionably determined the experiment's conduct and accounted in no small part for its longevity. When a vacancy opened at the helm of the Division of Venereal Diseases, the position was usually filled by a man who had worked on the study. Given the limited number of senior officers and the inbred promotion policies of the PHS, it could hardly have been otherwise.

Once he had assumed office, there was never any doubt that Dr. Vonderlehr would continue the experiment. Nine months of his life, nine grueling months of field work, were invested in it. He was absolutely convinced that the experiment had scientific merit. He was sure that the PHS was standing on the verge of important discoveries about the effects of untreated syphilis in Negroes, especially with regard to the cardiovascular system. Ending the study before they had learned more from it simply did not make good scientific sense.

Dr. Vonderlehr was totally blind to the fact that the experiment contained a fatal flaw: it had been hopelessly contaminated by treatment. In his desire to continue the study, he had glossed over the fact that all of the men had received a little treatment, arguing, in effect, that the men remained untreated "in the modern sense of therapy." As a study of the effect of undertreated syphilis, the experiment perhaps had some value; as a study of the effects of untreated syphilis, it was useless.

Dr. Vonderlehr's desire to continue the study stemmed from a combination of scientific interest and reformer's zeal. Finding severe manifestations of the disease in many of the men unquestionably strengthened his resolve to push on. From a purely scientific standpoint the pathologies were fascinating, but more was involved. As long as the medical profession and the general public dismissed syphilis as a trivial thing in the life of the Negro, there was not much hope for securing funding for public health programs to combat the disease. But if the U.S. Public Health Service could prove that syphilis injured blacks just as surely as it did whites, state legislatures (perhaps even Congress) might be persuaded to support programs modeled after the Rosenwald Fund's syphilis control demonstrations. The irony was unmistakable: A study of untreated syphilis might lead to the development of treatment programs.

But not for the men in the experiment. The summer of 1933 marked a watershed in the history of the Tuskegee Study of Untreated Syphilis in the Negro Male. Instead of ending, the study was to have a future, one that was to be open-ended. If Dr. Clark was the father of the experiment, Dr. Vonderlehr became its chief guardian and protector. He made certain that the men had not seen the last of the "government doctors."[53]

CHAPTER 9

"Bringing Them
to Autopsy"

DURING the summer of 1933 Dr. Vonderlehr moved with dispatch and purpose to keep the experiment alive. Neither his newly acquired duties as acting director of the Division of Venereal Diseases, nor the fiscal austerity imposed on the Public Health Service by the depression-inspired Economy Act could deter him. He spent a month and a half reviewing the appropriate literature and discussing the experiment with other officers. In mid-July he wrote Dr. Wenger outlining his thoughts for continuing the study and inviting suggestions on how best to proceed, emphasizing that "everyone is agreed that the proper procedure is the continuance of the observation of the Negro men used in the study with the idea of eventually bringing them to autopsy."[1]

Performing autopsies on the men introduced a significant addition to the experiment's protocol. It was obvious that pathologists examining diseased organs under a microscope could learn more that clinicians peering at X-rays; autopsies would enable the researchers to supplement and revise their clinical assessments, yielding data that the scientific community would regard as far more reliable than studies based solely on clinical observations.

Dr. Vonderlehr knew the autopsies would inject an element

132

of uncertainty about how long the experiment would last. Autopsies, he wrote Dr. Wenger, "may be impracticable in connection with some of the younger cases," but "those more advanced in age with serious complications of the vital organs should have to be followed for only a period of a few years." That estimate, of course, fell short of setting a definite cutoff date for terminating the experiment. He never fixed such a deadline. Nor is there any indication that he ever specified how many autopsies would be needed. These omissions could not help but lend an open-ended quality to the study, and there is every reason to believe Dr. Vonderlehr wanted it that way.[2]

Familiar groups were to be retained in the experiment. Following Dr. Clark's earlier approach, Dr. Vonderlehr told Dr. Wenger that he intended "to obtain the cooperation of the State and local health departments and, most important of all, the Tuskegee Hospital." To secure the aid of the latter, he proposed to offer Dr. Dibble an honorary appointment in the Public Health Service as "Acting Assistant Surgeon at $1 per annum." Dr. Dibble could then be asked to share the facilities of Andrew Hospital, to help perform the autopsies, and to act as an adviser/supervisor for the nurse who would keep tabs on the men in between visits of the "government doctors."[3]

Because he planned to send health officers to Tuskegee only once a year, Dr. Vonderlehr assigned a great deal of importance to the nurse's role. She would be the experiment's on-the-spot representative, the person with whom the subjects would have the most contact. Nurse Rivers was his choice for the job, and he told Dr. Wenger that he planned to "employ her on a two-thirds time basis, having her furnish [her own] transportation, for $1,000 a year." Guided by the need to maintain a shoestring budget, Dr. Vonderlehr estimated that "200 per annum additional [to Nurse Rivers's salary] would furnish incidental needs, such as small amounts of medicine, et cetera." Thus the total cost of the study (excluding the salary and travel expenses for health officers involved) came to only $1,200 per year.[4]

Choosing a field director presented a problem. Personnel cutbacks had reduced the division's staff in Washington from fifteen to twelve and two more positions were endangered. Since Dr. Vonderlehr could not get away or assign someone from the division's headquarters without placing additional strain on his staff, he asked Dr. Wenger if a member of the staff at Hot Springs could be spared for the assignment. So there would not be any questions about the authorization to conduct the experiment, Dr. Vonderlehr stated that he had sent Dr. Cumming a memorandum on the matter, adding: "I have reason to believe that this program will be approved by the Surgeon General."[5]

Despite these urgent promptings, Dr. Wenger refused to loan Dr. Vonderlehr a member of his staff. Dr. Wenger, too, was short on hands. But with advice, he was more generous. First and foremost, Dr. Wenger argued against employing Nurse Rivers. "I don't see that she can do anything else than use up gasoline making weekly calls on these patients, which do not seem to me to be necessary," wrote Dr. Wenger. Lavishing any more attention on the men while they were still alive struck him as an utter waste of time. "As I see it," he advised, "we have no further interest in these patients until they die."[6]

Rather than employing Nurse Rivers, Dr. Wenger advocated two other schemes for securing the autopsies. "When these patients die," he began, "some one of the dozen or more physicians in Macon County must sign a death certificate, which goes to the County Health Officer, Doctor Murray Smith. Doctor Smith could then notify Doctor Dibble who could make arrangements for the post-mortem." The alternative, he continued, was to secure the cooperation of Dr. Dibble and

> arrange with the doctors in Macon County to turn over to Doctor Dibble any of the demonstration cases applying to them for treatment. This would enable Doctor Dibble to keep more complete notes on these cases and in the event of death he would have more time to persuade the family to have a post-mortem performed.

Aware that the second plan depended on the support of the local physicians, Dr. Wenger added reassuringly, "I know the doctors of Macon County well enough to believe they will cooperate."[7]

There was a hitch with the second plan, one Dr. Wenger was quick to acknowledge: "If the colored population become aware that accepting free hospital care means a post-mortem, every darkey will leave Macon County and it will hurt Dibble's hospital." But there was a way around the problem. "This can be prevented," Dr. Wenger explained, "if the doctors of Macon

County are brought into our confidence and requested to be very careful not to let the objectives of the plan be known." In a sense Dr. Wenger's suggestion was predictable, for concealing the true objective of the study from the subjects was the policy the "government doctors" had followed all along. All that had changed was that Macon County's private physicians were to be made full-fledged accomplices in the Public Health Service's conspiracy.[8]

Concern over the experiment's scientific validity prompted Dr. Wenger's final recommendation. He advised against using Dr. Dibble or any of his interns at Andrew Hospital to perform the autopsies, warning: "Their findings would be of no more scientific value than if you or I did the post-mortem. So why not bring into the picture the pathologist at the U.S. Veterans Bureau Hospital? Then we will have a post-mortem record that is worth while[sic]." Dr. Wenger's candidate was Dr. Jerome J. Peters, the young black physician who had performed spinal punctures on the men.[9]

Dr. Vonderlehr's reactions to the suggestions were mixed. The idea of using death certificates submitted to Dr. Smith by local physicians struck him as totally impracticable. "This is definitely out of the question," he explained, "since most of the cases are buried before death certificates reach Doctor Smith's office." In addition, many of the men lived in contiguous counties, which meant that "their death certificates would not be forwarded to the local [Macon County] health unit even if it [the health unit] survived." Dr. Vonderlehr was more kindly disposed to the plan to obtain the cooperation of local physicians, but insisted "it would be necessary to obtain not only the cooperation of physicians in Tuskegee but in the adjoining towns and villages in Macon County and on its outskirts."[10]

Dr. Vonderlehr categorically refused to drop Nurse Rivers. "I feel," he asserted, "that unless someone is working locally with the idea of constantly keeping the welfare of the study in mind very little will be accomplished." Nurse Rivers would function "as a follow-up worker" who "would keep in contact with the average case only about once a year." She would "maintain a much closer touch with the patients showing a severe complication of syphilis who would be likely to meet their demise." Her work would not go unsupervised, for "about once a year some officer of the Service should [would] go to

Macon County and spend a few weeks with the idea of checking up on the nurse's work, doing short examinations on the more advanced cases and giving a placebo form of treatment to those desiring it."[11]

Dr. Vonderlehr agreed that Dr. Peters should perform the autopsies. In fact, he and Dr. Dibble had discussed the assignment earlier and had decided that "Doctor Peters as pathologist to the John A. Andrew Hospital would perform the necessary autopsies." The tissue samples were to be shipped to Washington, D.C., where they could be "studied at the National Institute of Health," a decision that reflected Dr. Vonderlehr's continuing desire to have the laboratory analyses performed by a facility of known excellence so the scientific community would have confidence in the experiment's findings.[12]

Dr. Wenger remained unconvinced that Nurse Rivers was vital to the study and recommended again against employing her. In her place, he suggested using county and state health workers. Lists of the subjects could be distributed to them and to the local physicians, all of whom could be relied upon to keep Washington informed.[13]

The only other alternative, as Dr. Wenger saw it, was for Dr. Vonderlehr to keep in contact by mail with the men directly from his office. According to this plan, Dr. Vonderlehr would devise a form letter (something on the order of a questionnaire), enclose a self-addressed stamped envelope, and ask the men to report to him once a month. Those who reported being ill then would be advised to see Dr. Dibble, who, in turn, could hospitalize them if necessary. "This last scheme seems to me most practical because these patients know and like you and I am sure the majority would send in a monthly report, since they would know that you are interested in them personally," wrote Dr. Wenger. With a sly reference to the spinal puncture letter that Dr. Vonderlehr had drafted, he added: "With your flair for framing letters to negroes this scheme seems most feasible."[14]

Ultimately, Dr. Vonderlehr rejected Dr. Wenger's counsel against employing Nurse Rivers, but his indebtedness to Dr. Wenger's other suggestions became abundantly apparent within the next few months. Taking the local physicians and health workers into their confidence, supplying them with comprehensive lists of the subjects, using form letters to communicate with the men — Dr. Wenger had been a fertile source of suggestions. Instead of treating those recommendations as mutually exclusive alternatives, however, Dr. Vonderlehr borrowed freely from them, patching together an intricate system for keeping tabs on the men and "bringing them to autopsy" that was to function well for nearly half a century.

In additon to working out the logistical problems associated with the autopsies, Dr. Vonderlehr devoted much of the summer of 1933 to securing the cooperation of groups vital to the experiment. First on his list was the Tuskegee Institute. In mid-July, he reminded Dr. Dibble of their previous discussions about continuing the experiment. "At the time," recalled Dr. Vonderlehr, "you expressed the opinion that the John A. Andrew Hospital might be willing to cooperate to the extent that free hospitalization would be arranged for the 400 individuals included in this study in case an illness occurred which was believed to be severe enough to eventuate in death." Once assured that the understanding still stood, Dr. Vonderlehr proposed to "at once take up with the Surgeon General the formal approach of the subject with Doctor Moton."[15]

Dr. Dibble replied that he was "certainly still interested in the project" and offered to raise the matter with Dr. Moton in order to "see what can be done." Cost was his primary concern. To hold expenses down, he suggested relying on the services of Nurse Rivers, aided, perhaps, by Dr. Smith and a few interns from Andrew Hospital. Dr. Vonderlehr was so heartened by this response that he immediately wrote back that he had taken steps "to place Miss Rivers in a part-time position with the Public Health Service" and pressed Dr. Dibble "for [the] Tuskegee Institute to employ her also part time," suggesting that their "agreement be a cooperative one so far as she is concerned."[16]

Late in July, Dr. Cumming, the surgeon general, wrote the principal of the Tuskegee Institute about Dr. Vonderlehr's desire to study at greater length "the effects of untreated syphilis on the human economy." The study that Dr. Vonderlehr had conducted during the past winter with the cooperation of Andrew Hospital, Dr. Cumming explained, "was predominantly clinical in character" and "points to the frequent occurrence of severe complications involving the various vital organs of the body and indicates that syphilis as a disease does a great deal of damage." Before these findings would be accepted by other physicians, however, additional proof was required. "Since clinical observations are not considered final in the medical world," Dr. Cumming explained, "it is our desire to continue observation on the cases selected for the recent study and if possible to bring a percentage of these cases to autopsy so that pathological confirmation may be made of the disease processes."[17]

No other arguments were made for conducting the experiment; no further discussion of the procedure to be employed was offered. He concluded by asking formally "that the support and cooperation of the Tuskegee Institute be given to this investigation."[18]

The PHS's nomenclature in presenting the experiment broke on racial lines. A curious protocol was employed, one that revealed a great deal about Dr. Vonderlehr's sense of the racial etiquette that would have to be followed in order to ensure the cooperation of the Tuskegee Institute's black leaders. When they corresponded among themselves or with other white physicians, the health officers invariably described the experiment as a study of the effects of syphilis on the "Negro male." But when they discussed the experiment with Dr. Moton and Dr. Dibble, they were careful to refer to it as a study of the effects of syphilis on the "human economy." The change in wording was significant, for it altered the appearance of the study from an investigation of race and disease to one of disease and people.

No one was fooled by the word game. Dr. Moton and Dr. Dibble both knew that black men alone would be studied. And yet nothing better illustrated the dilemma of black middle-class professionals who wanted to succeed in a society dominated by whites. The objective of whites was not to deceive blacks but to make it easier for them to engage in self-deceit. By politely and shrewdly refraining from stating what was obvious, the health officers permitted Dr. Moton and Dr. Dibble to preserve the fiction that the Tuskegee Institute was not lending biracial support to a racist experiment.

Without waiting for a reply from the Tuskegee Institute, Dr. Cumming informed Dr. Baker of his plans for resuming the experiment, formally soliciting the cooperation and approval of the Alabama Department of Public Health. Only a year earlier

Dr. Baker had responded to a similar request by insisting on a limited program of treatment. This time he demanded nothing of the Public Health Service and assured Dr. Cumming categorically: "This office will be very glad to cooperate in every way that it can."[19]

Dr. Vonderlehr was not idle while Dr. Cumming was negotiating with officials in Alabama. In addition to perusing the pertinent medical literature on syphilis and Negroes, he contacted a large number of experts in the field (including most of the members of the Cooperative Clinical Group), discussed his procedures and plans for the study, and invited their criticisms. Most responses were enthusiastic and encouraging in tone, providing clear evidence of considerable interest in the study within the scientific community. The only serious questions came from the American Heart Association, and here the objections centered on the scientific validity of the experiment.

In a letter to Dr. Stewart R. Roberts, the president of the American Heart Association, Dr. Vonderlehr sought confirmation of the diagnoses he had made of widespread syphilitic heart disease and help in distinguishing between complications that were caused by syphilis and those related to other heart diseases such as arteriosclerosis and hypertension. Dr. Vonderlehr admitted that he had been forced to rely on what he called "arbitrary measurements" of the heart in "separating the abnormal from the normal findings" and requested an official opinion "as to whether the separation is a proper one."[20]

The response was devastating. Dr. Vonderlehr's most important finding to date had been a high incidence of cardiovascular syphilis, and he had turned to the American Heart Association hoping to have his diagnoses confirmed. Instead, the spokesman for that organization, Dr. H. M. Marvin, totally rejected the scientific validity of the procedures and tests upon which the diagnoses had been based. While stressing that an official reply would have to await further consultation, Dr. Marvin pointedly observed: "I will say quite frankly that conclusions based upon the observations indicated in your letter would be regarded by me as of very little if any value," adding that the tests and procedures were "all open to serious criticism."[21]

The diagnoses, in Dr. Marvin's view, rested on hopelessly subjective observations, permitting Dr. Vonderlehr to peer at

X-rays and see syphilitic heart damage in cases where none existed. That view was later supported by a ten-member, blue-ribbon panel of specialists convened by the American Heart Association. The committee's report, issued in October 1933, was no less critical than had been Dr. Marvin's initial assessment.[22]

The American Heart Association's report did not shake Dr. Vonderlehr in the least. He dismissed it as an honest difference of opinion. In reply, he merely conceded that "the entire subject is open to discussion." Evidently, Dr. Vonderlehr still believed that his diagnoses were correct, that he had uncovered "a perfect goldmine" of cardiovascular syphilis, and that he was well on the way to proving that the disease affected blacks differently than whites. Had he been applying as a private individual to the American Heart Association for a grant to conduct the study, there is little reason to doubt that his proposal would have been declined. But as a member of the Public Health Service Dr. Vonderlehr commanded the funds necessary to conduct the experiment. He did not have to fear adverse reactions from a single group however prestigious or authoritative. He was relatively free to set aside negative assessments, and in this instance he did.[23]

Dr. Vonderlehr was more receptive to recommendations he thought were constructive. Introducing autopsies to the experiment's protocol was one example of his willingness to incorporate suggestions; his decision to add a control group was another. Late in July he wrote Dr. Dibble that the study should be expanded to admit "a number of control cases having no evidence of syphilis" and that the men "should be chosen from the groups previously included in our study last winter." Dr. Vonderlehr predicted, "it should be a very easy matter to pick out about 200 in the proper age group and bring them in for examination." The examinations were to be identical to those given to the syphilitic group, with one glaring, if eminently sensible, exception. "I do not anticipate performing spinal punctures on the controls," confided Dr. Vonderlehr. [24]

The control group was a crucial refinement, for it provided a basis for comparison that had been missing from the experiment. Periodic examinations of both groups, reinforced by autopsy reports on as many cases as possible, would enable the investigators to compare syphilitics with men who led similar lives yet did not suffer from the disease. The result would be a much clearer picture of how the disease affected people.

To recruit the control group Dr. Vonderlehr found it necessary to repeat his policy of deceit. Like the syphilitics, the controls were not to be informed about the study's true objective. They, too, would be told that the "government doctors" were returning to the community to examine people for "bad blood."

Dr. Vonderlehr would have preferred to examine the control group himself, or to have had Dr. Wenger examine them. Since neither could spare the time from other duties, the task fell to Dr. John R. Heller, a junior officer in the PHS's Division of Venereal Diseases whom Dr. Vonderlehr described as "an unusually intelligent young physician who has a clinical turn of mind." Dr. Heller thus became, as he later observed, "the first of many young health officers who were sent to Tuskegee to carry on the study."[25]

Born and reared in South Carolina, the son and paternal grandson of physicians, Dr. Heller received his medical degree in 1929 from Emory University, where he had been, as luck would have it, a classmate and friend of Dr. Murray Smith, the health officer of Macon County with whom he was to work closely for many years in connection with the experiment. Dr. Heller was concluding his second year of employment with the PHS when DR. Vonderlehr detailed him to Macon County in the fall of 1933. He had not, he later emphasized, been "in on the early discussions of the study" but had "merely followed the instructions . . . from Dr. Vonderlehr."[26]

As preparations for work on the control group neared completion, Dr. Vonderlehr became more and more disturbed that the Tuskegee Institute still had not formally agreed to the use of its medical facilities and staff. Throughout the summer and early fall, he presssed Dr. Dibble for a decision. Each time Dr. Dibble responded with assurances of his personal support followed by warnings that Dr. Moton might veto the project because of the Institute's precarious financial situation.

One stumbling block was the request that the Institute pay part of Nurse Rivers's salary. When cautioned that this might not be possible, Dr. Vonderlehr inquired if the Institute could provide her with room and board. The Institute would not be out any cash, and Nurse Rivers could earn her keep by working half time for the hospital and half time for the experiment. Dr. Dibble found the suggestion acceptable.

More difficult to grant were Dr. Vonderlehr's requests for hospitalizing terminally ill subjects and performing the autopsies at Andrew Hospital, for these involved staff time and some expense. When word had not arrived by the beginning of October, Dr. Vonderlehr took matters into his own hands and arranged a conference with Dr. Moton. They met in Tuskegee on October 20, 1933. At the end of the meeting Dr. Moton announced his decison: The Tuskegee Institute would cooperate fully. Terminally ill patients would be hospitalized in Andrew Hospital; autopsies would be performed there on as many cases as possible; and Nurse Rivers would be given room and board in exchange for half-time duty in the hospital. The remainder of her time was to be spent on the experiment.[27]

Dr. Dibble was delighted. He now had permission to participate in a study he thought had great scientific importance. His was to be a crucial role. In addition to admitting terminally ill cases and helping perform the autopsies, he also agreed to supervise Nurse Rivers's work with the men and happily accepted the appointment of "Special Consultant in the U.S. Public Health Service" at the honorific salary of one dollar per year.

Dr. Dibble was enthusiastic about the benefits the hospital promised to reap. "The prospects are very bright for an excellent clinic," he told Dr. Moton, "and it will certainly add greatly to the educational advantages offered our interns and nurses as well as the added standing it will give the hospital." The latter, in particular, appealed to Dr. Dibble, for joining federal and state authorities in a major research project might enable him to win recognition and prestige for himself and his hospital.[28]

Dr. Vonderlehr had good reason to be pleased; he had gotten everything he wanted from Dr. Moton. But a discovery made during his visit to Tuskegee lent a sense of urgency to getting on with the study. Opportunities for harvesting data were being lost: Three men included in the experiment had died recently, and not one had been brought to autopsy. "Two of these cases died a cardiac death," he wrote Dr. Wenger, "and it is therefore urgent that follow-up work on these cases be started immediately."[29]

A vital part of the follow-up work depended upon the state health department. During his trip to Tuskegee, Dr. Vonderlehr also visited Montgomery to enlist Dr. Gill's help in determining whether additional deaths had occurred unbeknownst to the Public Health Service. In addition, something had to be done to improve the intelligence system so that future deaths would be reported. In an effort to solve both problems, he gave Dr. Gill the names of the men in the experiment and asked him to "check this list against all death certificates reaching the Alabama State Board of Health" and to send the Public Health Service "a duplicate copy of the death certificate should one of the cases meet his demise." Dr. Gill promised to forward "the present list of deaths from Macon County" and declared: "In the future all deaths will be checked against this list and copies of these deaths sent to you." Dr. Gill kept his word. Over the years that followed the Alabama State Board of Health routinely supplied this information.[30]

Even more crucial was the cooperation that Dr. Vonderlehr worked to elicit from private physicians. Securing their support was not an easy task due to the sheer number who had to be won over. Dozens were involved. No purpose would have been served by concentrating solely on the physicians of Macon County because many of the men in the experiment actually lived in contiguous counties. In order to implement Dr. Wenger's suggestion about taking the local physicians into their confidence, Dr. Vonderlehr had to reach not only the physicians in Macon County but those in Lee, Bullock, Russell, and Tallapoosa counties as well.

Immediately following his successful meeting with Dr. Moton, he wrote the president of the medical society and the chairman of the board of health in each of the counties. He told them the Public Health Service was conducting "a study of the effects of untreated syphilis in the Negro in Macon County." Because the records to date revealed "an exceedingly high percentage of cases showing cardiovascular manifestations," he explained, the Public Health Service "desired to continue this study for some time in order that the clinical findings in the original work may be confirmed." Dr. Vonderlehr then requested a special joint meeting of the medical society and the board of health in each of the counties early in November so that he could talk with their members and explain how they could cooperate with the study. His willingness to undertake personally this arduous task testified to his zeal for the project.[31]

Dr. Vonderlehr returned to Alabama early in November to confer with the medical societies. In his letters arranging these meetings, he had stressed that the Alabama State Board of Health and Macon County Health Department were helping sponsor the experiment. Dr. Vonderlehr pursued this tactic at the ensuing meetings, seeking to allay fears from the private medical sector that the federal government might be acting unilaterally. According to Dr. Heller, who attended the conferences with him, Dr. Vonderlehr stated at the outset of each meeting that the Tuskegee Institute and the Veterans Hospital were full-fledged partners in the study. The audiences seemed to find this information reassuring. Indeed, Dr. Heller later maintained that it "practically assured the cooperation of the physicians in the surrounding area."[32]

The meetings with the local physicians were conducted as miniseminars on the experiment, with candor marking the discussions. "We told them essentially what we were doing," said Dr. Heller. "They understood it after it was explained to them as carefully as we could," he continued. "They understood what we were after, and were quite sympathetic and . . . encouraging to us." In fact, the wisdom of taking these local physicians into their confidence, of treating them like colleagues in the experiment, became more apparent with every group that was addressed. Dr. Heller remembered the audiences as being "very cooperative and very receptive," and recalled that many had "entered into the discussions" and were especially interested in "the medical aspects of it."[33]

No one questioned whether the experiment was ethical; no one even came close to doing so. "I don't recall any philosophical discussions at all," declared Dr. Heller. What emerged from his comments was the image of a profession whose members had closed ranks behind a study they were told had real merit. The experiment obviously had struck their sense of scientific curiosity, and it did not occur to anyone to suggest that it should not be conducted.[34]

Treatment was not discussed. Everyone at those meetings understood that the purpose of the experiment was to study untreated syphilis. Implicit in their approval was the pledge that they would not treat the men. Besides, there was no need to ask these physicians to withhold treatment; there was no real danger that they would provide it. The subjects were medically indigent. They had not received medical care in the past and there was no reason to think they would in the future.

But even if the men had been able to raise the money, there was little chance of obtaining effective treatment. According to Dr. Heller, the private physicians who practiced in the area were poor clinicians who were not skilled in administering arsphenamine and shied away from using it. The only treatment they were likely to prescribe were medicines that could be taken orally, and neither he nor Dr. Vonderlehr worried about this because they knew that it would not have much effect on syphilis.[35]

More was at stake in these conferences than informing local physicians about the experiment, securing their approval, and reaching a tacit agreement that the men would remain untreated: The Public Health Service needed their help, their active collaboration. Dr. Vonderlehr wanted them to serve as a conduit for funneling subjects to the autopsy table. Because tertiary syphilis is largely asymptomatic, he knew that the men would probably not seek medical assistance until they became critically ill—from whatever cause. The success of the experiment turned on what happened to them while they were dying. Those who died at home might well be buried before the news reached Tuskegee, and their autopsies would be lost forever. The best insurance was for them to expire in Andrew Hospital under the watchful eyes of Dr. Dibble and Nurse Rivers.

The help of the physicians was absolutely essential. At the meetings Dr. Vonderlehr distributed complete lists of the subjects and requested the physicians to check these names against their black male patients. Men on the list were to be referred routinely to Nurse Rivers, except those who were thought to be terminally ill. They were to be referred immediately to Dr. Dibble so that he could admit them at once to Andrew Hospital, where, hopefully, they would die and the autopsies could be performed.[36]

One by one, the medical groups agreed to cooperate fully. And with each pledge of support, Dr. Vonderlehr succeeded in closing the experiment more tightly around the men. The private physicians would be his diagnostic eyes; they would maintain the death watch; they would help bring the men to autopsy. Each pledge of support also meant that he had succeeded in shutting another door to treatment, reducing the possibility, however remote, that the men might obtain medical care. By the time he had finished the discussions, the subjects were sealed within the experiment, isolated from even the meager medical system that was open to their neighbors.

No doubt the physicians joined in the experiment with clear consciences. After all, what was being asked of them was sanctioned by health officials at the federal, state, and local levels, not to mention the black leadership of the Tuskegee Institute. But the fact that they did not perceive any ethical problems with the study does not in itself explain why they so willingly joined.

Their physical isolation may provide one answer. They were small-town and country doctors whose rural practices cut them off from the larger medical world, and they may have felt flattered to be asked to participate in a major scientific experiment. Many no doubt thought the study had scientific validity, that their fellow physicians could profit from the information it would yield.

Perhaps the most telling characteristic of the medical societies was the race of their members: They were all white. Alabama in the 1930s, the state of Scottsboro fame, was a segregated society, and professional organizations were no exception. All of the private physicians with whom Drs. Vonderlehr and Heller had spoken were white, and all of the subjects in the experiment were black. Avoiding professional contact with the men probably came naturally to doctors who routinely eschewed social intercourse with them, especially since withholding treatment in no way threatened the economic interests of the doctors. It cost them nothing because the men were poor, and there is no evidence that these white doctors were particularly solicitous about the health problems of black people who could not afford therapy on a fee-for-service basis.

What practical difference did the cooperation of the local physicians make in the lives of the subjects? It is true that ignorance and poverty had already decreed that most of them would not receive medical care. It is also true that the physicians in the area were not well qualified to administer effective treatment for syphilis even to those who requested and could pay for it.

But the agreement reached between the PHS and the local physicians had the effect of elevating a de facto situation into a policy. No longer were the men to be seen as potential patients; they had become perpetual subjects instead. Their status had changed dramatically; and in that sense they had become worse off than syphilitics in the area who were not in the study. Future developments in the public health movement might one day improve the quality of medical care that would be made available to them, but as long as the experiment continued no such possibility existed for the men on Dr. Vonderlehr's list. The status quo was to be preserved for them, placed beneath a microscope for scientific observation.

Dr. Vonderlehr returned to Washington following his successful discussions with the medical societies and county health boards, leaving Dr. Heller behind to select and examine the control group. The schedule called for Dr. Heller to work through the end of November and on through the first week or so of December and then break for the holidays, returning to Alabama to finish up after the first of the year. All went well. Fair weather prevailed, the roads remained open, and the vast majority of the men who were contacted cooperated. A few of those who reported had to be turned away because their blood tests now were positive, but for the most part the plan of using men from the old Rosenwald Fund survey worked smoothly.[37]

Once the news had spread that the "government doctors" had returned, men from the syphilitic group began appearing at Andrew Hospital. Dr. Heller commented that "every day now I have several of the 407 reporting for observation and 'pills.'" Though the men were supposed to remain untreated, Dr. Heller ignored the problem of contamination just as Dr. Vonderlehr had before him and gave the men small quantities of the protiodide pills they were seeking. Before long, however, he started handing out pink-colored aspirin tablets instead. This "pink medicine," as the doctors dubbed the aspirin, became an instant hit with the men. Most of them had never taken aspirin before and marveled at how it relieved their aches and pains. From then on, the "government doctors" routinely dispensed little bottles of "pink medicine" every time they examined the men. Within a few years, the "government doctors" also started dispensing iron tonic to the men. It, too, became much in demand. Perhaps no better placebos could have been used.[38]

Ironically, the only problem that developed with the control group stemmed from another federal agency's activities in the area. About three weeks after he began working, Dr. Heller reported to Dr. Vonderlehr:

> The project is moving along very smoothly now except for the C.W.A. [Civil Works Administration] which has literally disrupted the Ethiopian population as regards staying in one place very long. It was estimated this A.M. that no less than 3,000 men, 2,700 of whom were colored, were on hand at the Macon County Court House to register for jobs under the C.W.A. plan. Naturally, our clients down the way have forgotten all about such mundane things as appointments and have joined the wild scramble. The sheriff had to be called in to quiet them yesterday but they seem fairly orderly today. But we are slightly ahead of our quota to give us 100 by Dec. 9th and we will get them if we have to camp at the court house.

Despite such determination, Dr. Heller was not able to meet his goal and returned home to Nashville, Tennessee, in December, with only ninety-five examinations, a shortfall of five, which he blamed predictably on "the C.W.A. activities and inclement weather the last few days."[39]

A few days after Dr. Heller's departure one of the subjects became critically ill, providing the first opportunity for testing the system for securing autopsies that Dr. Vonderlehr had constructed with such painstaking care. The attending physician, Dr. Eugene S. Miller of Notasulga, Alabama, immediately contacted Dr. Dibble.

Dr. Vonderlehr must have smiled when he read what happened next. "Miss Rivers went to see him as soon as Doctor Miller notified us," wrote Dr. Dibble, "and brought him to the hospital." The man lost consciousness before arriving and died shortly after he entered the hospital, leaving Nurse Rivers the job of securing the family's permission for an autopsy. "She had some difficulty in getting a permit for Post signed," Dr. Dibble continued, "but she handled it very diplomatically, and we were able to get it." The autopsy was performed in strict compliance with the instructions Dr. Vonderlehr had laid down, with tissue samples from the brain, the spinal cord, and various organs, including the all-important heart, shipped immediately to the National Institute of Health. "Please let me tell you how much both Doctor Peters and myself [*sic*] enjoyed the autopsy," Dr. Dibble wrote Dr. Vonderlehr, "and if there are any additions for us to make in future cases, we will be very glad to make them."[40]

Dr. Vonderlehr was obviously pleased by how well his system had functioned and had nothing but praise to offer in reply. "Both you and Miss Rivers are to be commended for your alertness in obtaining this valuable information," he told Dr. Dibble, "and I feel that a start has been made in the most important and difficult portion of our study of untreated syphilis." Even more profuse was the appreciation he heaped upon the local physician who had been so helpful. After thanking Dr. Miller for his "thoughtful cooperation and kindness in recently referring . . . [the name of the deceased] to the John A. Andrew Hospital at Tuskegee Institute," Dr. Vonderlehr declared: "Such cooperation by the physicians of Macon County is the most important factor in bringing the study of untreated syphilis to ultimate success."[41]

Following the usual talks with state health officials in Montgomery, Dr. Heller returned to Tuskegee in February and resumed his search for controls. Speed was of the essence because he wanted to finish the examinations before the spring planting began. Nevertheless, he took the time to hold another round of meetings with physicians in the area. He emerged convinced that they would maintain the vigil and that more autopsies would be forthcoming. "No further deaths have come to our attention," he wrote Dr. Vonderlehr in March, "though I have my eye on several who could qualify for a place on Drs. Dibble and Peters' Table."[42]

Dr. Heller's confidence was not misplaced, for more referrals and more autopsies soon followed. In fact, a physician in East Tallahassee even sent a subject to Dr. Dibble who was not terminally ill but merely had an unusually severe case of ulcerated syphilis on his right arm. Publicly, Dr. Vonderlehr was delighted over this evidence of how well the referral system was working and offered to send the doctor a copy of the man's biopsy report. Privately, however, he still had a few doubts about the system, which he confessed in a letter written to Dr. Dibble:

I realize that we are asking individual physicians engaged in general practice in Macon and adjoining counties to be more than ordinarily alert in a matter which, while it may be of scientific interest to them, will bring them no financial reward. The entire follow-up scheme is a very interesting experiment and is, I am certain, well worthwhile.

If anything, Dr. Vonderlehr probably sold the local physicians short; helping science was apparently the only reward they wanted. Years after the study ended, Dr. Heller could not recall a single physician who had requested a referral fee for sending subjects to Dr. Dibble.[43]

By the middle of March a weary Dr. Heller had selected his final subject and the two-hundred-man control group was complete. The examination records were shipped to Washington, where Dr. Vonderlehr and several of his colleagues, aided again by Dr. Moore who evaluated the men's chest X-rays, spent several busy weeks poring over the data. The materials were then carefully filed away for future use. Together with the records on the syphilitics, they would provide the basis for determining how healthy men fared in comparison with those who had the disease.

One final task remained to be done to activate Dr. Vonderlehr's meticulously constructed system for bringing the men to autopsy. Late in the spring of 1934, he sent comprehensive lists of the subjects and the controls to the state health authorities, Drs. Dibble and Smith, all the local physicians, and Nurse Rivers.

Of all the lists that were distributed, none was to receive more use than the one that went to Nurse Rivers. And over the decades that followed, she gave Dr. Vonderlehr ample reason to be pleased he had overridden Dr. Wenger's objections against employing her.

CHAPTER 10

"The Joy of My Life"

THE first few autopsies upset Nurse Rivers. Drs. Peters and Dibble actually performed them, but she was required to assist. "I hadn't had that experience," she stated. "It wasn't an easy thing to see them do those autopsies." In fact, she reacted to them much like a layman. Cutting dead men open, removing their vital organs, brains, and spinal cords, seemed "crude" to Nurse Rivers, and because she felt squeamish she found it hard to fulfill all that was expected of her, especially securing permission for the autopsies from the men's families. "I wasn't sold on autopsy," she admitted, "so I had a problem selling it to other people."[1]

Nurse Rivers worked hard to overcome her personal feelings. She considered herself a professional woman, a nurse who could do what the doctors ordered. Assisting with the autopsies and obtaining permission from the families were among the most important of her duties, and she was determined to do her job well. She wanted to cast a happy reflection on the nurses' training program at the Tuskegee Institute and on Dr. Dibble for recommending her to Dr. Vonderlehr. Gradually, her distaste for the autopsies decreased and then vanished entirely, making it easier to deal with the relatives of the men. "I would come to find out that I was worse off than the family," she recalled. "The family would immediately say, 'All right, Nurse Rivers.'" Indeed, she went on to compile an incredibly high consent rate. During the first twenty years of the experiment, she approached 145 families and all but one granted permission.[2]

Nurse Rivers's success was no accident. With only slight variations she followed the same procedures with each family. Immediately after a subject had died, she would break the news personally to the next of kin, who, in most instances, was the man's wife. Her sense of timing was acute. "I wouldn't go right on in to the autopsy," she explained, "and I'd stay with the family because they would expect me to come and console them." Hours would pass with nothing more than sobs of grief breaking the silence.[3]

Often the family would create the opening. Faced with the loss of a loved one, they turned to her for some explanation. Many feared that they might be suffering from the same sickness and sought reassurance that they, too, would not die. But if such convenient lead-ins were not forthcoming, Nurse Rivers was prepared to initiate the subject of autopsies herself.[4]

The request was always conveyed in highly personal terms and with great sensitivity to the family's wishes, for Nurse Rivers had a gift for using the right language. "Now I want to ask you a favor," she would entreat the wife soon after they both had stopped crying. "You don't have to do it; we don't have to do it." She would then explain that the doctors wanted to learn what had caused the man's death, but instead of mentioning the word "autopsy" she employed a term that was sure to be understood. "You know what an operation is," Nurse Rivers would say reassuringly. "This is just like an operation, except the person is dead."[5]

Yet the word "operation" sometimes triggered fears of disfigurement. "This was all that they were concerned about," Nurse Rivers recalled. "They didn't want somebody thinking that the body had been opened up." Whenever concerns of this sort arose, she would promise the family that the doctors would not harm the body, declaring: "You won't know when he's dressed that he's had an operation!"[6]

That reply took care of the chest and abdomen, but failed to ease fears about the head. Thus, Nurse Rivers found it necessary to describe in graphic detail how the doctors would cut into the back of the skull, pull the hair over the face, remove the brain, and then put the hair carefully back into place. No trace of the procedures would be visible because the men would be lying on their incisions in their coffins.[7]

Moreover, Nurse Rivers assured the families that the autopsies would be kept absolutely confidential. In fact, she turned back on them the responsibility for any leaks that might occur, stating, "Nobody will know that body has been opened. If anybody knows it besides me, you, and the doctor, you've got to tell it."[8]

Nurse Rivers made certain the doctors were aware of the families' concern about disfigurement. "I'm going to tell you just one thing," she remembered saying half jokingly to Dr. Peters as the autopsies were beginning. "If you mess up that body, you won't get another." Not getting more autopsies, of course, would have threatened the experiment's future, and if it folded, Nurse Rivers knew she would either have to find new employment or return to Andrew Hospital as the supervisor of night nursing, a position she disliked heartily. "I'd be out a job," she complained to Dr. Peters, adding with a chuckle: "You got your job, don't mess with me."[9]

Beginning in 1935 her work became easier because the PHS began offering burial stipends in exchange for permission to perform the autopsies. The idea seems to have originated in a request for a cash payment from the widow of the first subject on whom an autopsy was performed. Accordingly to Nurse Rivers, the woman asked "for a hundred and fifty dollars for her husband's body as we performed an autopsy." Though the request was politely refused, Dr. Vonderlehr was quick to perceive in burial stipends an excellent means of enticing the families.[10]

In October 1934 the PHS submitted a formal request to the Rosenwald Fund for $500, with the understanding that the application would be renewed every year for the next ten years in order to provide ten burial stipends annually, each of $50. Sensing that the foundation might not wish to be identified publicly with the study, Dr. Cumming wrote to Davis: "If you do not desire to use the name of the Rosenwald Fund in this study this could be arranged I am sure." The Rosenwald Fund turned down the application. The request was rejected, Davis explained, not because the Fund objected to the experiment, but because it had been forced to adopt a strict policy against supporting new proposals. "I hope very much that there is some way in which the $500 can be secured for carrying through the projects," he concluded.[11]

The PHS had better luck with the Milbank Memorial Fund, a highly respected medical foundation in New York. In May 1935 the Fund awarded $500 to the PHS to pay the burial expenses of the men whose families consented to autopsies. In his first report back to the foundation, Dr. Cumming stated that the $50 that had been set aside for each death had been "sufficient to meet both the cost of burial and incidental expenses connected with the autopsy" and asked that the Fund "continue to support this study to the extent of providing for a maximum of ten autopsies per year at 50.00 each, or a total of $500.00." The request was approved. Indeed, the Fund renewed the grant every year for nearly four decades, increasing the amount of its annual appropriations as necessary to keep up with rising costs.[12]

The burial stipends were a strong incentive for cooperating with the experiment. "For the majority of these poor farmers such financial aid was a real boon," declared a PHS report published in 1953, "and often it was the only 'insurance' they could hope for." According to the report's principal author, Nurse Rivers, Macon County's black people "didn't have anything for burials."[13]

Nurse Rivers saw the burial stipends as a godsend for people who could not afford decent funerals. The cash payments also provided protection against losing the autopsies of men who did not die in the hospital. "They would let me know when somebody died," she observed, "because in those early days fifty dollars was a whole heap of money for a funeral." Occasionally, one of the men might balk, complaining that he needed help while he was still living, not after he was dead, but whenever this occurred, explained a PHS report: "She appealed to him from an unselfish standpoint: What the burial assistance would mean to his family, to pay funeral expenses or to purchase clothes for his orphaned children." Most of the families accepted the offer without hesitation, considering themselves fortunate to receive burial aid. Nurse Rivers, too, felt personally grateful because the money kept her from having to face them empty-handed. "I could go to them and ask for an autopsy because I knew the fifty dollars was coming."[14]

Nurse Rivers's interest in the families did not end once they had granted permission for the autopsies. She attended every funeral service and often sat with the relatives of the deceased. "I was expected to be there," she said. "They were part of my family."[15]

Her success rested in large measure on the rapport she had with the families, relationships that were close and ongoing. Keeping in touch with the men was essential, for if contact were broken, autopsies might be lost. In the early years of the experiment, there was a tendency to underestimate the difficulties that would confront Nurse Rivers as a follow-up worker. "The Negro in Macon County appears to be an individual who remains in the same place over a period of many years," wrote Dr. Cumming. "Old Negro men are frequently met who report that they were born within a mile or two of the meeting place and have never moved out of the County." He saw Macon County as a hermetically sealed laboratory, an ideal setting for studying syphilis "not presented in many places in the civilized world today."[16]

The view from Macon County was not quite that simple, as Nurse Rivers soon discovered. Monitoring hundreds of men was difficult, even when they stayed put. Many did not. Scores of the men led peripatetic lives, changing residencies within the area again and again. Others, hoping to find employment, left Alabama and joined the black migration to northern cities such as Cleveland, Detroit, Chicago, and New York. But whether they remained in one place or moved about, Nurse Rivers was responsible for tracking them and nurturing their interest in the experiment. And, as the years passed, those duties taxed all the persistence, stamina, and resourcefulness she could muster.

Nurse Rivers struggled to maintain accurate records on the men and devoted a great deal of time and energy to keeping her files updated. But despite her best efforts, many could not be accounted for at any given time. Some disappeared entirely, never to be heard from again. Others floated in and out of the study, returning one year only to drop out of sight the next. In fact, it was not uncommon for subjects who were listed as dead to reappear on the streets of Tuskegee very much alive.

Men who stayed in the vicinity posed the fewest problems because their movements could be tracked easily, making it possible to stay in touch by mail. But while form letters were

an efficient means of announcing impending visits by "government doctors" or the like, they were no substitute for face-to-
face meetings with a medical worker. More and more, Nurse
Rivers came to rely on personal contacts.

Home visits became an important part of her follow-up activities. Through them, she came to know the men and their
families well. "Miss Rivers would come by and check on us
between times we see the doctors," recalled one of the men.
"Yes, sir, she sure would. Come in and visit with us and talk to
us and ask us how we doing," the man continued. "Sometime
she'd feel our pulse, see how our pressure was doing . . . . It was
very nice," he added gratefully. Similar testimonials make it
clear that the PHS did not exaggerate when it reported: "A single home visit is worth more than a dozen letters on impressive
stationery."[17]

Nurse Rivers visited the ill more frequently. A subject who
was sick in bed for two weeks on one occasion remembered her
making "three or four different trips" to his home. To keep herself abreast of illnesses, she relied upon direct notifications by
physicians, the men's families, and the men themselves. The
men were especially helpful. In addition to contacting her
about themselves, they reported on each other, giving Nurse
Rivers eyes and ears everywhere. She did her best to be omni-
present because sick men could take a turn for the worse at any
moment, and it was her job to be there just in case a trip to
Andrew Hospital seemed advisable. Men who were amazed to
see her appear unannounced at their sickbeds often inquired
how she had learned of their illnesses. "Oh, a little bird told
me," Nurse Rivers would reply with a smile.[18]

The routine of home visits and sick calls made for a relaxed
pace, but the tempo picked up dramatically for a few weeks
each year when the "government doctors" reappeared. Nurse
Rivers set the exact dates, matching their visits to the cycles of
agrarian life, usually late January or early February so as not
to interfere with preparations for spring planting. She sent letters telling the men when and where to meet the "government
doctors."

"Annual roundups" was what the health officers called
their excursions back to Alabama. A different team of doctors
conducted the roundups most years. Leaving the checkups to
Drs. Vonderlehr and Heller would have provided continuity in

clinical personnel, but they had to give up the field work because they rose rapidly in the PHS and could not interrupt
other duties for two or three weeks each year. Junior officers
performed the examinations instead. During the lifespan of the
experiment, several generations of young health officers who
were involved with treating syphilis in other populations were
sent to Tuskegee to sharpen their diagnostic skills and obtain
experience managing uneducated rural people.

Working with so many different physicians did not make
Nurse Rivers's job any easier. Each new team had to be introduced to the men as strangers. "Some doctors were liked by all
the patients; others were liked by only a few," a Public Health
Report admitted. Similarly, some doctors seemed to enjoy
working with the men, while others could not wait to leave.
Standing between the physicians and the subjects was Nurse
Rivers. Perhaps most people would have found being caught in
the middle uncomfortable or even unpleasant, but she accepted
the role with philosophical detachment. "Some people rub
other people wrong," she observed; "there's got to be somebody
who can serve as a cushion."[19]

Several of the physicians were harsh and condescending,
projecting airs of authority and superiority that threatened to
inject overt racial tensions into the experiment. "I always observed the doctor's approach to these people because we had to
be very, very careful with them because they were sensitive to
the white man," observed Nurse Rivers. She had vivid memories of subjects coming to her and saying: "Nurse Rivers, I
don't like that man. He don't know how to talk to you." Whenever this occurred, she explained: "Immediately, I would go to
that doctor and I would say to him: 'Doctor, maybe I can help
you a little bit. . . . I think some of the patients don't understand your reactions. They don't like to be stormed at or yelled
to.' " After pausing a few moments for the message to sink in,
Nurse Rivers would tell the doctor that she was sure that he
could get all the men to cooperate. Then she would add with as
much firmness as the occasion warranted: "Now if you have
any problems and they don't understand and you don't understand just let me know and we'll work that out."[20]

Wise offenders took her meaning and changed their de-
meanor on the spot. Nurse Rivers recalled one young doctor in
particular, however, who tried to make excuses, claiming not

to realize that his behavior had been offensive. Though the incident had occurred years earlier, her back stiffened, her eyes
narrowed, and her lips tightened when she discussed her response: "I said [to the doctor]: 'You don't have to pet them; you
don't have to beg them. Just talk to them man to man. Just talk
to them; they understand. You don't have to get on your knees
to them, but just be polite to them. Just talk to them like
they're people.' " A few moments passed, then the physician
apologized.[21]

A few of the doctors went to the opposite extreme, assuming
an exaggerated tone of concern and politeness. Their approach
backfired, too. The men spotted them as "phonies" and reacted
negatively to their ingratiating manner. "You know," observed
Nurse Rivers, "sometimes you can kind of go overboard trying
to be nice and when you do, you mess up." Her solution was to
tell the doctors to act naturally, to be themselves. Any other
approach might drive the men away; "and I was terribly determined that we would not lose patients," she stated.[22]

For their part, the physicians came to respect her knowledge of human relations and to value her advice. One health
officer probably spoke for his colleagues when he described
Nurse Rivers as "a good right hand, an excellent person." What
commended her most, he confessed, was that she "would indicate to me the things that she thought I could or couldn't do
with them. . . . . She would not let me fall into any pitfalls. She
was very careful about keeping me out of trouble."[23]

If Nurse Rivers served as a "cushion," she also served as a
"bridge" between the doctors and the men. The health officers
occasionally complained that the men were uncooperative or
responded to instructions too slowly. She handled these situa-
tions by paraphrasing what the doctors had said so the men
would understand exactly what the doctors wanted. Nothing
angered the health officers more than subjects who refused to
be examined because they did not feel sick. The doctors inter-
preted this attitude "as rank ingratitude for a thorough medical workup which would cost anyone else a large amount of
money if sought at personal expense." On those days, the PHS
report explained, "the nurse reminded the doctor of the gap
between his education and health attitudes and those of the
patients."[24]

Rushing through examinations without giving the men

time to talk about their aches and pains was a serious offense for young clinicians to commit. The men felt neglected, uncared for. But instead of confronting the doctors whenever this occurred, they turned to Nurse Rivers, who listened to their complaints and offered soothing explanations. "She tried always to assure them that the doctor was a busy person interested in many things, but that they really were first on his program," declared the public health report.[25]

Though the men probably believed these reassurances, many wondered why the same doctors seldom returned. "They sent a different crew every year when they sent a doctor," a subject observed. "You never did see them others no more." Another man, whose eight years of schooling made him one of the best-educated subjects in the experiment, expressed his suspicions more strongly: "I tell you the only thing on down through the years that made me think on my way was that we never had the same doctor. . . . That's why I maybe begun to wonder ." Struck by the absence of older faces among the doctors, he added: "They were young men and that's what made me curious. I said [to myself]: 'I wonder if they were doing their intern or practicing on us or what?' But nobody ever said nothing."[26]

Few questions of this sort ever reached the doctors. The men preferred to devote their discussions to matters of health rather than personnel changes. Besides, the familiar figure of Nurse Rivers remained a constant, appearing like an old friend at each roundup. Her presence no doubt made the rotation among the doctors seem less important.

Most of the men never raised questions about the experiment, at least not outside their own circle. To them Nurse Rivers offered no explanations; one of her characteristics was knowing when to remain silent. "She never did tell us nothing about what they [the doctors] was doing," complained one subject bitterly. But when the men did raise questions, they asked them of Nurse Rivers. She parried each with consummate skill, varying her responses to match her listeners and imparting only as much information as the moment demanded.[27]

Often her replies merely echoed what the men had been told at the beginning. "The answer she would give me was: 'You just got bad blood and we is trying to help you,' " a subject recalled. While generally vague and elusive, Nurse Rivers

also knew how to trade upon the men's ignorance and need for
medical care to fashion explanations for the experiment that
they would find compelling. One subject who complained of
being in chronic poor health and asked why he should remain
in the study remembered her replying: "You may be suffering
with something you don't know it, and if you go through this
study then you'll know what's wrong with you and you'll know
how to remedy [it]."[28]

The relationship that evolved between Nurse Rivers and
the men played an important role in keeping them in the experiment. More than any other person, she made them believe that
they were receiving medical care that was helping them. "She
knew them [and] they knew her and trusted her," stated Dr.
Heller. "She would keep them satisfied that our intentions
were honorable and that we were out for the good of the patient."[29]

How well she did her job is evident from the comments of
the subjects. "We trusted them because of what we thought
that they could do for us, for our physical condition," said one
of the subjects. "We were unable to do anything for ourselves
physically." When asked about his participation in the experiment, another man replied: "We [were] just going along with
the nurse." He, too, definitely believed that he was benefiting
from the study for he added: "I thought they [the doctors] was
doing me good."[30]

If the men trusted and respected Nurse Rivers it was no less
true that she became genuinely devoted to them. Among all the
researchers, she alone came to know the men as individuals.
She visited in their homes, ate at their tables, sat at their sickbeds, and mourned at their funerals. Her life became inter-
twined with theirs, and a bond that transcended friendship developed between them. A young woman when the experiment
began, she grew old with the men who survived. In a real sense,
she shared their lives and they became her life. After watching
her interact with the men and their families, one of the "government doctors" observed that for her "the Study has become
a way of life."[31]

Evidence of their close relationship can be seen in the ease
with which the men joked around Nurse Rivers. Over the years
they spent many hours together riding to and from Tuskegee to
meet with the "government doctors." A lot of story telling went

on during those rides, and the men did not let Nurse Rivers's sex get in the way. "When they wanted to talk and get in the ditch," she explained, "they'd tell me: 'Nurse Rivers, we all men today.'" She approved heartily of this solution because once they had all become men, the subjects would say anything, delighting her with their ribald humor. She remembered one ride in particular in which a man turned to his friend and demanded to know why the doctors had asked him to take off *all* his clothes in the examination room. Before the man could reply, another passenger chimed in: "Well, he ain't got nothing you ain't got. . . .If it is [different], I want to follow you the next time." At that point Nurse Rivers shouted, "Lord, have mercy!" and asked the men to all be ladies again. "If you get women and men [together]," she explained again, "well, you have to be careful about what you say. See?"[32]

"Oh, we had a good time. We had a good time," repeated Nurse Rivers. "Really and truly, when we were working with those people . . . that was the joy of my life."[33]

To one health officer associated with the study, the relationship that developed between her and the men seemed warm, even caring: "They felt like they belonged to her and she belonged to them. They all knew her by first name, had great respect, and, I think, real affection for Nurse Rivers." Another health officer was sure that the feeling was mutual; indeed, that for Nurse Rivers the sentiment ran deeper: "She really loved those people, knew them, every one, knew everything they did, [was] interested in everything, and they could go to her at any time." Moreover, when Nurse Rivers spoke of the men, declared the health officer, "she talked about them as if they were her family."[34]

For most of her life the men in the experiment were the closest thing Nurse Rivers had to a family in Tuskegee. Her blood relatives lived elsewhere. She did not marry until she was well into her fifties, and when she finally did wed, she remained within the experiment, marrying Julius Laurie, an orderly at Andrew Hospital and the son of one of the controls. After her marriage the "government doctors" addressed her as "Mrs. Laurie," but to most of the men in the study she remained "Nurse Rivers."

Nurse Rivers's ability to recognize the men on sight helped the PHS prevent them from obtaining treatment. During the first few years of the experiment there was no real danger that the men would receive medical care. But in 1937 the Rosenwald Fund decided to renew its support of syphilis control programs and sent a black physician, Dr. William B. Perry of the Harvard School of Public Health, to Macon County. Fearing that the resumption of treatment activities might endanger the experiment and aware that Dr. Perry needed help badly, Dr. Vonderlehr shrewdly arranged to have Nurse Rivers assigned as his assistant. Dr. Perry agreed to cooperate fully with the experiment, and he and Nurse Rivers worked together for several months. Her presence at the treatment clinics no doubt guaranteed that the men in the experiment were not treated.[35]

Nurse Rivers was called upon to perform the same task a year or so later when another treatment program threatened to make health care available to the men. Shortly after Dr. Thomas Parran became surgeon general of the Unites States in 1935 and, due largely to his dynamic leadership, the PHS launched a nationwide campaign to eradicate venereal diseases. Detailing federal health officials to local health departments to develop effective education and treatment programs was an integral part of this campaign, and in 1939 a PHS mobile treatment unit was assigned to Macon County. Dr. Vonderlehr immediately took action to have Nurse Rivers attached to the unit. He did so, he explained, in order to "facilitate the follow-up of patients included in our study of untreated syphilis." According to a black physician who was involved with public health work in Macon County between 1939 and 1941, however, Nurse Rivers did more than follow up men in the experiment. "When we found one of the men from the Tuskegee Study," recalled Dr. Reginald G. James, "she would say: 'He's under study and not to be treated.'"[36]

Men in the experiment told similar stories. Because of Nurse Rivers, they were prevented from receiving medical care at the rapid-schedule treatment clinics that were introduced by the PHS in the late 1930s and early 1940s. Experimental in nature, these clinics offered an intensive, accelerated schedule of treatments with neoarsphenamine and bismuth, reducing the prescribed therapy period from a year or more down to a week or less. Rural patients were transported to urban clinics where they remained in residence until the treatments were completed. A subject in the experiment, who was waiting to board a bus with other blacks (the clinics were, of course, seg-regated) bound for Birmingham, was snatched out of line by Nurse Rivers. "You can't go down; you can't take them shots," he remembered her saying.[37]

Another subject made it all the way to Birmingham only to be denied treatment. A call must have been made from Tuske-gee, for the morning after he arrived a nurse announced to the entire group that there was a man at the clinic who did not belong there. When she called out his name, the bewildered subject immediately stood up and identified himself. "She said, 'Well, come here, come here. Why are you up here? You're not supposed to be. You're under Nurse Rivers in Macon County,'" the man recalled. "I said, 'They told me to come,' And they put me on the bus and sent me back."[38]

Nurse Rivers was not troubled by the duties she performed. Indeed, she never thought much one way or the other about the ethics of the experiment. She saw herself as a good nurse, one who always did what the doctors ordered. Not once did she advocate treating the men. In fact, she never raised the matter for discussion. She did not do so, she explained, because "as a nurse, I didn't feel that that was my responsibility. That was the doctors.'" Any other response would have been unthink-able for a nurse of her generation, argued Nurse Rivers, be-cause "as a nurse being trained when I was being trained we were taught that we never diagnosed; we never prescribed; we *followed* the doctor's instructions!"[39]

If anything, Nurse Rivers was comfortable not treating the men during the early years of the experiment. Neoarsphenamine and bismuth were the drugs of choice then, and she was concerned about the problem of side effects. "I saw so many reactions with these medications," she stated, stressing in particular the case of a woman who "died before she could get up out of the chair and we could get her on the stretcher." Similar experiences left her cool toward the drugs, no doubt making it easier to accept withholding them from the men. "I didn't feel good about neo and all this stuff," she de-clared.[40]

An apparent contradiction ran through Nurse Rivers's res-ervations. There was no denying that neoarsphenamine and bismuth occasionally produced harmful reactions, but they re-mained in use for the very good reason that physicians thought that the benefits of the drugs outweighed the dangers. If, as Nurse Rivers seemed to imply, the men in the experiment were better off not being treated, what is to be said for the thousands of patients whom she helped treat with the drugs? Was a disservice done to those patients by treating them? Certainly not. Those patients received the best care public health officials could offer under the circumstances. It seems clear that Nurse Rivers seized upon her doubts about the drugs (perhaps more in retrospect than at the time) as an excuse to justify not treating the men.

Rationalizing the denial of penicillin was more difficult. Within a few years of its discovery in the early 1940s, penicillin was hailed a wonder drug by medical authorities around the globe. Relatively inexpensive, safe for most patients, fast-acting and incredibly effective, penicillin gave physicians the best treatment for syphilis the world had ever known.

Nurse Rivers did not give penicillin a second thought, at least not in connection with the men in the experiment. By the time it became widely available more than a decade had passed since the men had been given any form of treatment for syphilis. A momentum had developed; not treating them had become routine.

Ironically, Nurse Rivers's real concern was that the men had become a privileged group. Compared with their neighbors, she saw them as "the cream of the crop" in terms of the health care they received. She formed that attitude in the early years of the experiment and maintained it for the remainder of her professional career. When the study began, the black population in many parts of Macon County lived outside the world of modern medicine. Though hookworm, pellagra, tuberculosis, and syphilis (to mention only a few diseases) were endemic in the area, many people went from cradle to grave without ever seeing a physician.

In Nurse Rivers's view the experiment lavished medical attention on those fortunate enough to be selected. Instead of being neglected, the men were examined by a team of physicians every year, received free aspirin for their aches and pains and "spring tonic" for their blood, and had their own nurse to look after them. "They didn't get treatment for syphilis, but they got so much else," she stated. Arguing that medicine is as much art as it is science, she also explained the therapeutic value of what the subjects thought was being done for them. "They enjoyed having somebody come all the way from Washington or Atlanta down here [to Tuskegee] and spend two weeks riding up and down the streets looking at them, listening to their hearts and [having] somebody to take their blood pressure and this sort of thing," she declared. "That was as much help to them as a dose of medicine."[41]

What troubled Nurse Rivers more than anything was the plight of people who came to her begging to be admitted to the study. "There were so many people who wanted just a physical examination, and nothing else," she stated. They had listened to the men tell stories about the wonderful care they were receiving from the "government doctors" and wanted help, too. "They'd come and tell me, 'Nurse Rivers, my blood was bad,'" she recalled. Most of the time she replied, "You have to go and talk to the doctor about that." But occasionally she would succumb and shuffle a few outsiders in with the others just so they could be examined and get a little medicine. She did so because she knew how much it meant to them and because she did not have the heart to turn all of them away. "That was the only thing that worried me," she lamented, "that there were so many people in need of the same thing yet they were not eligible for the program."[42]

Women posed a special problem in this regard. There was no way to slip them in, and they "got mad that they couldn't go" because "they were sick, too." The wives of the subjects were especially difficult. "I had one tell me, 'Nurse Rivers, here you come after John and I'm sick, too!' I said: 'Well, honey, I can't take you. I have to do what the doctors tell me.'" For every woman who accepted this reply, however, another would say: "Nurse Rivers, you just partial to the men." The doctors finally rescued her by instructing Nurse Rivers to tell the women that only men were allowed in the examination room because the patients were required to undress. If women were brought in, a female doctor would have to attend them, and one was not available. "So this was our alibi for getting through," explained Nurse Rivers.[43]

With outsiders pleading for admission and the subjects grateful to be in, Nurse Rivers had moral certainty that the study was benefiting the men. She persisted in that belief long after the introduction of new health programs in Macon

County had destroyed any foundation for it in fact. The treatment clinics these programs set up were not dispensing aspirin. They administered syphilis-fighting drugs for little or no charge to everyone who needed treatment. Nurse Rivers failed to see that the men in the experiment had gradually become the outsiders, that keeping them out of the clinics had transformed them into a deprived group. Instead, she remained captive of attitudes formed during the early years of the experiment. Events outstripped her ability to make associations or to fathom their meaning.

Nurse Rivers devoted her life to the experiment with a clear conscience. For her the men were the experiment, and she saw herself as serving them well. She had been trained to follow the doctors' orders and to take good care of her patients. Nothing in her nurse's training had prepared her to recognize that there could ever be a tension between doing what the doctors instructed and looking after the best interests of her patients. Her former teachers at Tuskegee, the private doctors in the area, and the PHS officers who served as her supervisors were all involved in the experiment. It never occurred to her to question their judgment.

Another professional hierarchy impinged upon Nurse Rivers: the division between medical practitioners and medical scientists. The stature of scientists in American society was high when the Tuskegee Study began, and her career paralleled advances in medical research that further increased their prestige. Nurse Rivers never pretended to be able to judge the scientific merits of the study. Her background was in clinical medicine, and as a practitioner she did not have the specialized training to challenge the authority of scientists. Far from fretting over the scientific validity of the study, Nurse Rivers accepted the expertise of her supervisors. "I'm not a scientist," she admitted freely. "I never thought much about it."[44]

Sex roles reinforced her ethical passivity. Most physicians were male, most nurses were female, and, within medicine as within American society, the men dominated. Deference to male authority figures formed a pattern in Nurse Rivers's life. Her father was the principal influence of her early years; Dr. Dibble molded her professionally and hand-picked her for the experiment; and all the supervisors under whom she worked were male. While she would not hesitate to argue with a physi-

cian in defense of the subjects, in most instances she did as she
was told.

Race was the final authority symbol in Nurse Rivers's
world. She was black and the physicians who controlled the
experiment were white. Indeed, the medical profession was
dominated by whites. While the participation of the Tuskegee
Institute lent an element of biracial support, it was still true
that the men who directed the experiment were white. Blacks
might conduct the day-to-day operations, but they reported to
white authorities in Washington and their contribution was
checked by whites during the annual roundups. The state and
local health departments, aided by white physicians in the
Tuskegee area, acted as local monitors, reinforcing the black
net erected to catch the subjects for autopsies.

And yet if Nurse Rivers was subject to the authority of race,
she never realized that the men were its victims. She knew that
only black men were selected as subjects, that they were chosen because they were ill, that they were systematically de-
ceived and lied to, that they were denied treatment, and that
syphilis killed many of them. But she could still say: "It didn't
affect me as a civil rights issue" and could declare: "I don't
think it was a racist experiment."[45]

The Oslo Study was the key. Nurse Rivers was aware that
the Tuskegee experiment was designed to provide a black contrast to the Oslo Study and she understood its overall purpose
was to prove that whites and blacks responded differently to
syphilis. This suggested that the races were being treated
equally. She completely ignored all the distinctions between
the studies. To her, all that mattered was that physicians had
once studied untreated syphilis in whites. "They didn't treat
those folks in Norway," she asserted. "This is the way I saw it:
that they were studying the Negro just like they were studying
the white man, see, making a comparison."[46]

Class consciousness offers the best explanation of her denial
that the experiment was racist. The dilemma confronting her
was the same for all the black professionals who were involved
in the experiment: on the one hand scientific energy and
money were to be devoted to the study of diseased blacks, long
ignored by science and medicine; but, on the other hand, the
whole notion of framing the experiment as a study of "the diseased" instead of "disease" smacked of racism. The social gap

that existed between her and the men made Nurse Rivers less sensitive to the full implications of attempting to prove that blacks really were different from whites. Class consciousness, stoutly reinforced by professional loyalties, served as the functional counterpart of race in placing her and the other black clinicians on the side of the white researchers. As upwardly mobile blacks they did not seem to feel personally threatened by working to prove still another way in which blacks could be labeled "different."

If Nurse Rivers avoided the difficult confrontation with racism posed by the experiment, she did not shirk her duty to the subjects as she saw it. To the physicians the men remained subjects, but to her they were patients. Her supervisors had decreed that the men would remain untreated for syphilis. That decision set the limits of what she could do. But within the confines of doing as she was told, Nurse Rivers struggled to preserve her professional integrity and personal humanity vis-à-vis the men.

Nurse Rivers spent her life tending all their ailments unrelated to syphilis, and she delivered excellent care to their families. The dual nature of her appointment made this possible. The experiment was only half her job; the other half consisted of regular public health work. When she was not busy with the men, she recalled, she spent her time looking after "my mamas, my old folks, and my babies." Much of her activity centered in the public schools and in the maternity clinic that opened in Tuskegee during the 1940s, but a good deal of her time was spent traveling across the county overseeing midwives, visiting shut-ins, and delivering prenatal and postnatal care.[47]

Relief work formed an important part of her routine. She would beg food and clothing from church and civic groups in Tuskegee and then distribute the items to needy families in the hinterland. No less than their neighbors, the families of men in the experiment had Nurse Rivers to thank for many kindnesses.

In a sense, Nurse Rivers managed to combine both parts of her job. The subjects were scattered across the county and she would visit them while out tending other business. "I saw the men while I saw the women," she explained. Over time the two parts of her job seemed to meld, and Nurse Rivers came to regard herself as the nurse who took care of everyone—in or out of the study. Not all of the men wanted to share her, though. On one occasion a subject saw her leaving a neighbor's home and stopped her, demanding to know why she had visited the neighbor instead of him. When she protested that she had not known that he was ill and needed visiting, the man replied: "No, ma'am, I wasn't sick, but you us nurse; you belong to us." In her heart, she probably agreed.[48]

Her years of service won national recognition. On April 18, 1958, Eunice Rivers Laurie became the third annual recipient of the Oveta Culp Hobby Award. Named after the first secretary of the Department of Health, Education, and Welfare, the award is the highest commendation HEW can bestow on an employee. She had an inkling that she was being brought to the nation's capital to receive an award, but beyond that she knew nothing. She made the journey by train, first-class Pullman service (segregated, of course) with meals served in her coach, and was very excited when she arrived in Washington. "She stood in the Department's big auditorium, motionless and bewildered, tears filling her eyes as Assistant Secretary Edward Fors Wilson announced she had won the coveted award," described a reporter for the *Washington Post*. "I was scared to death," she recalled. "[I] got up there crying."[49]

As she listened to the nice things that were being said, Nurse Rivers could not help feeling a little embarrassed and out of place: "People were lovely there and I appreciated it very much and yet I wondered if I was worthy of all of this." She had never thought of herself as an extraordinary person. As far as she was concerned, her work was just "a day-to-day job," and she did not expect to receive an award for merely performing her duty. "I was a public health nurse," she insisted, "I wasn't doing it for an honor or anything of that kind. I was doing it for humanity, for the sake of humanity."[50]

Though the experiment was not mentioned by name at the ceremony, Eunice Rivers Laurie was given the Oveta Culp Hobby Award for her role in the Tuskegee Study. She received a framed certificate praising her for "notable service covering 25 years during which through selfless devotion and skillful human relations she has sustained the interest and cooperation of the subjects of a venereal disease control program in Macon County, Alabama." It was signed by Marion Fulsom, the secretary of HEW. She hung it on the living room wall of her home in Tuskegee, proudly displayed between a photograph of Martin Luther King and a plaque on which the Florence Nightingale Pledge was inscribed.

Nurse Rivers continued to work for several years after receiving the award. In her final years, she stated, people often stopped her on the streets and said: "Nurse Rivers, how in the world you still following them old people?" Her reply was always the same: "Yes, I'm following them. They're friends of mine and I'm trying to keep up with them so that the department can keep up with them. . . . I love those people. I enjoy going out there and sitting down and talking to them." Old age forced Nurse Rivers to retire in 1965, but she continued to come out of retirement for a few weeks to help with the annual roundup every year until the experiment ended.[51]

CHAPTER 11

"Even at Risk
of Shortening Life"

THE PHS officers who began the Tuskegee Study devoted their careers to eradicating syphilis. For their generation syphilis was a dreaded disease, much as cancer became to post–World War II Americans. The PHS officers were field-oriented professionals to whom scientific experiments were of secondary interest. Administrators and clinicians rather than scientists, their primary concern was developing a national campaign to combat venereal diseases.

The PHS officers who worked in the VD Division called themselves "syphilis men," so great was their identification with their jobs. They were crusaders, true believers. Safeguarding the public's health was their mission, and as zealots they had a tendency to overstate the challenges they confronted. Labeling syphilis "the great killer" they proclaimed the gospels of prophylaxis, prompt diagnosis, and early treatment. To them it was the most insidious of diseases. "When a person had syphilis [in those days]," quipped a former PHS officer, "just everything that happened after that was attributed to syphilis—syphilitic ingrown toenails, syphilitic moustache, syphilitic baldness, what have you."[1]

PHS officers did not ignore the health of black Americans. They had worked with the Rosenwald Fund to survey the syph-

ilis rates in several black communities, and they had helped
staff portable clinics to bring treatment to blacks in rural
areas. Their efforts established the pattern for the national
campaign that Dr. Parran launched a few years later when,
once again, mobile clinics were dispatched in the South. And,
at a time when white physicians in private practice eschewed
professional contact with black physicians, the PHS's officers
employed black doctors. Drs. Vonderlehr and Wenger, in particular, promoted black hiring and used their influence repeatedly to arrange attractive residencies for young black physicians and to secure advanced medical training in the nation's
leading medical schools for older black staff members.[2]

In short, the PHS officials behind the Tuskegee Study were
racial liberals by the standards of the 1930s. Within the medical profession, they were truly progressive. They began the experiment because they were interested in black health, in
studying the effects of syphilis on black people. Macon County,
as they never tired of repeating in their private and published
writings, offered a ready-made laboratory for the experiment,
one they thought would have been impossible to duplicate anywhere else in the country. The health officers also believed that
syphilis in blacks was fundamentally a different disease from
syphilis in whites. The experiment, they hoped, would tell scientists precisely what the differences were.

Administratively, the Tuskegee Study was an easy project
to run, making few demands on PHS officials. The mechanism
for following the subjects and securing autopsies functioned
reasonably well, with most of the work done by health professionals in Macon County. The experiment was also cheap to
maintain. Nurse Rivers was the only staff member assigned
full time to the study, and her salary was never high. The
Milbank Fund paid the burial stipends. Other expenses were
easily absorbed by the PHS as routine operating costs.[3]

External events occasionally impinged upon the experiment during its early years, but the PHS officials showed remarkable skill in handling the problems as they arose. This
was especially true of matters that could be taken care of in
Macon County. The local medical establishment either cooperated with the Tuskegee Study or took no notice of it. Nationally, the experiment developed a following among syphilologists through published reports. The study went on its way

without much notice from the nonmedical world. Indeed, the PHS officers enjoyed virtual immunity from lay interference until public disclosure ended the experiment.

The Tuskegee Study had few detractors within the PHS and over the years it came to have a great many friends. Most discussions of the experiment revolved around ways of improving it scientifically. On the few occasions when someone did challenge the study directly, a defender invariably pointed out how long it had been going on, how much work the PHS had invested, and how science would benefit if the study continued. The results were to increase its bureaucratic momentum, making it largely self-perpetuating, and to strengthen everyone's resolve to improve the experiment scientifically.

Dr. Vonderlehr faced the first challenge to the study's continuation while he served as the director of the Division of Venereal Diseases (1935 – 43). Feeling that more attention needed to be devoted to the study and too busy to do it himself, Dr. Vonderlehr selected Dr. Austin V. Deibert to take charge. In the fall of 1938, Dr. Deibert went to Tuskegee intent upon staging something a good deal more important than a roundup. His assignment was to give the men thorough physical examinations. With the exception of a ten-year hiatus that included the period of World War II, the examinations were repeated approximately every five years thereafter.[4]

No sooner had Dr. Deibert begun the examinations than he was surprised to discover that the allegedly untreated syphilitic subjects had actually been receiving varying amounts of neoarsphenamine and bismuth. He immediately wrote to Dr. Vonderlehr and demanded to know why a study of untreated syphilis was being conducted on men who had been treated. To restore the experiment's scientific integrity, he suggested dropping the treated syphilitic subjects from the study and replacing them with new syphilitic subjects who were truly untreated.[5]

Dr. Vonderlehr was agreeable. He admitted that the men had been treated, but insisted it had been unavoidable. He explained that in the beginning there was no plan to make the experiment permanent. Also, it would have been difficult to hold the men's interest without giving them a little treatment. "In consequence," he stated, "we treated practically all of the patients with early manifestations and many of the patients

with latent syphilis." Dr. Vonderlehr endorsed the idea of replacing the men who had been treated, but he did not specify
how much treatment it took for a subject to be considered
treated. Since all of the syphilitic subjects had received at least
a modicum of neoarsphenamine or bismuth, he was apparently
concerned only with those men who had received quite a few
shots of arsphenamine.[6]

Dr. Deibert expected to discover a high concentration of
cardiovascular disease among the younger men. Instead, he
found relatively few severe cases in this age group. The impli-
cation seemed to be that the men had received some benefits
from the small amounts of treatment that Dr. Vonderlehr had
given them. Dr. Deibert wrote:

> The paucity of clinical findings still alarms me, but I feel that the
> inadequately treated group accounts for this. The majority of this
> group falls into the 25 to 35 year age group and that none of them
> have developed aortitis fortifies my belief that even a very little
> treatment goes a long way in avoiding cardio-vascular complica-
> tions, tho admittedly it is a trifle too soon to make a definite state-
> ment to that fact.[7]

Several years earlier, Dr. Vonderlehr had winked at the
problem of contamination, but it was not possible for him to
ignore Dr. Deibert's warning that the spontaneous course of
the disease might have been altered by treatment of the younger men. He now agreed the treated cases would have to be replaced. "If it is not possible to add the number of untreated
syphilitic Negro males included in the study," he wrote, "it
will, of course, be necessary to exclude all of those who were
treated some years ago in the future." Arguing that no purpose
would be served by studying these men, Dr. Vonderlehr added:
"I doubt the wisdom of bothering to examine the treated individuals carefully because we already have in the clinics of the
Cooperative Clinical Groups a considerable number of Negro
males in the proper age groups who have received inadequate
treatment and who are under observation." In other words, clinicians elsewhere (especially Dr. Joseph Earl Moore of Johns
Hopkins) had already compiled data on the effects of undertreated syphilis.[8]

Had Dr. Deibert taken these instructions literally, he would
have had to eliminate the entire syphilitic group from the

study. Instead, he ignored the fact that all of the men had received at least a little treatment, apparently adopting Dr. Vonderlehr's view that treatment was a problem in only a handful of the men.

Once he became interested in the work, Dr. Deibert quickly lost his compunctions about keeping the treated group in the study. Tactical considerations offer one explanation for his change of heart. He informed Dr. Vonderlehr that he had continued to examine the treated cases and planned to persist unless instructed to stop. "For psychological reasons I feel that these cases should be maintained: an 'esprit de corps' has been built up and if they be discarded, their fellow members on the 'list' will become suspicious," wrote Dr. Deibert. "It would then take a great deal of explaining and I am at a loss, as is Nurse Rivers, as to what to say."[9]

Dr. Deibert also confessed that the partially treated subjects had struck his investigator's fancy. "My clinical appetite is whetted by the maintenance of this group," he wrote Dr. Vonderlehr. "They provide another factor 'X' in the study." He predicted that the "inadequately treated group should prove valuable not only from the final pathological standpoint but clinical and serological as well." Though Dr. Vonderlehr had argued only a few weeks earlier that the treated men should be dropped, he reversed himself and granted Dr. Deibert permission to keep them in the study, provided it could be done "without great difficulty." He also reiterated his approval of the idea of adding new subjects to reinforce the syphilitic group.[10]

Fear of spinal taps was a major obstacle in the path of recruiting new subjects. "After the word passes along sufficiently that we are not giving 'back shots' they come out of the canebrakes," Dr. Deibert wrote Dr. Vonderlehr. "I hope I know something of the psychology of the negro," he continued, "but at any rate I try my best to send them forth happily shouting the praises of the clinic to their friends at home."[11]

Dr. Deibert planned to use men who were in the experiment to recruit new subjects. "To inject new blood into this study," he reported to Dr. Vonderlehr, "letters are now in the mail to all of the examined patients urging them to tell their friends that the clinic is being enlarged and we are optimistically hoping to 'screen out' 150 more suitable candidates." The need for new subjects had assumed greater urgency, he explained, because the physical examinations had revealed that not more than a hundred and twenty-five men in the diseased groups could be considered untreated. "To be significant," Dr. Deibert warned again, "the study must be stabilized by new men."[12]

Early in the examinations, Dr. Deibert discovered a problem in the control group. "About a dozen of the controls now have positive serology," he wrote Dr. Vonderlehr. Unlike the men who had long-standing infections, those with newly acquired syphilis were certainly contagious. Yet there was no discussion of treatment in the letters that passed between Tuskegee and Washington. Instead of dropping the men from the study and treating them for their recently acquired infections, Dr. Deibert simply transferred them to the other side of the ledger. According to published reports, the twelve controls who were found to have syphilis in 1939 were switched to the syphilitic group.[13]

But the large-scale rebuilding of the syphilitic group advocated by Dr. Deibert never materialized. After concluding his examinations of the original subjects, Dr. Deibert was able to add only fourteen new syphilitic subjects to the study group. Why his ambitious plans failed remains a mystery. Offering no details on the nature of the difficulties he had encountered, he informed Dr. Vonderlehr shortly before leaving Tuskegee that "the addition of an appreciable number of new cases must be deferred to a later date as conditions are not favorable at the present time."[14]

Although Dr. Murray Smith, the county health officer, continued to talk about bringing in new subjects for the next few years, no new subjects were added to the syphilitic group after 1939; neither were any dropped. Despite the concern that treatment had rendered many of the men useless to the experiment, subsequent investigators kept them in the study, preserving Dr. Deibert's "X" factor to the end.[15]

By the 1938 checkup, inertia was working to keep the experiment stable. The tasks were so well delineated that they could be carried on by new personnel, with or without full knowledge of the ramifications of the study. The role of the Tuskegee Institute as fiscal agent for the burial stipends is the best example. Beginning in 1939 the autopsies were performed in local funeral homes instead of the Tuskegee Institute's Andrew Hospi-

Unidentified subject and Nurse Rivers in cotton field. (*Center for Disease Control, Atlanta, Ga.*)

Obtaining STS specimens. From left: unidentified subject, Nurse Rivers, David Albritton, Dr. Walter Edmondson, unidentified subject. (*Center for Disease Control, Atlanta, Ga.*)

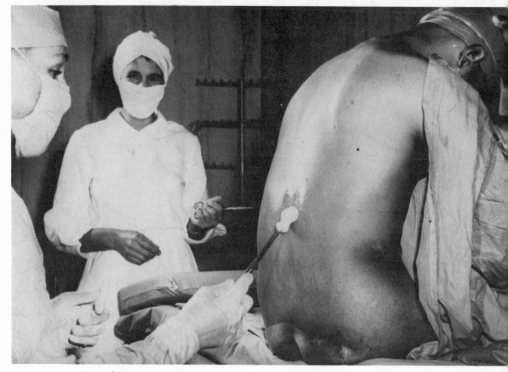

Spinal tap, 1933. From left: Jesse J. Peters, Nurse Rivers, and unidentified subject. (*Center for Disease Control, Atlanta, Ga.*)

Below left: Case of ulcerated cutaneous syphilis on left leg, photographed from rear. (*Center for Disease Control, Atlanta, Ga.*) Below right: Case of ulcerated cutaneous syphilis on right arm (*Center for Disease Control, Atlanta, Ga.*)

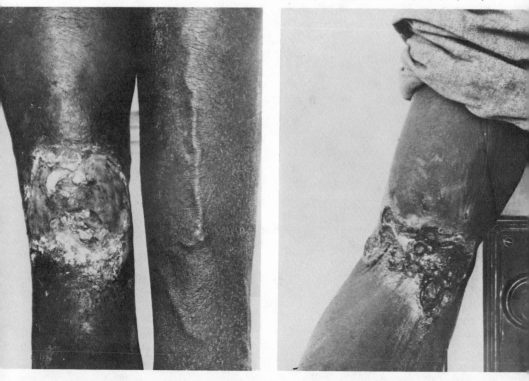

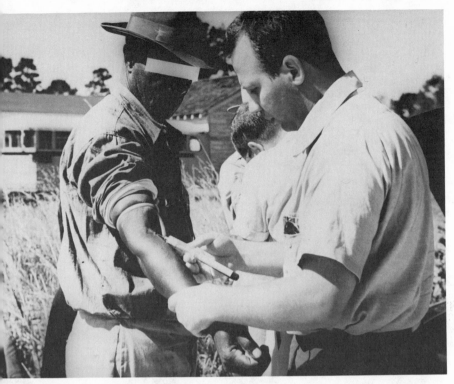

Blood test in annual roundup, early 1950s; unidentified subject and Dr. Edmondson. (*Center for Disease Control, Atlanta, Ga.*)

Eye examination. (*Center for Disease Control, Atlanta, Ga.*)

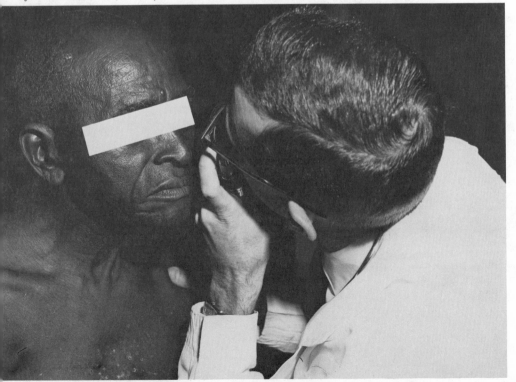

Annual roundup for solitary subject, early 1950s. (*Center for Disease Control, Atlanta, Ga.*)

From left in top photo, Mr. Albritton, Dr. Edmondson, Nurse Rivers, and unidentified subject. In bottom photo, Mr. Albritton takes blood sample.

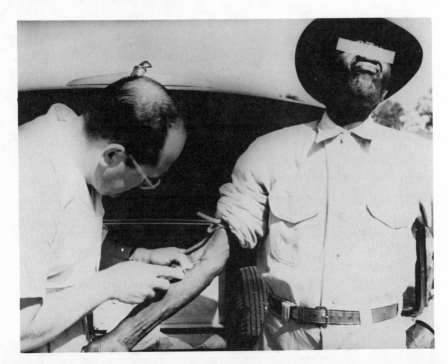

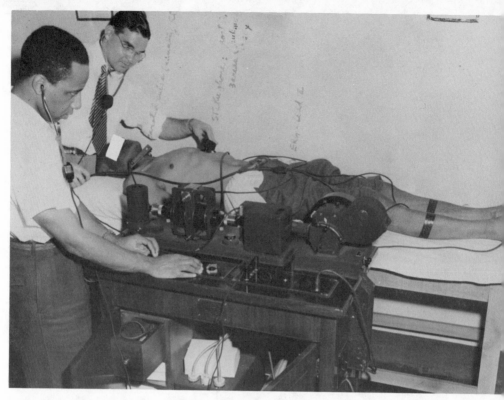

Cardiographic evaluation, early 1950s. From left, Mr. William Bouie, Dr. Stanley H. Schuman, unidentified subject. (*Center for Disease Control, Atlanta, Ga.*)

Mr. Bouie and Dr. Schuman performing X-ray examination on unidentified subject. (*Center for Disease Control, Atlanta, Ga.*)

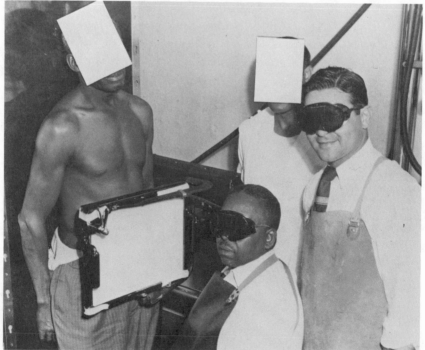

PHS officers, early 1950s. Standing, from left: Nurse Rivers, Lloyd Simpson, Dr. G.C. Branch, Dr. Stanley H. Schuman. Seated, from left: Dr. Henry Eisenberg, Dr. Trygve Gjestland (visitor from Scandinavia). (*Center for Disease Control, Atlanta, Ga.*)

Twenty-five year certificate, distributed in the late 1950s to each of the surviving subjects. (*Center for Disease Control, Atlanta, Ga.*)

U. S. PUBLIC HEALTH SERVICE

This certificate is awarded to

In grateful recognition of 25 years

of active participation in the

Tuskegee medical research study.

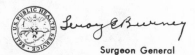

Awarded 1958

Surgeon General

Peter Buxtun testifying at the Kennedy hearings, March 1973. (*Courtesy Peter Buxtun*)

From left: Senator Edward M. Kennedy and Peter Buxtun, March 1973. (*Courtesy Peter Buxtun*)

tal. Two years later, Dr. Smith tried to convince Dr. Vonderlehr that the Macon County Health Department should replace the Tuskegee Institute as the fiscal agent for the Milbank Fund. "The officials at Tuskegee Institute are not the same ones that you and I had such fine cooperation with a few years ago," wrote Dr. Smith. "They know nothing about the study, they do nothing for the patients, and for two years autopsies have been done in undertaker parlors."[16]

According to Dr. Smith, the Tuskegee Institute's new principal, Dr. J. A. Kenny, had no knowledge of the experiment yet had to approve all requests before the Institute would release any payments from the Milbank Fund's burial grants. "If you will allow us [the Macon County Health Department] to disburse the fees, it will give us a closer tie-in with the families and undertakers, whereas at present they feel that Tuskegee Institute is giving them this help," wrote Dr. Smith. "They have lost sight of the fact that the Health Department is still doing its part in keeping the study going along according to plans."[17]

Dr. Vonderlehr turned down Dr. Smith's request. Explaining that the application designating the Tuskegee Institute as fiscal officer for the coming year had already gone off to the Milbank Fund, Dr. Vonderlehr recommended working to develop better cooperation with the Tuskegee Institute. In short, the Tuskegee Institute continued to handle the payment of burial stipends.[18]

Outside events alone threatened to impinge upon the study. Until World War II erupted, Nurse Rivers, with the aid of local and state health authorities, had successfully cut the men off from earlier treatment programs, but the war created a situation in which representatives of the lay public were making certain that syphilitic men in Macon County got treated. Approximately two hundred and fifty of the syphilitic subjects were under forty-five years of age in 1941 and became "A-1" registrants. Once the physical examinations they had received for induction into the armed services revealed syphilis, the men started getting letters from their local draft board ordering them to take treatment. In the spring of 1942, Dr. Smith informed Washington of the problem and requested instructions.[19]

Aware that Dr. Smith was a personal friend of J. F. Segrest, the chairman of the local draft board, Dr. Vonderlehr recommended a meeting with Mr. Segrest in which he would be told all about the experiment, with special emphasis on its scientific importance. Since the men were all over thirty-five and would probably never be called into active duty, Dr. Vonderlehr predicted: "It is entirely probable that if you place a list of the male Negroes included in this study in Mr. Segrest's hands he will cooperate with you in the completion of the investigation." Several weeks later Dr. Smith reported that the board members had agreed to exclude the men in the study "from their list of draftees needing treatment." Apparently, the arrangement worked well, for by the end of the summer he boasted to Dr. Vonderlehr: "So far, we are keeping the known positive patients from getting treatment."[20]

Preventing the men from receiving treatment had always been a violation of Alabama's public health statutes requiring public reporting and prompt treatment of venereal disease cases. In 1943 these regulations were superseded by the Henderson Act, an extremely stringent public health law inspired by the wartime emergency. The law pertained to tuberculosis as well as venereal diseases and required state and local health officials to test everyone in the state between the ages of fourteen and fifty and treat those who were found to be infected. Under the auspices of the law, health officials conducted the largest state-level testing and treatment program in the history of the nation. But just as the men in the Tuskegee Study were exempted from earlier treatment programs, the Henderson Act was never applied to them. State and local health officials continued to cooperate with the study.[21]

Two other developments made 1943 an important year in the history of the experiment: Dr. Heller succeeded Dr. Vonderlehr as the director of the Division of Venereal Diseases and the PHS started administering penicillin to syphilitic patients in several treatment clinics across the country. As director (1943–48) Dr. Heller occupied a strategic position from which to deal with developments that might have ended the study, and in each instance proved himself a loyal friend to the experiment.

Had Dr. Heller wished to end the experiment by giving the men penicillin, he could have done so. Yet penicillin presented no more of an ethical issue to Dr. Heller than earlier treatment had. When asked to comment years later, he could not recall a single discussion about giving the subjects penicillin. It was withheld for the same reason that other drugs had been held back since the beginning of the experiment: Treatment would have ended the Tuskegee Study. Dr. Heller asserted: "The longer the study, the better the ultimate information we would derive." The men's status did not warrant ethical debate. They were subjects, not patients; clinical material, not sick people.[22]

Ironically, the PHS officials saw improved health programs and the discovery of penicillin as additional reasons for continuing the experiment. In his annual report to the Milbank Fund at the end of 1943, Dr. Parran based his request for continued support on the claim that the study had become "more significant now that a succession of rapid methods and schedules of therapy for syphilis had been introduced, and the finding of syphilis has become practically a routine periodic testing of the citizenry." These developments increased the experiment's value, he explained, because it now could be used as a "necessary control against which to project not only the results obtained with the rapid schedules of therapy for syphilis but also the costs involved in finding and placing under treatment the infected individuals."[23]

Once the value of penicillin became firmly established, the PHS insisted that it was all the more urgent for the Tuskegee Study to continue. The 1951 report to the Milbank Fund argued that improved therapy had made the experiment a never-again-to-be-repeated opportunity. The widespread use of wonder drugs for a variety of ailments had practically eliminated the possibility of finding another large group of syphilitic patients. The report declared that the information the study was yielding "can never be duplicated since penicillin and other antibiotics are being so widely used in the treatment of other diseases thereby affording a definite treatment for syphilis."[24]

If penicillin failed to change Dr. Heller's views on treating the men, he was equally unmoved by the moral concerns about human experimentation that developed during the Nuremberg trials. He saw no connection whatsoever between the Tuskegee Study and the atrocities committed by Nazi scientists. "I, like most everybody else, was horrified at the things that were practiced upon these Jewish people, such as doing experiments while the patients were not only alive but doing such things as would cause their deaths," he later recalled. "All of these sorts of things were horrendous to me and I, like most everyone else, deplored them." He did not make any associations between Tuskegee and Nuremberg, Dr. Heller insisted, "because to me there was no similarity at all between them." The health officers who assumed responsibility for the study after Dr. Heller no doubt agreed with that assessment. There is no evidence that the Tuskegee Study was ever discussed in the light of the Nuremberg code, the ten basic conclusions or principles on human experimentation that emerged from the trials.[25]

And yet there was a similarity between the Nazi experiments and the Tuskegee Study, one which went beyond their racist and medical natures. Like the chain of command within the military hierarchy of Nazi Germany, the Tuskegee Study's firm entrenchment in the PHS bureaucracy reduced the sense of personal responsibility and ethical concern. For the most part doctors and civil servants simply did their jobs. Some merely "followed orders"; others worked for "the glory of science."

It made little difference who was at the helm. When Dr. Heller left the Division of Venereal Diseases in 1948 to become the director of the National Cancer Institute, the Tuskegee Study was fifteen years old. He and Dr. Vonderlehr, with the aid and approval of Dr. Parran, the surgeon general, had kept it going through the national syphilis campaign, World War II, the development of penicillin, and public reaction to the Nuremberg trials. Indeed, under their guidance and patronage, the experiment had evolved into something of a "sacred cow" within the PHS.

The new generation of senior officials who took charge of the experiment, men such as Dr. Theodore J. Bauer (director, 1948–52), Dr. James K. Shafer (director, 1953–54), Dr. Clarence A. Smith (director, 1954–57), and Dr. William J. Brown (director, 1957–71) had grown to maturity in the PHS with the Tuskegee Study. Many of them had been personal friends and protégés of the study's organizers. Most had conducted roundups as junior officers or had at least heard their superiors deliver papers on the experiment at professional meetings. A closely knit group of career officers, they had watched the study become a living tradition. In short, the study had become routine and they had grown accustomed to it.

Thus, the transfer of power to new senior officials in the late 1940s and on through the 1950s posed no real threat to the Tuskegee Study. Unable to look with new perspectives, the health officials who inherited the study could not review it objectively. Familiarity had co-opted them before they assumed command. The experiment never received a fresh review.

A test case came immediately after Dr. Heller departed. In July of 1948, Dr. Theodore J. Bauer, the newly appointed director of the Division of Venereal Diseases, received a sharply critical memorandum on the experiment from Albert P. Iskrant, the chief of the Office of Statistics of the division. Iskrant's reading of the three articles that had been published by 1948 left him skeptical and troubled about the scientific merits of the study and somewhat uneasy about its moral implications as well. After objecting to several procedural and conceptual weaknesses in the study's protocol, Iskrant asked whether the subjects had been "tested in accordance with the Alabama law, and if so, were any of the study group placed under treatment?" In addition, he echoed Dr. Deibert's charge of a decade earlier that the experiment had been contaminated by treatment. Noting references to treatment of the supposedly untreated syphilitics, he declared: "Perhaps the most that can be salvaged is a study of inadequately treated [syphilis]." Significantly, Iskrant did not recommend that the study be ended; merely that efforts be made to improve it scientifically.[26]

No action was taken on Iskrant's memorandum, but within a few years everyone agreed that the study was beset with problems. No one knew the exact number of subjects (different figures were given in practically every published report); the records were incomplete and poorly organized; attendance had fallen off at the annual roundups; numerous subjects could no longer be accounted for; and the issue of contamination remained unsettled.

In 1951 the PHS launched a full-scale review of the procedures that had been followed to date. The review was conducted by the two officers who had assumed responsibility for the Tuskegee Study, Dr. Sidney Olansky and his assistant, Dr. Stanley H. Schuman, both of the PHS's Venereal Disease Research Laboratory in Chamblee (a suburb of Atlanta), Georgia. They contacted the study's organizers and all of the senior officers who had worked on it down through the years, soliciting their views on whether the study should be continued and how it could be improved.

The old guard was unanimous in recommending that the study go forward. Dr. Heller confessed that he had little to offer in the way of concrete suggestions, but stated that he still believed "in the original concept of following up these individuals" and urged his successors to "get as many as possible back in the active file and learn as much about them as you possibly can." Dr. Wenger made the point even stronger: "We know now, what we could only surmise before, that we have contributed to their ailments and shortened their lives," he wrote. "I think the least we can say is that we have a high moral obligation to those that have died to make this the best study possible." Another senior official declared: "We have an investment of almost 20 years of Division interest, funds, and personnel," as well as a "responsibility to the survivors for their care and really to prove [to them] that their willingness to serve, even at risk of shortening life, as experimental subjects [has not been in vain]. And finally a responsibility to add what further we can to the natural history of syphilis."[27]

Following these consultations, Drs. Olansky and Schuman conferred with specialists from several fields who assembled in Tuskegee. High on the agenda was the issue of contamination, but the health officers framed the discussions in such a way as to prejudice the answer. Instead of reviewing the therapy the men had received since 1932, the stated aim of their inquiry was: "To learn how much treatment this group of supposedly untreated syphilitics has received since the widespread introduction of antibiotics." In other words, they limited the scope of their review and refused to confront the problem squarely.[28]

The results were predictable. Subsequent references to treatment in the published literature insisted that the men could still be considered untreated because they had not received enough treatment to cure them. Thus, Dr. Vonderlehr's successors joined him in denying that the Tuskegee Study was contaminated.[29]

Drs. Olansky and Schuman were especially eager to rekindle the subjects' enthusiasm for the study. Their plan emphasized the need to increase the "reservoir of good will in our patients" by distributing a little medicine for everyday ailments, maintaining close contact with the follow-up workers, stressing the burial stipends, and lecturing to the men in small groups "on the importance and significance of this study, reinforced by a photograph of each group." Provided that the matter was handled skillfully, they thought it might even be possible to persuade the men to consent to lumbar punctures (spinal taps) once again. "Good will (i.e., interest in the patient as a person) and group psychology (i.e., undergoing all the procedures as a group) will be our chief aids in securing L.P.'s," they wrote.[30]

The researchers also tried to promote coordination and data sharing between the Tuskegee Study and the Oslo Study. As luck would have it, Drs. Olansky and Schuman were working to revitalize the experiment when the venerable Norwegian study was also being reviewed. Dr. Trygve Gjestland, the current director of the Oslo Study, happened to be visiting in the United States in 1951, and in November he was asked to join them in Tuskegee to review the experiment.

Dr. Gjestland remained in Tuskegee for a week. Noting that he was immediately struck by "the remarkable socioeconomic and racial differences between the rural Alabama Negro farmers and the fair-skinned Norwegians," eyewitnesses to his visit later reported: "As the first men trooped into the hospital for examination, Dr. Gjestland and the examiners felt as if they were witnessing a strange and historic procession." Before departing, he offered detailed suggestions for improving the study, the most important of which were reorganizing and updating the records and reviewing the criteria for clinical diagnoses of syphilis and syphilitic heart disease.[31]

Predictably, the health officials emerged from the 1951 review convinced that the experiment should go forward. The consultations and discussions had taken months to complete, but the hard questions had not been asked. No one had pushed the issue of contamination; no one had questioned whether the study was ethical. Instead, the talks had centered on procedural improvements, ignoring a host of issues that might have ended the study then and there.

The review did generate a major overhaul of the experiment. In 1952, the files were reorganized, a team of statisticians transferred the autopsy reports to punch cards, and a single set of diagnostic standards was adopted. No personnel changes were made in Tuskegee. Nurse Rivers was retained and Dr. Peters was kept in charge of the autopsies, a service he continued to render until his retirement in the early 1960s. To improve the quality of his work, Dr. Peters received a new set of instruments in 1952, replacing what one health officer called "over-age tools resembling some high grade Neanderthal equipment."[32]

The fourth major examination of the subjects, conducted in 1952, boasted the most thorough medical scrutiny of the men to date. In addition, the researchers launched an extensive effort to reach men who had moved out of the area. Working with the names and addresses supplied by Nurse Rivers, the PHS employed its national network to full advantage for the first time. Dr. Bauer, the division director, furnished state and local health officials across the country with the names and addresses of subjects in their vicinities and asked his colleagues to bring the men in for examinations. He sent each health officer an examination kit and in some instances arranged for PHS officers to bring thè subjects to the clinics and hospitals. No health department refused the request, and Dr. Bauer received especially good cooperation from health officials in Chicago, Cleveland, Detroit, and New York. During the next two decades, Dr. Bauer's practice of using state and local health departments to keep the men in the study became standard operating procedure.

A new reason for continuing the experiment emerged during the 1952 examinations: The Tuskegee Study promised to become an important investigation of aging. The subjects were either old or middle aged (the youngest was forty-four in 1952), presenting researchers with the opportunity to follow the process of aging as well as the effects of syphilis. After examining more than a hundred subjects and assisting Dr. Peters with a few autopsies, Dr. Schuman declared that he had been "most stimulated by the problems involved in distinguishing syphilitic changes from the aging process." As he neared the end of the examinations, Dr. Schuman announced even more emphatically: "As far as I am concerned, this Tuskegee project is only half-realized. Its possibilities are only developing. Its conclusions will probably shed as much light on our understanding of the factors in aging and heart disease as in the problems of syphilis."[33]

Dr. Schuman's comments were consistent with earlier published reports. An article that appeared on the study in 1946 revealed that the life expectancy of syphilitics who were between the ages of twenty-five and forty-five when the experiment began was 20 percent lower than controls in the same age group. After age forty-five, the article explained, the marked disparity in life expectancy between the two groups decreased gradually with age. The meaning was clear: Syphilis shortened the lifespan of its victims appreciably, but it did most of its damage while the men were still relatively young.[34]

Later reports on the Tuskegee Study elevated the importance of aging to official PHS dogma. In a 1954 article, the researchers declared that "the effects of the natural aging process reflected in both study groups tend to overshadow any difference due to the syphilitic process in the older groups." A report published the same year predicted: "In the years to come, the force of mortality associated with aging will tend to obscure the possible effects of syphilis." And in 1964 still another article stated that the syphilitic group had only a few more abnormalities than the control group, "a finding expected since syphilis would be expected to have taken its toll earlier. After the age of 55 the processes of aging emerge and seem to become the significant factors in both groups."[35]

By focusing on aging as well as syphilis, Drs. Schuman and Olansky added a new rationale for continuing the experiment until the last man had died. In the future the study would require even greater patience (an article published in 1954 estimated that it would take at least another twenty years for all the men to die, an estimate that proved conservative) because the remaining syphilitics had already survived the period of highest risk. Moreover, the older the experiment became and the longer the survivors were able to live with the disease, the more difficult it would become for future researchers to see that the experiment was harming the men. The benign view that PHS officers came to have of the experiment in the 1950s and 1960s stemmed, in no small part, from the longevity of the survivors.[36]

No doubt the belief that the experiment was not harming the men contributed to the pleasure that young officers derived from the yearly visits to Tuskegee. According to senior officials, the junior officers who were sent on the roundups liked the assignment. Dr. Olansky recalled one health officer in the

1950s who became "so enamored of those people that he wanted to go back and study them again." The civil rights movement did nothing to change their enthusiasm. Long after the public had become disturbed over racial injustices in the South, the PHS still had staff members who were eager to conduct the roundups in Alabama. Dr. William J. Brown, the director of the Division of Venereal Diseases from 1957 to 1971, stated that he had no difficulty getting health officers to work on the experiment, including physicians who had grown up in the North. Dr. Brown observed: "These young physicians out of the East enjoyed going down. . . . They liked to go down there and see these people and examine them."[37]

The health officers enjoyed the roundups, at least in part, because of the warm receptions they got from the subjects. References to grateful, happy men form a constant theme in the reports of health officers throughout the forty-year history of the experiment. "They were always very cheerful; they were always very glad to see us," recalled Dr. Olansky. The men appreciated the aspirin and iron tonic that were handed out, he explained, and often tried to show their gratitude by giving the "government doctors" gifts. "They brought cornbread, cookies, whatever they had that they could make," Dr. Olansky added, "and they were very, very pleased if you ate it—most pleased."[38]

The junior officers got more than token presents out of the roundups. Most were young doctors with little clincial experience. The trips to Tuskegee gave them a chance to sharpen their diagnostic skills by observing the complications of late syphilis. Thus, in addition to collecting blood samples and stimulating the subjects' interest, the roundups served as a training program for young officers.

The trips also provided welcome respites from other duties. Treating syphilitic patients was boring work, especially after the discovery of penicillin. The roundups permitted the doctors to escape the routine of treatment clinics and savor, if only for a few weeks, the intellectual excitement of becoming researchers on a scientific experiment, one that their superiors regarded as very important. Moreover, for physicians with scientific ambitions, the Tuskegee Study afforded opportunities to publish and advance their careers.

Like their predecessors, the health officials who guided the experiment during its second twenty years proved adept at maintaining the interest of the subjects. In 1958, for example, they distributed certificates of appreciation and cash payments of twenty-five dollars to the men—one dollar for each year of the study. Printed on heavy paper, bearing the seal of the United States Public Health Service, signed by the surgeon general, Dr. Leroy E. Burney, and resembling Sunday school attendance awards, the certificates thanked the men by name for "25 years of active participation in the Tuskegee medical research study." The certificates were a big hit. Two years after the award ceremony, Nurse Rivers was still trying to get copies for the men who had not been present, describing one man as "very much disturbed" that he had not received his. "That reminds me," she complained humorously, "I did not receive my certificate!"[39]

In the early 1960s, the researchers changed the season for the roundups from winter to summer so the subjects and the health officers could enjoy better weather during their meetings. The men had grown older, many had retired, and there was less reason to be concerned about interfering with their work. The health officers also started distributing small cash payments, one or two dollars per man, on a regular basis as inducements for the men to cooperate.

As time passed officials simply assumed that the study would continue until the last subject had died. It was as though the PHS had converted Macon County and the surrounding areas into its own private laboratory, a "sick farm" where diseased subjects could be maintained without further treatment and herded together for inspection at the yearly roundups. The health officer who conducted the 1970 roundup even spoke of "corraling" the men for study. The work made no emotional demands on the health officers because the contact they had with the subjects did not require them to develop person-to-person relationships. They never got to know them as patients or as people.[40]

Instead, the health officers behaved like absentee landlords, issuing orders from afar, demanding strict accountings for day-to-day affairs, and appearing in Tuskegee only when needed. From their standpoint the operation of the "sick farm" was nearly ideal. They were free to analyze data and to write articles; a few weeks of frantic activity each year on the roundups was all they had to do in Alabama. Time, disease, and Nurse Rivers took care of the rest.

CHAPTER 12

"Nothing Learned Will Prevent, Find, or Cure a Single Case"

BARRING public disclosure, the only pressure that might have forced PHS officials to end the Tuskegee Study voluntarily would have been the adoption of federal guidelines on human experimentation. Discussions by PHS and NIH officials about the need to regulate human experimentation in extramural research programs dated from 1945. Little came of these early deliberations. The Nazi experiments had practically no effect on them because American officials tended to dismiss the German studies as the isolated acts of deranged scientists—sheer madness that would never again be repeated.

Low-key discussions on human experimentation continued within the PHS and NIH into the 1950s and 1960s, largely because officials thought that the government agencies that promoted scientific research should encourage academic and private industry investigators to adopt guidelines creating a system of self-regulation for scientists. The civil rights movement no doubt added to the pressure for reform during the 1960s by calling attention to the plight of minority groups, as did the consumers' rights movement by demanding better service and more public accountability from the professions. The first federal law that explicitly imposed controls on human experimentation came in response to the thalidomide tragedy.

The Pure Food and Drug Act Amendments of 1962 sought to protect the public by ordering doctors to inform their patients when they were being given drugs experimentally.

Additional impetus for government regulation came from the international front. The Declaration of Helsinki, issued by the World Health Organization in 1964, served notice that American government agencies were out of step with international medical developments in failing to take action to protect the subjects of scientific experiments. The Declaration of Helsinki announced a series of guidelines that were much less legalistic than the Nuremberg Code and far more concerned with the ethics of human experimentation. Endorsed by practically all of the leading medical organizations in the United States, the code contained provisions on informed consent that were especially stringent.

An NIH report in 1964 further strengthened the case for action. The result of years of inquiry, the paper revealed that within the American medical profession there were no generally accepted codes on clinical research. The legal status of studies involving human subjects remained ambiguous at best, and wide variations existed in official attitudes toward human experimentation. The potential for abuse became clear with the exposure of a shocking experiment. During the review of their own report on human experimentation, NIH officials learned of an ongoing study in which medical scientists in the United States had injected live cancer cells into patients. Distressed by this revelation and mindful of the need to fill an apparent void, government health officials began work drafting flexible guidelines that would keep federal control of research to a minimum, while creating the appearance of decisive action.[1]

On February 8, 1966, the surgeon general's office issued Policy and Procedure Order Number 129, outlining the PHS's first guidelines on clinical research and training grants. The guidelines established a system of peer review exercised by a standing panel of colleagues at an investigator's institution. Members of the committee had the responsibility of reviewing all proposals from their institution and submitting an "assurance of compliance" to the PHS.[2]

Critics accused the review panels of being weighted in favor of the investigators, and the PHS responded by revising the guidelines in 1969. Henceforth, the panels had to include members with nonscientific backgrounds. In 1971, the surgeon general attempted to clarify the policy again, requiring review panels to include people who were capable of judging projects by community standards. In practice, however, the 1969 and 1971 revisions had little effect. The heart of the regulations remained peer review, and the government made no attempt to apply rigid rules to diverse research proposals. Instead of drafting a substantive moral or ethical code, health officials preferred to rely upon procedural guidelines to be applied by a system of decentralized review committees.[3]

Significantly, none of the guidelines contained provisions that applied to the PHS's own research programs. Nothing in the guidelines, except, of course, their spirit, obliged the PHS to meet the same standards as its grantees. Thus, none of the health officers connected with the Tuskegee Study expressed any ethical concern until critics started asking questions.

In June 1965, Dr. Irwin J. Schatz, a staff member of the Henry Ford Hospital in Detroit, became the first member of the medical profession to object to the Tuskegee Study. After reading one of the published reports on the experiment, he wrote the primary author of an article published in 1964:

> I am utterly astounded by the fact that physicians allow patients with a potentially fatal disease to remain untreated when effective therapy is available. I assume you feel that the information which is extracted from observations of this untreated group is worth their sacrifice. If this is the case, then I suggest that the United States Public Health Service and those physicians associated with it need to reevaluate their moral judgments in this regard.

Dr. Schatz never received a reply. His letter was tucked away in the files of the Center for Disease Control with a note stapled to it by Dr. Anne Q. Yobs (coauthor of the report that had prompted his attack) containing this explanation: "This is the first letter of this type we have received. I do not plan to answer this letter."[4]

Peter Buxtun was not so easily dismissed. Born in Prague, Czechoslovakia, in September 1937, Buxtun was brought to the United States as an infant on the eve of World War II by his Jewish father and Catholic mother who fled Europe to escape the Nazis. He was reared on a ranch in Oregon, later graduating from the University of Oregon with a major in political science. Following a hitch in the army where he received training as a psychiatric social worker, Buxtun was hired in December 1965 as a venereal disease interviewer and investigator by the PHS in San Francisco.

Soon after going to work at the Hunt Street Clinic, Buxtun heard the Tuskegee Study discussed by coworkers one day at lunch. He had difficulty believing the stories. "It didn't sound like what a PHS institution should be doing," he stated. Since he was required as part of his job to write a short paper on venereal disease or epidemiology every two months, Buxtun decided to do his next assignment on the Tuskegee Study and asked the Center for Disease Control for reprints of articles that had been published on the experiment. When the copies arrived, he recalled, "I went through them and was even more disturbed." He found the discussions of syphilitic heart disease especially troublesome, and the more he read the more it became obvious that the subjects did not have much medical knowledge and did not know what was being done to them. "That was what really stuck in my craw," he declared.[5]

In early November 1966, Buxtun sent Dr. William J. Brown, the director of the Division of Venereal Diseases, a letter (registered mail) expressing grave moral concerns about the experiment. He asked whether the purpose of the experiment was to obtain information "on the syphilitic damage which these men were being allowed to endure." He also inquired if any of the men had been treated properly and whether any had been told the nature of the study. And finally, he asked, "are untreated syphilitics still being followed for autopsy?"[6]

Weeks passed and nothing broke the silence from the CDC. Dr. Brown drafted a two-page reply but never mailed it. Instead, he asked a colleague from the CDC who happened to be going to San Francisco over the Christmas holidays to drop by the Hunt Street Clinic and discuss the experiment with Buxtun. The two men met and Buxtun tried to explain his moral objections, all the while feeling that the visitor thought that he was a bit crazy. "He was still somewhat puzzled but said he would take my views back to Dr. Brown," Buxtun recalled.[7]

A few months later Buxtun was invited to attend at government expense a conference on syphilis research at CDC. Once he arrived, however, it became clear that no provisions had been made for him to attend the sessions and that the real reason he had been brought to Atlanta was to discuss the Tuskegee Study. Late in the afternoon he was introduced to Dr. Brown, who escorted him to an executive conference room with a big mahogany table surrounded by a dozen or so chairs. The room was large and very dignified in decor, displaying an American flag and the PHS flag at one end. In addition to Dr. Brown, Buxtun encountered the emissary who had talked with him in San Francisco and Dr. John Cutler, a health officer with intimate knowledge of the study.

According to Buxtun, Dr. Cutler began to harangue him the moment they were seated. "He was infuriated," stated Buxtun. "He had obviously read my material, thought of me as some form of a lunatic who needed immediate chastisement and he proceeded to administer it." Dr. Cutler then launched an impassioned defense of the experiment, stressing, in particular, how it would benefit physicians who were treating syphilitic blacks.[8]

Buxtun was neither intimidated nor impressed. The men were not volunteers, Buxtun insisted, "they were nothing more than dupes and were being used as human substitutes for guinea pigs." He stated that the PHS had a duty to consider the moral implications of the study and suggested that legal advice be sought. Moreover, Buxtun warned that if the story fell into the hands of a yellow journalist, it could be used to damage the entire PHS, including its worthwhile programs.[9]

Buxtun left the meeting with "a very inconclusive feeling," he stated, "as though I had dropped a bomb into their laps and nobody knew quite what to do about it." He returned to San Francisco, expecting to be fired. When he was not, Buxtun settled back into his work. He did not anticipate hearing from Atlanta immediately. Instead, he thought the health officers would take care of things "in their own professional and bureaucratic way." Months passed and nothing happened.[10]

In November 1967, Buxtun resigned voluntarily from the PHS. The next fall he enrolled in law school at Hastings. Still troubled by the experiment, he wrote Dr. Brown a second letter in November 1968. Two years had passed since his first inquiry. During the interlude several American cities had exploded into race riots, and Buxtun had grown more alarmed and pessimistic about the racial implications of the experiment. "The group is 100 percent Negro," he declared. "This in itself is political dynamite and subject to wild journalistic misinterpretations." The racial composition of the study group also supported "the thinking of Negro militants that Negroes have long been used for 'medical experiments' and 'teaching cases' in the emergency wards of county hospitals." Denying that the subjects were volunteers, he characterized them as "uneducated, unsophisticated, and quite ignorant of the effects of untreated syphilis." The excuses and justifications that might have been offered for starting the study in 1932 were no longer relevant. "Today it would be morally unethical to begin such a study with such a group," he declared. "Probably not even the suasion of belonging to the 'Nurse Rivers Burial Society' would be sufficient inducement." Buxtun closed by expressing the hope that the subjects had been treated or would be soon.[11]

This time Buxtun got results. Dr. Brown showed the letter to his boss, Dr. David Sencer, the director of CDC, and for the first time in the history of the experiment health officials realized that they had a problem on their hands. They did not think that they were doing anything wrong, but they were worried that people who did not understand medical research might make trouble if the press became involved. They saw the experiment as a public relations problem that could have severe political repercussions.

On February 6, 1969, Drs. Sencer and Brown convened a blue-ribbon panel to discuss the Tuskegee Study. The conference was held at CDC, in the same conference room where health officials had met with Buxtun two years earlier. This time the participants were all physicians. The committee consisted of three medical professors, the state health officer of Alabama, and a senior officer from the Milbank Memorial Fund. In addition to Drs. Sencer and Brown, the PHS had several high-ranking officers in attendance. Dr. Olansky, who had left the PHS by this time and was employed by the Emory University Clinic, was called in as a special resource person to discuss the early years of the experiment. No one with training in medical ethics was invited to the meeting, none of the participants was black, and at no point during the discussions that followed did anyone mention the PHS's own guidelines on human experimentation or those of other federal agencies.

Following the introduction of panelists, Dr. Sencer delivered a brief description of the Tuskegee Study and then told the group that the PHS needed their help in deciding whether to terminate or continue it. When the study began, he explained, there was no concern about racial discrimination and withholding treatment from the men did not pose any problems. In recent years, however, questions had been raised and the study had become a political liability. "We want your advice in making a decision," he told the panelists. "We are here to discuss this problem."[12]

Dr. Brown then took over the meeting, focusing attention on the study as it was organized in 1932; the fate of the participants down through the years; and the current condition of the survivors. The original study group had been composed of 412 black men with syphilis and 204 black male controls, he told the panelists. According to the most recent figures, 56 syphilitic subjects and 36 controls were still living, a total of 373 men in both groups were known to be dead, and the remaining subjects could not be accounted for. Dr. Brown stated that 83 of the syphilitic subjects had shown evidence of the disease at time of death, but stressed that he personally believed that syphilis had been the primary cause of death in only 7 of the men. The ages of the survivors, he revealed, ranged from 59 to 85, with one subject claiming to be 102.[13]

Once the meeting was opened for discussion, Dr. J. Lawton Smith, associate professor of ophthalmology at the University of Miami, quickly emerged as the leading proponent of continuing the study. That was hardly surprising. He had a personal interest in seeing the experiment go forward. Not only had he known about the study for years, he had actually been to Tuskegee to examine the subjects in connection with his own research. Describing the eye examinations he had performed on the men in 1967, Dr. Smith stated that he had taken fundus (the part of the eye opposite the pupil) pictures, boasting that "20 years from now, when these patients are gone, we can show their pictures."[14]

Dr. Smith thought that the time had come to change the study's emphasis. "First, stress pathology, get away from serology," he urged his colleagues. "You will never have another study like this; take advantage of it." He even volunteered to return to Tuskegee, to go to the subjects' homes, explain the experiment to them, and examine them again. "This is a golden moment," Dr. Smith declared. "Turn this Study into pathology studies."[15]

Dr. Gene Stollerman, in contrast, cared more for the survivors than the experiment's scientific potential. He was chairman of the Department of Medicine at the University of Tennessee and the only member of the panel who did not have previous knowledge of the Tuskegee Study before being asked to review it. It quickly became apparent that he was also the only panelist who saw the subjects as patients and thought that they had a right to be treated.

Dr. Stollerman sought repeatedly to shift the discussions to the PHS's moral obligation to treat the men. He rebelled against the scientific focus of the meeting. For him the experiment raised moral questions, and he was troubled by the committee's insistence on discussing the survivors as a group of subjects rather than individual patients. He urged his colleagues to establish criteria for treatment, to give the men complete examinations, and to decide whether or not to treat each patient on a case-by-case basis. Unless the men were treated, he warned prophetically, there were certain to be criticisms of the study.[16]

Dr. Stollerman's recommendations found little support among his colleagues. Instead of addressing his moral concerns, they turned the meeting into a medical debate on whether treatment would do more harm than good. No one attempted to gauge the degree of risk on a case-by-case basis or even suggested that this might be a good idea. Instead, the physicians lumped the men together and cited the severe complications that could result from penicillin therapy (Herxheimer reactions, fibrillations, etc.) as absolute dangers. Dr. Olansky, whose name appeared as the principal author and coauthor of more publications on the study than any other investigator, was especially forceful in voicing his concern over the damage treatment might inflict on the men.[17]

The ad hoc committee also heard testimony that treatment probably would not help the men. Citing a recent study by Dr. Smith, Dr. Brown noted that although penicillin could cure syphilitic lesions it often failed to kill the spirochetes that were encased in certain tissues of the body. "I doubt if you could cure them," Dr. Smith observed gravely. Dr. Myers further discounted treatment by suggesting (without a word of explanation) that the subjects probably would not accept therapy even if it were offered. "I haven't seen this group," he admitted, "but I don't think they would submit to treatment."[18]

In the end, the ad hoc committee overrode Dr. Stollerman and recommended against treatment—at least not for the present. Predictably, that decision ended debate on the Tuskegee Study's future: It would continue. The physicians had approached the experiment as a medical affair, and once a medical judgment had been made against treatment, they saw no point in stopping the study. Except for Dr. Stollerman, they perceived no conflict between their own scientific interest in the experiment and attempting to decide what was best for their subjects. The doctors thought that the Tuskegee Study had scientific importance and that much remained to be learned. Since they had convinced themselves that the men could not benefit from treatment, it followed in their minds that science should be permitted to learn all it could.

With the experiment's future settled, the ad hoc committee turned its attention to protecting the PHS. Having the men give their "informed consent" in writing would have been ideal, but that would have required explaining the experiment to them in language they could understand, with special emphasis on the risks to which they had been exposed. No one brought up the possibility that the men might listen and understand all too well. Instead, most of the committee argued at the outset that it was impossible to obtain "informed consent" from men of such limited education and low social status. In their judgment, the men were incapable of understanding the facts of the experiment and forming their own conclusions.

The other possibility was to seek the approval of the Macon County Medical Society, obtaining, as it were, a type of "surrogate informed consent" from local doctors. Dr. Myers warned that the society's racial composition had completely changed in recent years, transforming it from an all-white organization into a nearly all-black one. Still, he had found them very reasonable to work with, Dr. Myers admitted, adding that the fears of real trouble-making had not come to pass. He recommended bringing the local doctors up to date on the experiment so that in the future federal and state health authorities could "work very closely with them and keep them informed of everything we do." Seconding the idea, Dr. Smith suggested sending someone to explain the experiment to the society's members. "They might think the same [as we do]," he declared. "If the local physicians agree there is no need for treating these patients, this would be good public relations."[19]

Reinvolving the Macon County Medical Society was indeed critical to protecting the PHS. Over the years, relations with the local doctors had been neglected, for once Nurse Rivers's network was firmly established they had become relatively unimportant to the experiment. The physicians with whom Drs. Vonderlehr and Heller had collaborated were either dead or retired, and a new generation had replaced them, one that had little knowledge of the experiment.

Dr. Sencer soundly endorsed reestablishing contact so that the PHS could benefit from a time-honored principle of the medical profession: namely, that "good medicine" in any community is defined by the physicians who practice there. If the PHS succeeded in establishing rapport with the Macon County Medical Society, he told his colleagues, there would be no need to answer criticisms. Thus, without being aware of what they had done, the ad hoc committee and the health officials brought the Tuskegee Study full circle. Like the experiment's organizers, they saw local doctors as crucial allies without whose help the study could not go forward. Ironically, Dr. Sencer and his colleagues were as hopeful of winning the support of black physicians in 1969 as the experiment's organizers had been of white physicians in 1932.[20]

Dr. Myers suggested that before any overtures were made to the local medical society it would be wise to discuss the experiment with the county health officer, Dr. Ruth R. Berrey, a former missionary to Nigeria whom he described as "very competent." Cautioning that Dr. Berrey might lean toward treatment, he told the group: "She loves the people in the area. She's very good to them." Still, trying to win her over was worth a try, he thought, because she was "very interested in research" and enjoyed good relations with the local doctors. Dr. Myers left no doubt that her support might help persuade them to sanction the study.[21]

Virtually everyone agreed that the study needed to be upgraded scientifically. Greater efforts needed to be expended to locate subjects who had been lost to the study, and the PHS had to be prepared to devote more money and more personnel to the experiment's final years. There was even talk of providing some free medical care for men who were in need of treatment. Dr. Sencer stated that Nurse Rivers would have to be replaced with someone younger so that follow-up work could be resumed and the men who showed signs of active syphilis could be treated. The others were to remain untreated.[22]

Early in the discussions Dr. Myers had warned that no new actions could be taken on the experiment without the whole program folding, but as the meeting drew to an end the group became more optimistic. Before adjourning, Dr. Sencer asked Dr. Kiser, the Milbank Fund's representative, to comment on the racial and political overtones of pushing forward. "This is not a Study that would be repeated now. The public conscience would not accept it," Dr. Kiser replied. "If you combined treatment with the present study, I am impressed with the plan—but I don't know whether the Fund would up the ante." Dr. Sencer closed by assuring everyone that the PHS would be guided by their recommendations and that he, personally, planned to "lean heavily on Ira [Myers]."[23]

A few weeks later Dr. Myers discussed the Atlanta meeting with his colleagues on the Alabama State Board of Health. They listened carefully and then voted unanimously to refer the entire matter to the Macon County Medical Society. He then spoke with Dr. Berrey. According to Dr. Myers, she had heard no criticisms of the experiment and had doubts if the local medical society even knew it existed, but she hoped the doctors would be sympathetic. With the local ground work completed, Dr. Myers forwarded the names of the officers of the society to the CDC, suggesting that Dr. Brown contact them directly to arrange an audience.[24]

The 1969 meeting with the Macon County Medical Society ended in total victory for the PHS. Dr. Sencer dispatched Dr. Brown and two other federal officers, Drs. Leslie Norins and Alfonso H. Holguin, to Tuskegee, and Dr. Holguin, who was spokesman for the PHS delegation, explained the experiment in detail to the society's members. According to Dr. Brown, the directors listened attentively and immediately "volunteered cooperation and approval and support." Indeed, just as their white predecessors had done nearly four decades earlier, Macon County's black physicians promised to assist the PHS. "They actually agreed," Dr. Brown continued, "if they had a list of the individuals that they would not knowingly give them antibiotics . . . but would refer them locally to the health department and to Nurse Rivers." Needless to add, each of the local doctors was given a list.[25]

Apparently, no one thought to question the morality of withholding treatment that was not specifically limited to syphilis. Antibiotics, it must be stressed, are given for a wide variety of infections.

The PHS also reestablished something of its former working relationship with medical personnel at John A. Andrew Hospital, thus restoring another element of biracial support for the experiment. Following the retirement of Dr. Dibble, none of the staff there had been involved directly with the study, though the Tuskegee Institute had continued to serve as fiscal agent for the Milbank Fund's burial stipends. In April 1970, Dr. Joseph G. Caldwell, the health officer in charge of the annual roundup that year, met with both the administrator and the medical director of Andrew Hospital and contracted to have the men's X-rays done in the hospital's new three-story building. Mr. Luis A. Rabb, the administrator of the hospital, not only agreed to cooperate but insisted on giving Dr. Caldwell and Nurse Rivers Laurie a personally guided tour of the new building. No doubt the men who were examined there a few weeks later found the hospital impressive. They must have had a sense of déjà vu upon returning to the campus of the Tuskegee Institute.[26]

In September 1970, Mrs. Elizabeth M. Kennebrew, a black woman, went on the PHS payroll as the nurse assigned to the Tuskegee Study. Realizing that she was being asked to fill some rather large shoes, one of her supervisors later wrote to her reassuringly: "The excellent rapport which Mrs. Laurie had with these patients cannot be achieved overnight, but I believe a regular system of visitation will aid you in doing this." Toward that end, he instructed her to "make personal contact with every patient being followed in the Tuskegee area at least once every 2 months," adding that "patients who are hospitalized for any reason should be followed daily with visits." Nurse Kennebrew settled easily into the routine and

reported to her superiors in Atlanta: "Most of the patients seem
to look forward to my visits because they get either pain pills
and/or tonic."[27]

Armed with the approval of the local doctors, a revitalized
working relationship with the Tuskegee Institute, and a new
nurse, the PHS entered the 1970s determined to continue the
experiment until the last subject had died. Despite the ad hoc
committee's discussions, none of the men was treated for syphilis and the experiment's focus remained the same—following
the men to their graves to trace the effects of untreated syphilis. All that changed was the zeal with which the PHS pursued
the men.

Not since the early 1950s had health officials expended so
much energy searching for subjects who had been lost to the
experiment. They outdid themselves in devising schemes for
finding the men. One health official persuaded the assistant
postmaster in Tuskegee to help with the search, while another
officer turned to private enterprise for assistance: He paid a
retail credit association thirty dollars a man to track down the
more difficult cases. Amid the flurry of activities, there was
even talk of employing a full-time person at CDC to supervise
and coordinate the study's final years, including editing a monograph that would report all the findings in a single volume,
with various chapters contracted to experts not affiliated with
the PHS.[28]

Moreover, reports from the field indicated that the Tuskegee Study had lost none of its power to fascinate young clinicians. Echoes of Dr. Vonderlehr's enthusiastic letters could be
heard in 1970 in the words of Dr. Caldwell, who uncovered a
man, long missing from the study, with "classic aortic insuffi-
ciency and syphilitic heart disease." According to Dr. Caldwell,
the man "even had deMusset's sign and capillary pulsations
which none of the other patients with AI [aortic insufficiency]
have had." (In deMusset's sign, the valve of the left ventricle to
the patient's heart is badly eroded and will not close properly.
Thus, when the heart contracts, the valve leaks, causing the
blood to rush back through the artery to the head with such
force that the patient's head snaps back.) "It is unfortunate
that it took us all of 29 years, however, to locate and examine
him again," wrote Dr. Caldwell. "This has destroyed much of

the potential of being able to follow the development of this complication of syphilis."[29]

In addition to descriptions of syphilitic pathologies, the reports were filled with comments on social conditions. Like the experiment's organizers, the health officers of the 1970s were shocked by what they saw in Macon County. To Dr. Caldwell local conditions were "unbelievably primitive." He told of visiting a subject who "had not even electricity and lived 2–3 miles from the nearest dirt road or neighbor." One of the man's two mules had died within the past month just over the rise in front of his "hut," and due to his old age and disabilities he had not been able to dispose of the carcass. "The stench of our examining room (his hut) was unbelievable," wrote Dr. Caldwell, "and two mice which kept scampering about the room added to the local color." While the "government doctors" examined her husband, the man's wife, who was in her late sixties, stayed outside in a field, plowing a few acres for watermelons with their remaining mule. To complete the examination, Dr. Caldwell took the man and his wife to Tuskegee, a trip the health officer stated was "without doubt the delight of the year for both of them."[30]

Despite the similarity between these reports and the comments made by the experiment's organizers nearly four decades earlier, the health officers of the 1970s did not view the study in the same light. The self-confidence of the predecessors had been replaced by self-consciousness. For beneath the façade of "work as usual" there was a growing uneasiness, a perception that things had changed. The health officers had not come to the conclusion that the Tuskegee Study was morally wrong. Rather, they feared the consequences if the experiment became known publicly. The day had passed when medical researchers could ignore the public's concern over the protection of human subjects, and they knew it.

Thus, the PHS officials became more and more apprehensive about disclosure and felt restrained. When an old friend inquired about recent publications, Dr. Brown replied: "The climate in recent years (disfavor of research involving human volunteers as well as racial tension) has not been conducive to wide publicity of the Tuskegee findings." He was even more candid in confessing his reluctance to sanction new articles to the Milbank Fund, explaining, "We feel that the analysis of the data assembled to date should await a more favorable national climate."[31]

Apprehension gave rise in one instance to a modicum of critical thinking. Late in 1970 Dr. James B. Lucas, the assistant chief of the Venereal Disease Branch, finally said what no other PHS officer had uttered: The Tuskegee Study was incongruous with the goals of the PHS. Worse yet, the experiment was "bad science" because it had been contaminated by treatment. "Nothing learned will prevent, find, or cure a single case of infectious syphilis or bring us closer to our basic mission of controlling venereal disease in the United States," Dr. Lucas declared. Moreover, the experiment's value had been undermined, he explained, "because effective and undocumented treatment has been given to the vast majority of the patients in the syphilitic group" for most had received penicillin "in the 'happenstance' manner while under treatment for other conditions."[32]

Dr. Lucas stated that the impact of this inadvertent treatment would be almost impossible to assess "but without question the course of untreated syphilis (which the study was supposed to have delineated) has been radically altered." As a result, he concluded: "Probably the greatest contribution that the Tuskegee Study has made and can continue to provide has been documented sera for study in our laboratory," the sole use for which was "evaluating new serologic tests." Thus, Dr. Lucas admitted that the Tuskegee Study's principal contribution to medical science has been keeping laboratories supplied with blood samples for evaluating new blood tests for syphilis, such as precipitation tests like the Hinton, which had replaced the Wassermann. The benefit seems small when one remembers that some of the blood donors later died from syphilis.[33]

Like his predecessors, however, Dr. Lucas opposed ending the experiment. The PHS had "both an implied and expressed obligation" not to abandon "the remaining syphilitic patients." Stressing that the "long continued assignment of Mrs. Laurie and now Mrs. Kennebrew to Tuskegee demonstrates our good faith and sincerity," Dr. Lucas insisted that the PHS was obligated to preserve its "present level of observation as long as a significant number of patients remain alive." He therefore recommended that the experiment "be continued along its present lines with periodic clinical observation and serologic surveillance." Conceding that "outside experts" might "prefer not to be associated with this study because of its sensitive nature," Dr. Lucas saw no reason why the PHS could not continue to publish reports by using its own medical officers."[34]

In the end it was Peter Buxtun (aided by the press) who stopped the Tuskegee Study. Dr. Brown had delayed answering his second letter until after the ad hoc committee had met. He then informed Buxtun that a committee of highly competent professionals drawn from outside the government had reviewed all aspects of the experiment and had decided against treating the men, a decision Dr. Brown insisted was "a matter of medical judgment since the benefits of such therapy must be offset against the risks to the individual." In response, Buxtun made no attempt to challenge the committee's medical authority, freely conceding that "most of the physical damage and early death has been suffered, and advanced age prevents treatment of the survivors." Instead, he reviewed the facts of the experiment, tracing step by step how the men had reached the state that they could no longer be helped and could "no longer exercise the choice of ending their days free from syphilis." Urging Dr. Brown to see that there were legal and moral issues at stake as well as medical ones, he concluded by asking: "What is the ethical thing to do? Compensate the survivors? Compensate the families of all the subjects? Or should NCDC await the quiet demise of the survivors and hope that will end the matter?"[35]

Buxtun was not surprised when his questions went unanswered. He had written to vent his anger and frustration, not really expecting a reply. Yet, concern over the experiment haunted him all through law school. In addition to discussing the study with friends, he told his story to several law professors. They were sympathetic but offered little encouragement that anything could be done, stating that the statute of limitations had expired in the vast majority of cases of men who had died. One professor did suggest sending a long letter to the American Civil Liberties Union, complete with reprints of the articles and copies of the correspondence. "I regret to say that I neglected to do that because I was up to my rear in alligators with law work at that time," Buxtun recalled.[36]

Early in July 1972 Buxtun finally told his tale to someone who was willing to do more than listen politely—Edith Lederer, a longtime friend who worked as an international affairs reporter with the Associated Press in San Francisco. He had mentioned the experiment once before, but she had not seemed to grasp what he was saying. This time, however, she hung on every word, devouring the letters and articles that Buxtun produced as proof.

Lederer showed copies of the materials to her superiors at the Associated Press and asked to be assigned to the story. To her disappointment, she was told that the Tuskegee Study would have to be turned over to an investigative reporter in the East, someone who would be closer to the sources and had experience with government agencies. She immediately thought of her friend, Jean Heller, a highly regarded young reporter who worked for the research bureau of the Associated Press in Washington, D.C. She sent the materials on the Tuskegee Study to Heller and, in effect, dropped the story in her lap, tied with a pretty bow.

Heller could not begin her investigation immediately because she had to cover the Democratic National Convention in Miami. Once George McGovern was nominated, however, she returned to Washington and went to work filling in the gaps that existed in Buxtun's materials. A little digging uncovered additional medical articles on the experiment, but her best source of information proved to be officials at the CDC. While she did not go to Atlanta, Heller received straightforward, matter-of-fact answers to her questions—however sensitive or ostensibly damaging to the PHS. Spokesmen there even provided estimates of the number of men who had died from the various complications of late syphilis. In short, the health officials acted like men who had nothing to hide.[37]

True to their goal of pursuing the subjects until the last one had died, PHS officers were still conducting the experiment when Heller broke the story on July 25, 1972, in the *Washington Star*. Ironically, another ghost out of a public servant's medical past appeared simultaneously. The Tuskegee Study had to compete for headlines with the sensational disclosure that Senator Thomas Eagleton of Missouri, Senator McGovern's running mate, had a medical history of bouts with depression requiring hospitalization and shock therapy. A high-ranking official in the Department of Health, Education, and Welfare confessed privately to Heller that he was relieved when the Tuskegee Study and the Eagleton affair hit the front pages of the nation's newspapers on the same day. "He kept us beneath the fold," the official sighed.[38]

Epilogue

THE day after the story broke, Dr. Merlin K. Duval, the assistant secretary for health and scientific affairs of the Department of Health, Education, and Welfare, told reporters that he was "shocked and horrified" by the Tuskegee Study. "Although the study was begun in 1932 and although the opportunity to bring treatment to the men has long since passed," Dr. Duval declared, "I am today launching a full investigation into the circumstances surrounding it." He promised a special effort to determine "why the study was permitted to continue past the time when penicillin became the effective drug of choice against the disease."[1]

A spokesman for Dr. Duval explained that the treatment for syphilis prior to the discovery of penicillin was often fatal, a fact that he implied might well have justified the withholding of treatment during the 1930s when the study began. The same spokesman stressed that the forthcoming investigation would try to make certain that other medical experiments using human subjects would not be permitted to continue "to the point where the benefits to the patients no longer outweigh the risks."[2]

For several weeks Dr. Duval's statement set the tone for the government's official response to the experiment's disclosure.

Spokesmen up and down the chain of command at HEW head-quarters in Washington carefully avoided efforts to defend or justify the experiment directly. Instead, they echoed the public outcry condemning the study. Denunciations even came from the PHS officers at the Center for Disease Control in Atlanta, the agency that was in charge of the Tuskegee Study during its final years. To Dr. Donald Printz, an official in the Venereal Disease Branch of the CDC, the experiment was "almost like genocide" and he did not shrink from declaring that "a literal death sentence was passed on some of those people." Yet how-ever much they condemned the study, health officals usually softened their criticisms by insisting that the study began when attitudes toward human experimentation were different and when the treatment was worse than the disease. They also maintained that the men were now beyond medical help, thus strongly implying that no real harm had been done by continu-ing the study in recent years.[3]

There were several troubling assumptions hidden in these arguments. Dr. Duval's assertion that "the opportunity to treat the men had long since passed" seemed to relieve the current administration from any responsibility for continuing to with-hold treatment from the men, when, in point of fact, no effort had ever been made to determine on an individual basis whether any of the men might benefit from treatment. Dr. Duval also ignored completely the initial decision to withhold arsphenamine and bismuth, the "drugs of choice" at the time the experiment began. He offered absolutely no proof that phy-sicians in 1932 thought that the treatment was worse than the disease.

Indeed, officials presented no evidence that the pros and cons of treatment were ever discussed by the experiment's or-ganizers. Similarly, current expressions of shock and indigna-tion had the effect of putting distance between present officials and the generation of health officers who had initiated the study, yet said nothing about the responsibility modern offi-cials had to bear for continuing the experiment. Finally, the promised review put the government in the position of investi-gating itself. As an instrument for preempting public action, a government investigation might have had some value, but could health officials truly be trusted to pass judgment on themselves?

Following the lead of federal officials, the Tuskegee Institute issued a press release stating that it was "deeply concerned" about the experiment. The Institute acknowledged
that its medical facilities and personnel had been used in the
study, but emphasized that cooperation had been limited to
the 1930s when the surgeon general of the United States had
personally requested the Institute's participation in the experiment as part of a larger treatment program. Referring to the
subjects as "voluntary participants" in an experiment that was
designed "to develop new and more effective treatment programs," the Institute maintained that the study "was acceptable under the clinical conditions prevailing 40 years ago,
when the drugs available for treatment . . . were dangerous and
their long-term effectiveness had not been established."[4]

The Institute claimed it had lost contact with the experiment by the time penicillin became available in the 1940s.
Both the treatment program and the study of untreated syphilis had been removed from Andrew Hospital and "were fully
based in the Macon County Health Department" by 1946. From
that date to the present, the Institute declared, "there has been
no active medical program at Tuskegee Institute's John A. Andrew Hospital connected with this USPHS study." While tech-
nically true, that statement ignored the fact that the Institute
had given its tacit approval to the experiment by permitting its
facilities and medical personnel to be used repeatedly over the
years. Indeed, a few days before the Institute released a formal
statement, the administrator of Andrew Hospital, Luis Rabb,
told reporters that the subjects had been X-rayed at the hospital two years earlier, but denied that this constituted direct
involvement because the hospital's X-ray facilities were available to anyone.[5]

The Veterans' Administration Hospital in Tuskegee, whose
pathologist, Dr. Peters, had performed some of the autopsies
until his retirement in 1963, also tried to distance itself from
the study. Dr. Robert S. Wilson, the hospital's director, denied
that his institution had been directly involved, though he could
not rule out the possibility of indirect participation at some
past date since some the subjects may have been veterans.
"The Veterans' Administration would not condone or approve
of such as this," Dr. Wilson told reporters.[6]

The other collaborating agencies staked out similar positions. Dr. Ira L. Myers, the state health officer of Alabama, told reporters that his department had simply helped the PHS observe and evaluate the subjects. He repeated the familiar argument that the study had been started when "there was not much in the way of treatment for syphilis." The subjects had participated "on a volunteer basis," he explained, and he insisted that the men had been "followed pretty carefully to be sure that no one had been denied care." In his view the flap was totally unjustified. "Somebody is trying to make a mountain out of a molehill," Dr. Myers declared.[7]

Yet Dr. Myers neglected to mention that the state board of health had refused to commit itself three years earlier when the PHS had sought advice about whether to stop or continue the experiment. Dr. Myers was not available for comment when the *Montgomery Advertiser* announced that it had uncovered records of the February 1969 meeting in which the board had voted unanimously to refer the Tuskegee Study without comment to the Macon County Health Department.[8]

The Macon County Medical Society responded to the experiment's disclosure with expressions of concern and pledges of help. Dr. H. W. Foster, the society's president, told reporters that he was under the impression that the PHS would stop the experiment immediately. For its part, the society had voted unanimously "to identify the remaining living members of this study and make available forthwith appropriate therapy."[9]

A few days after that statement was released, however, the *Montgomery Advertiser,* pursuing its story on the state board of health, contacted spokesmen for the society and asked whether it had in fact approved the experiment back in 1969. Dr. S. H. Settler, the society's secretary, acknowledged that they had met with representatives of the PHS in 1969 and admitted agreeing to the study's continuation. He denied, however, that they had been informed about the withholding of treatment, a claim the PHS spokesmen who had talked with the group promptly challenged. Dr. Alfonso H. Holguin and Dr. William J. Brown told the *Advertiser* that the local doctors had been apprised of the nature of the experiment and had agreed that the men should not be treated.[10]

While its partners retreated into official silence following their initial statements, the federal government moved forward with an investigation. Bowing to public opposition against its promised internal review, the government reversed itself and appointed a nine-member citizens panel, five of whom were black, to investigate the experiment. Dr. Duval announced on August 24, 1972, that the Tuskegee Syphilis Study Ad Hoc Panel would be headed by the distinguished black educator, Broadus Nathaniel Butler, president of Dillard University in New Orleans.[11]

The racial composition of the ad hoc advisory panel was designed to allay fears of a whitewash. "I wanted a panel that would be sympathetic to the public point of view rather than the scientific or factual point of view, so I loaded it with angry blacks," Dr. Duval insisted a year after forming the panel. "My purpose was an exercise in self-flagellation if you will," he added. "I knew we were going to pay a penalty for Tuskegee, and I figured we should take the whole penalty—that way there could be no criticism."[12]

Despite his eagerness to "take the whole penalty," Dr. Duval severely restricted the scope of the inquiry. Had he desired a comprehensive investigation, he would have permitted the panel to frame its own questions. Instead, he directed the panel to:

1. Determine whether the study was justified and whether it should have been continued when penicillin became generally available.
2. Recommend whether the study should be continued at this point in time, and if not, how it should be terminated in a way consistent with the rights and health needs of its remaining participants.
3. Determine whether existing policies to protect the rights of patients participating in health research conducted or supported by the Department of Health, Education, and Welfare are adequate and effective and to recommend improvements in these policies if needed.[13]

Dr. Duval clearly wanted the panel to concentrate on the issue of informed consent and the decision to withhold penicillin from the men. He made no mention of the initial decision to withhold salvarsan and bismuth, and he did not confront the issue of racism by charging the panel to explain why the experiment was limited to blacks. Dr. Duval was sensitive to the need to proceed expeditiously, however. He ordered the panel to conclude its investigation and issue a final report by December 31, 1972, unless he personally approved an extension. (Acting upon a subsequent request from the panel, he did in fact grant an extension through the end of March.)[14]

Working in separate teams to attack each of its three charges, the ad hoc panel held a dozen meetings, collected scores of affidavits, interviewed numerous witnesses, visited Tuskegee, and reviewed a pile of documents that one panelist put at "just short of three feet high." A decision on the second charge came quickly. Late in October, the panel notified Dr. Duval that the experiment "should be terminated immediately," with the men receiving "the care now required to treat any disabilities resulting from their participation."[15]

While Dr. Duval promised to implement these recommendations "as rapidly as possible," months of delay ensued as federal health officials and lawyers debated whether the government had the authority to provide comprehensive health care for the men. The ad hoc panel, on the verge of releasing its final report, finally broke the impasse by appealing directly to Casper Weinberger, the secretary of HEW. Secretary Weinberger announced on March 3, 1973, that he had instructed the PHS to provide all necessary medical care for the survivors of the study. Ironically, the only legal way he could authorize treatment was to reopen the experiment so that the men could receive health care as part of the official study.[16]

The ad hoc panel's first report, issued in late April 1973, was highly critical of the entire study. While acknowledging that "scientific justification for a short-term demonstration study in 1932 cannot be ruled out," the panel judged that the experiment was "ethically unjustified in 1932." That decision rested on the government's failure to obtain the informed consent of the participants in a study of a disease with a known risk to human life. The panel stated unequivocally that "penicillin therapy should have been made available to the participants . . . as of 1953 when penicillin became generally available" and strongly implied that treatment with arsenicals and mercury should have been administered earlier. Finally, to the surprise of no one, the panel argued that existing protections for the human subjects of experiments were not effective. The panel offered procedural and substantive recommendations for safeguarding subjects, the most important of which was the

creation by Congress of a permanent body to regulate all feder-
ally sponsored research on human subjects.[17]

Though useful as a public forum, the ad hoc panel had no
legal standing. An advisory body with a limited investigative
mandate, it did not address itself to any of the legal questions
arising from the experiment. Scores of men had died from a
disease that could have been cured. Some had gone blind,
others insane. Had any laws been broken? Were physicians and
scientists who had conducted the study in any way liable for
their actions? For their omissions? Were the subjects entitled
to compensation?

Shortly after word of the experiment broke, Governor
George Wallace's office announced it would seek to determine
whether any of Alabama's state laws requiring treatment for
communicable diseases had been broken. No legal action followed this announcement, though the experiment clearly violated state health laws passed in 1927, 1943, 1957, and 1969.
Without attempting to assign legal responsibility to any individuals, Alabama's senators, James B. Allen and John D.
Sparkman, coauthored a bill to authorize federal payments up
to $25,000 for each participant in the Tuskegee Study. In their
view, the federal government had an ethical responsibility to
compensate the survivors and their families.[18]

There were strong indications that the men would sue if the
government did not volunteer compensation. Shortly after the
story broke, Charles Pollard, one of the survivors, approached
Fred Gray for legal advice concerning the experiment. Pollard
turned to him only in part because Gray had done some routine
legal work for him in the past. Along with everyone else in Macon County, he knew that Gray was Tuskegee's most prominent
black lawyer and one of Alabama's leading civil rights activists.

Gray had first won national recognition in 1955 by defending Rosa Parks for refusing to relinquish her bus seat to a white
man in Montgomery. An ordained minister of the Church of
Christ, as well as a lawyer, he represented Martin Luther King
in the Montgomery bus boycott case that followed. Over the
next quarter of a century, he helped build one of the most successful black law firms in Alabama and argued several important cases before the United States Supreme Court. Personally
unassuming and soft-spoken, Gray managed to combine civil

rights activities and a profitable legal practice. In 1970, he was elected to the Alabama State House of Representatives, the first black Democrat to join white legislators in Montgomery since Reconstruction.

Gray delayed bringing suit for nearly a year, hoping the government would volunteer compensation and medical care. During the interlude, Senator Edward M. Kennedy offered the Alabama lawyer a public forum from which to present his case. Long recognized as one of the Senate's leading authorities on health care, Kennedy had expressed his outrage over the experiment when the story first broke. In February and March of 1973, he held a series of hearings on human experimentation before the subcommittee on health of the committee of labor and public welfare. Testimonies were received from top-ranking government bureaucrats, leading scientists, high-powered academics, and concerned citizens on topics ranging from psychosurgery to involuntary sterilization. More than any other case, however, the Tuskegee Study dominated the hearings.

All sides got to tell their stories. Peter Buxtun recounted his efforts to persuade the PHS to stop the experiment voluntarily; Dr. David Sencer, the director of the Center for Disease Control, served as spokesman for the PHS; and Dr. Jay Katz, a professor in the Yale University School of Law and a member of the Tuskegee Syphilis Ad Hoc Advisory Panel, argued persuasively against the ability of the current system of institution-based peer review panels to provide adequate protection for human subjects in experiments.

The most poignant testimonies, however, came from two survivors of the Tuskegee Study, Charles Pollard and Lester Scott. It was the first chance any of the subjects had been given to tell their stories to any agency or branch of government, and the two men did so with dignity and candor.

Pollard and Scott unfolded a forty-year saga of lies and deceit, of unlettered men who had trusted and been betrayed by educated men. Each, in turn, related how he had answered the PHS's call for blood tests; how he had been told his blood was bad; and how he had cooperated for forty years with doctors who said they were treating him. Both emphasized they wanted nothing more to do with the PHS or any of its doctors. When asked by Senator Kennedy what the government should do for them now, Scott replied: "They ought to give us compensation or something like that, where we can see other doctors and continue our health."[19]

Gray was adamant on this point. The men did not want to be placed back in the hands of an agency that had repeatedly "refused to treat them," he declared in his testimony before the committee. "They have no faith, trust, nor confidence that the Public Health Service will properly examine them and give them proper treatment." PHS physicians could not be trusted to make unbiased medical decisions, Gray charged, because their primary concern "would be to cover up their unlawful conduct during the past forty years." The only solution was for the government to give the men adequate compensation, enough to permit them to "select their own physicians, hospitals, and medical technicians who will give them medical attention."[20]

Senator Kennedy was clearly angered by what he heard. He called the Tuskegee Study "an outrageous and intolerable situation which this Government never should have been involved in." The tragedy was compounded by the government's failure to provide health care to the men immediately after the study was disclosed, an injustice that had been left standing for eight months despite the ad hoc panel's recommendation that health care be made available and despite Dr. Duval's assurances that it would be. Kennedy noted with approval Secretary Weinberger's announcement (issued just a few days before witnesses on the Tuskegee Study began testifying) pledging comprehensive health care for the men without further delay, but warned that his subcommittee would be watching to see if the promises were kept. "We are going to stay after it," he told the survivors and their attorney.[21]

The Kennedy hearings presaged a national review of federal guidelines on human experimentation, a review in which opponents of existing regulations used the Tuskegee Study as a rallying cry for reform. The result was a complete revamping of HEW regulations on human experimentation. The new guidelines established specific criteria for research projects involving human subjects and mandated a larger role for humanists on institutional review panels. More than any other experiment in American history, the Tuskegee Study convinced legislators and bureaucrats alike that tough new regulations had to be adopted if human subjects were to be protected.[22]

For the men in the Tuskegee Study, of course, the new regulations came too late. Uppermost in their minds were treatment and compensation. In the wake of Senator Kennedy's hearings, the government moved rapidly to provide complete health care to all the men—both those who had syphilis and those who did not. Beginning in April 1973, the CDC undertook the mammoth job of tracking down the survivors to inform them in person and in writing that the government would pay all of their medical expenses for the remainder of their lives. Field representatives urged the men to obtain comprehensive medical examinations at once by physicians of their choice and to proceed immediately with appropriate medical care. To help the attending physicians, the CDC provided a checklist of tests and procedures recommended by a panel of distinguished physicians with no previous contact with the experiment.[23]

The CDC also restored old services. Henceforth, the government (not the Milbank Fund) would pay burial stipends, a key benefit under the experiment. Significantly, no mention was made of the autopsies. Instead, they were quietly dropped as a condition. And, as a final irony, the CDC reappointed Nurse Kennebrew to look after the survivors who lived in and around Macon County. Her assignment, as in bygone days, was to visit the men periodically and make certain they were receiving proper medical care for all their ailments. Not until two years after medical services were supplied for the men were provisions made for their families. In 1975 the government extended treatment to the subjects' wives who had contracted syphilis and their children with congenital syphilis.[24]

A few of the men were suspicious and categorically refused to take advantage of their new health program, but most did so eagerly. Armed with special identification cards instructing physicians and druggists to send all bills directly to the CDC for payment, the men selected their own physicians, had themselves examined, and began enjoying the luxury of total health care. That included vigorous therapy for tertiary syphilis. Despite the PHS's long-standing argument that treatment might prove harmful, no cases of drug reactions or any other complications were reported among the syphilitic survivors who were given penicillin.[25]

The government's failure to offer a cash settlement as part of its health plan made a lawsuit inevitable. Attorney Gray recognized from the outset that it would be a difficult and complex case, and he did not hesitate to seek help in preparing for trial. After being turned away by several private firms, he obtained help from two Columbia University law professors, Michael Sovern and Harold Edgar. They provided legal assistance on a wide range of fronts. Unexpected aid also came from another source. Jim Jones, a young historian who was preparing a book on the Tuskegee Study, contacted Gray and turned over mounds of materials he had uncovered on the experiment. Jones also helped with subsequent research on the case.

On July 23, 1973, nearly a year to the day after Jean Heller broke the story, Gray filed a $1.8 billion class-action civil suit in the United States District Court for the Middle District of Alabama. Gray demanded $3 million in damages for each living participant and the same amount for the heirs of the deceased. He also requested a permanent injunction enjoining the defendants from continuing the Tuskegee Syphilis Study or any experiment on human subjects without their full knowledge and informed consent. Beginning with the United States of America, he named as defendants the Department of Health, Education and Welfare, the United States Public Health Service, the Center for Disease Control, the state of Alabama, the state board of health for Alabama, and the Milbank Fund. In addition, Gray cited the heads of most of the agencies that were named in the suit, charging them in their official capacities. Three former PHS officers were charged individually as part of a blanket suit against all PHS officers who had personally conducted the study.

The Tuskegee Institute, for which Gray served as the general counsel, was not named in the suit. Neither was the Veterans Hospital. The local health department and the Macon County Medical Society also escaped legal notice. In fact, no predominantly black institution was named in the suit. The same was true of individuals; all of the individually named defendants were white. No black physicians were mentioned; neither were any black nurses.

Gray obviously preferred to deal with black and white issues, and he hit the issue of race hard in the lawsuit. Noting that "only black men were used as subjects in the study," he called the experiment "a program of controlled genocide." The suit alleged that the study had violated rights guaranteed to the men under the "Fifth, Ninth, Thirteenth and Fourteenth Amendments to the Constitution of the United States and Article I, Section 6 of the Alabama Constitution of 1901." Among the damages Gray alleged the men had suffered were:

> physical and mental disability, affliction, distress, pain, discomfort, and suffering; death; loss of earnings; racial discrimination; false and misleading information about their state of health; improper treatment or lack of treatment; lowerence of tolerance to other physical and mental illnesses; use as subjects in human experimentation without informed consent; the maintenance of Plaintiff-subjects as carriers of a communicable disease that can cause harm to others, including birth defects in children born of mothers to whom the disease has been communicated and the shortening of their lives.[26]

The case never came to trial. In December 1974, the government agreed to pay approximately $10 million in an out-of-court settlement. The plaintiffs agreed to drop further action in exchange for cash payment of $37,500 to every member of the class of "living syphilitics" who was alive on July 23, 1973; $15,000 to the heirs of each of the "deceased syphilitics"; $16,000 to every member of the class of "living controls" who was alive on July 23, 1973; and $5,000 to the heirs of each of the "deceased controls." Gray's fee was to be subtracted from the payments. The heirs of the deceased participants had to be determined and paid in accordance with the Alabama laws of descent and distribution. In addition to the cash settlement, the government agreed to the continuation of its ongoing medical and burial programs and promised to use its best efforts to help locate the men and their heirs. A time limit of three years was set to file claims for payment, after which any remaining funds would revert to the United States.[27]

The amount of Gray's legal fee was left for Frank M. Johnson, Jr., the judge, to decide. Judge Johnson awarded him 12.5 percent of the cash settlement. As an added incentive for Gray to be diligent in locating the survivors and the heirs of the deceased, Judge Johnson ruled that Gray be paid 10 percent of the $10 million settlement immediately, with the remaining 2.5 percent to follow as the missing plaintiffs were found. The fee agreement awarded Gray approximately a million dollars in legal fees.[28]

The task of tracking down the men, which was Gray's responsibility, proved difficult. There were fewer than a hundred and twenty known survivors in 1974, leaving more than five hundred subjects (most presumed to be dead) to be accounted for. In many instances all Gray had to go on was a name. With no further means of identifying the men, he had no choice but to place ads in newspapers across the county and then wait for the avalanche.

Immediately after the ads were printed, long lines began appearing every morning in front of his law office in Tuskegee. Many thought the government was simply giving away money to any black man who could prove he had had syphilis. Others were there for less innocent reasons. People with no legitimate claim whatsoever came from distant states (one from as far away as Europe), hoping to convince Gray that they had relatives among the study's victims. Several women tried to file statements claiming they had been participants and a few white residents of Tuskegee even joked that they had relatives who had been subjects.[29]

Many of the deceased men had large families, leaving ten to twelve children behind as heirs. The job of sorting through their claims was compounded by the need to distinguish between legitimate and illegitimate offspring, for Alabama's laws did not permit children born out of wedlock to inherit any portion of their fathers' estates. According to Billy Carter, an attorney who worked for Gray locating survivors and heirs, the settlement produced deep divisions between legitimate heirs and their half brothers and sisters. Many of these people had lived together as families, Carter explained, but when he offered to divise a voluntary arrangement whereby the legitimate heirs could share the money with the others, no one accepted the offer.[30]

Perhaps the most distressing thing Gray and Carter encountered was the lack of social and economic mobility among the heirs. "There were more people who had to execute documents by making marks than I'll ever see for the rest of my life," Carter recalled. "It didn't matter whether they had gone to Cleveland or stayed right here, so many of them were illiterate and uneducated." Many of the heirs did not even know their family members' last names, referring to them only by nicknames such as "Kid" and "Coon." Carter added: "The sad thing is that it could happen all over again. These people could just as easily be conned and taken advantage of as their fathers and grandfathers in the syphilis study."[31]

Had the subjects of the Tuskegee Study been taken advantage of? The PHS officers who had been directly involved in the experiment thought not. There was nothing in their public statements to indicate even an ounce of contrition. No apologies were tendered; no one admitted any personal wrongdoing. On the contrary, the health officials who had exercised direct responsibility for the experiment made it clear that they had acted in good conscience. If anything, they probably felt maligned and abused by the public's reaction and betrayed by the government's failure to defend the study. Had they been given an opportunity to retrace their steps, there is little doubt they would have conducted the experiment again.

Nurse Rivers Laurie had a more ambiguous reaction. Years after the experiment had ended, she refused to believe it had harmed the men. "I still don't feel that we misused the patients [I mean] the people," she observed. All projects involved human errors, Nurse Laurie explained, and this was no exception. "We probably made some mistakes," she confessed. In her view, withholding treatment in the 1930s had not been a mistake because "we were getting such reactions that . . . we would have lost patients." She had more doubts about penicillin; withholding it might have been an error, she admitted. But foremost in her mind was informed consent. When asked to explain what mistakes had been made, she volunteered, "The doctors didn't tell the patients they did have syphilis."[32]

The survivors of the experiment were confused and divided in their views. A large number, to be sure, were sickened by the years of deception and expressed hatred and contempt for the "government doctors" following the disclosure. One man, who no doubt spoke for many of his fellows, dismissed the entire study as "a bunch of hogwash." But others had a less clear view of what had happened and had great difficulty making any sense of the study. After commenting that he and his friends had been used as "guinea pigs," another survivor confessed: "I don't know what that means. . . . I don't know what they used us for." The same man added: "I ain't never understood the study."[33]

Notes

Chapter 1. "A Moral Astigmatism"

1. *New York Times*, July 26, 1972, pp. 1, 8.
2. Because of the high rate of geographic mobility among the men, estimates of the mortality rate were confusing, even in the published articles. PHS spokesmen in 1972 were reluctant to be pinned down on an exact figure. An excellent example is the Interview of Dr. David Sencer by J. Andrew Liscomb and Bobby Doctor for the U.S. Commission on Civil Rights, Alabama State Advisory Committee, September 22, 1972, unpublished manuscript, p. 9. For the calculations behind the figures used here, see *Atlanta Constitution*, September 12, 1972, p. 2A.
3. During this primary stage the infected person often remains seronegative: A blood test will not reveal the disease. But chancres can be differentiated from other ulcers by a dark field examination, a laboratory test in which a microscope equipped with a special indirect lighting attachment can view the silvery spirochetes moving against a dark background.
4. At the secondary stage a blood test is an effective diagnostic tool.
5. Dr. Donald W. Prinz quoted in *Atlanta Journal*, July 27, 1972, p. 2; *Birmingham News*, July 27, 1972, p. 2.
6. *New York Times*, July 27, 1972, p. 18.
7. Dr. Ralph Henderson quoted in ibid.; *Tuskegee News*, July 27, 1972, p. 1.

8. *New York Times*, July 27, 1972, p. 2.

9. Eunice Rivers, Stanley Schuman, Lloyd Simpson, Sidney Olansky, "Twenty Years of Followup Experience in a Long-Range Medical Study," *Public Health Reports* 68 (April 1953): 391 – 95. (Hereafter Rivers et al.)

10. Ibid., p. 393.

11. Dr. John D. Millar quoted in *Birmingham News*, July 27, 1972, pp. 1, 4; *Atlanta Journal*, July 27, 1972, p. 2.

12. Prinz quoted in *Atlanta Journal*, July 27, 1972, p. 2.

13. Millar quoted in *Montgomery Advertiser*, July 26, 1972, p. 1.

14. Ibid.; Prinz quoted in *Atlanta Journal*, July 27, 1972, p. 2.

15. Millar quoted in *Montgomery Advertiser*, July 26, 1972, p. 1; *New York Times*, July 28, 1972, p. 29.

16. Dr. Edward Lammons quoted in *Tuskegee News*, August 3, 1972, p. 1.

17. Prinz quoted in *Atlanta Journal*, July 27, 1972, p. 2; Millar quoted in *Montgomery Advertiser*, July 26, 1972, p. 1.

18. *St. Louis Dispatch*, July 30, 1972, p. 2D.

19. *Time*, August 7, 1972, p. 54; *Chicago Sun Times*, July 29, 1972, p. 23.

20. *News and Observer*, Raleigh, North Carolina, August 1, 1972, p. 4; ABC Evening News, August 1, 1972.

21. Their reactions can be captured at a glance by citing a few of the legends that introduced newspaper articles and editorials that appeared on the experiment. The *Houston Chronicle* called it "A Violation of Human Dignity" (August 5, 1972, Section I, p. 12); *St. Louis Post-Dispatch*, "An Immoral Study" (July 30, 1972, p. 2D); *Oregonian*, an "Inhuman Experiment" (Portland, Oregon, July 31, 1972, p. 16); *Chattanooga Times*, a "Blot of Inhumanity" (July 28, 1972, p. 16); *South Bend Tribune*, a "Cruel Experiment" (July 29, 1972, p. 6); *New Haven Register*, "A Shocking Medical Experiment" (July 29, 1972, p. 14); and Virginia's *Richmond Times Dispatch* thought that "appalling" was the best adjective to describe an experiment that had used "Humans as Guinea Pigs" (August 6, 1972, p. 6H). To the *Los Angeles Times* the study represented "Official Inhumanity" (July 27, 1972, Part II, p. 6); to the *Providence Sunday Journal*, a "Horror Story" (July 30, 1972, p. 2G); and to the *News and Observer* in Raleigh, North Carolina, a "Nightmare Experiment" (July 28, 1972, p. 4). The *St. Petersburg Times* in Florida voiced cynicism, entitling its editorial, "Health Service?" (July 27, 1972, p. 24), while the *Milwaukee Journal* made its point more directly by introducing its article with the legend "They Helped Men Die" (July 27, 1972, p. 15).

22. R.H. Kampmeir, "The Tuskegee Study of Untreated Syphilis," *Southern Medical Journal* 65 (1972): 1247–51.
23. Ibid., p. 1250.
24. *Philadelphia Inquirer*, July 30, 1972, p. 4H; *Montgomery Advertiser*, August 12, 1972, p. 13; letter to the editor signed A.B., *Evening Star*, Washington, D.C., August 10, 1972, 18A; for examples of a similar reaction, see the *Gazette*, Charleston, West Virginia, July 30, 1972, p. 2D, and Salley E. Clapp to Dr. Merlin K. Duval, July 26, 1972, Tuskegee Files, Center for Disease Control, Atlanta, Georgia. (Hereafter TF-CDC).
25. *Providence Sunday Journal*, July 30, 1972, p. 2G; for the same view, see *Evening Sun*, Baltimore, Maryland, July 26, 1972, p. 26A.
26. Roderick Clark Posey to Millar, July 27, 1972, TF-CDC; *Daily News*, July 27, 1972, p. 63; see also *Milwaukee Journal*, July 27, 1972, p. 15; *Oregonian*, July 31, 1972, p. 16; and Jack Slater, "Condemned to Die for Science," *Ebony* 28 (November 1972), p. 180.
27. *Atlanta Journal*, July 27, 1972, p. 2; *Campus Digest*, October 6, 1972, p. 4.
28. *Afro-American*, August 12, 1972, p. 4. For extended discussions of the race issue, see Slater, "Condemned to Die," p. 191, and the three-part series by Warren Brown in *Jet* 43, "The Tuskegee Study," November 9, 1972, pp. 12–17, November 16, 1972, pp. 20–26, and, especially, November 23, 1972, pp. 26–31.
29. *Los Angeles Times*, July 27, 1972, Part II, p. 6; *New Courier* also stated, "No other minority group in this country would have been used as 'Human Guinea Pigs,' " and explained, "because those who are responsible knew that they could do this to Negroes and nothing would be done to them if it became known," August 19, 1972, p. 6
30. *Greensboro Daily News*, August 2, 1972, p. 6; *Gazette-Telegraph*, Colorado Springs, August 3, 1972, p. 8A; *Washington Post*, July 31, 1972, p. 20A. See also *Arkansas Gazette*, July 29, 1972, p. 4A.
31. *Los Angeles Times*, July 27, 1972, p. 20A.
32. *Washington Post*, July 31, 1972, p. 20A.
33. *Birmingham News*, July 28, 1972, p. 12; *Gazette-Telegraph*, August 3, 1972, p. 8A; *Greensboro Daily News*, August 2, 1972, p. 6A.
34. *Atlanta Constitution*, July 27, 1972, p. 4A.
35. *New Haven Register*, July 20, 1972, p. 14; *News and Observer*, August 1, 1972, p. 4; for similar views see *Desert News*, Salt Lake City, Utah, July 26, 1972, p. 10A; and *Colorado Springs Telegraph*, August 3, 1972, p. FA.

Chapter 2. "A Notoriously Syphilis-Soaked Race"

1. Holmes cited in Gerald N. Grob, *Mental Institutions in America: Social Policy to 1875* (New York, 1973), p. 3.
2. John S. Haller, Jr., "The Negro and the Southern Physician: A Study of Medical and Racial Attitudes 1800–1860," *Medical History* 16 (1972): 239–44. See also Mary Louise Marshall, "Plantation Medicine," *Bulletin of the Medical Library Association* 26 (1938): 115–28; "Samuel A. Cartwright and States' Rights Medicine," *New Orleans Medical and Surgical Journal* 93 (1940): 74–78.
3. Todd L. Savitt, "Sickle Cell and Slavery: Were Blacks Medically Different from Whites?" (Paper presented at the Southern Historical Association Meeting, November 1975), pp. 1–15.
4. Albert Deutsch, "The First U.S. Census of the Insane (1840) and Its Use as Pro-Slavery Propaganda," *Bulletin of the History of Medicine* 15 (1944): 469–82. See also Gerold N. Grob, *Edward Jarvis and the Medical World of Nineteenth-Century America* (Knoville, 1978), pp. 70–75.
5. Quoted in Haller, "Negro and Southern Physician," p. 242.
6. William Dosite Postell, *The Health of Slaves on Southern Plantations* (Baton Rouge, 1951), pp. 50–54, 66.
7. James McIntosh, "The Future of the Negro Race," *Transactions of the South Carolina Medical Association* 41 (1891): 186. For other statements of the golden age thesis, see F. Tipton, "The Negro Problem from a Medical Point of View," *New York Medical Journal* 43 (1886): 570; J. Wellington Byers, "Diseases of the Southern Negro," *Medical and Surgical Reporter* 43 (1888): 735; Edward Henry Sholl, "The Negro and His Death Rate," *Alabama Medical and Surgical Age* 3 (1891): 340; Hunter McGuire and G. Frank Lydston, "Sexual Crimes Among the Southern Negroes—Scientifically Considered—An Open Correspondence Between," *Virginia Medical Monthly* 20 (1893): 105–107, 112–14, 120; J. F. Miller, "The Effects of Emancipation Upon the Mental and Physical Health of the Negro of the South," *North Carolina Medical Journal* 38 (1896): 285–94; J. T. Walton, "The Comparative Mortality of the White and Colored Races in the South," *Charlotte Medical Journal* 10 (1897): 291–94. After the turn of the century the theme continued to be important in the increasing emphasis on environmental causes for the black health problem. See D'Orsay Hecht, "Tabes in the Negro," *American Journal of Medical Sciences* 126 (1903): 708; Henry McHatton, "The Sexual Status of the Negro—Past and Present," *American Journal of Dermatology and Genito-Urinary Diseases* 10 (1906): 6–8; Thomas W.

Murrell, "Syphilis in the Negro: Its Bearing in the Race Problem," *American Journal of Dermatology and Genito-Urinary Diseases* 10 (1906): 305–306, and "Syphilis and the American Negro: A Medico-Sociologic Study," *Journal of the American Medical Association* 54 (1910): 846–47; Howard Fox, "Observations on Skin Diseases in the Negro," *Journal of Cutaneous Diseases* 26 (1908): 109; H. H. Hazen, "Syphilis in the American Negro," *Journal of the American Medical Association* 63 (1914): 463; Roy L. Keller, "Syphilis and Tuberculosis in the Negro Race," *Texas State Journal of Medicine* 19 (1924): 498.

8. For special emphasis on the supervision of morality, see Mcguire and Lydston, "Sexual Crimes," pp. 105–107, 112–14, 170; Hecht, "Tabes in the Negro," p. 708; McHatton, "Sexual Status," pp. 6–8; and Murrell, "Syphilis in the Negro," pp. 505–506. The view of the black family under slavery found in late-nineteenth-century medical literature was, of course, biased and oversimplified, vastly exaggerating both the benevolence and the control of masters. For recent historical interpretations of the effect of slavery on black family life, see Herbert G. Gutman, *The Black Family in Slavery and Freedom, 1750–1925* (New York, 1976); Eugene Genovese, *Roll, Jordan, Roll: The World the Slaves Made* (New York, 1974); and Robert Fogel and Stanley Engerman, *Time on the Cross: The Economics of American Negro Slavery*, 2 vols. (Boston, 1974).

9. John S. Haller, Jr., *Outcasts from Evolution: Scientific Attitudes of Racial Inferiority, 1859–1900* (Urbana, Ill., 1971), pp. 40–44, and "Race, Mortality, and Life Insurance: Negro Vital Statistics in the Late Nineteenth Century," *Journal of the History of Medicine* 25 (1970): 247–61.

10. Byers, "Diseases of the Southern Negro," p. 737.

11. See especially ibid., p. 735; McIntosh, "Future of the Negro Race," p. 186; McGuire and Lydston, "Sexual Crimes," pp. 105–125; Hecht, "Tabes in the Negro," p. 708; McHatton, "Sexual Status," p. 9; Murrell, "Syphilis in the Negro," pp. 305–307, and "Syphilis and the American Negro," p. 847; Fox, "Observations," p. 109; Hazen, "Syphilis in the American Negro," pp. 463–64. For other articles stressing black immorality, see Frank Jones, "Syphilis in the Negro," *Journal of the American Medical Association* 42 (1904): 32; Eugene R. Corson, "Syphilis in the Negro," *American Journal of Dermatology and Genito-Urinary Diseases* 10 (1906): 241, 247; Daniel David Quillian, "Racial Peculiarities as a Cause of the Prevalence of Syphilis in Negroes," *American Journal of Dermatology and Genito-Urinary Diseases* 10 (1906): 277–79; E. M. Green, "Psychoses Among Negroes—A Comparative

Approach," *Journal of Nervous and Mental Diseases* 41 (1914): 703–708; Kenneth M. Lynch, B. Kater McInnes, and G. Fleming McInnes, "Concerning Syphilis in the American Negro," *Southern Medical Journal* 8 (1915): 452; M. L. Graves, "Practical Remedial Measures for the Improvement of Hygiene Conditions of the Negro in the South," *American Journal of Public Health* 5 (1915): 212. Such explanations continued into the 1920s; see, for example, Ernest L. Zimmerman, "A Comparative Study of Syphilis in Whites and in Negroes," *Archives of Dermatology and Syphilology* 4 (1921): 73–74; David L. Belding and Isabelle L. Hunter, "The Wassermann Test: VI. The Influence of Race and Nationality Upon Routine Wassermann Tests in a Maternity Hospital," *American Journal of Syphilis* 9 (1925): 126, 130; Franklin Nicholas, "Some Health Problems of the Negro," *Journal of Social Hygiene* 8 (1925): 281–85; S. W. Douglas, "Difficulties and Superstitions Encountered in Practice Among Negroes," *Southern Medical Journal* 19 (1926): 736–38; and C. Jeff Miller, "Comparative Study of Certain Gynecologic and Obstetric Conditions as Exhibited in the Colored and White Races," *American Journal of Obstetrics and Gynecology* 26 (1928): 662–63; Groesbeck Walsh and Courtney Stickley, "Arsphenaminĕ Poisoning Occurring Among Negro Women," *American Journal of Syphilis and Neurology* 19 (1935): 324–25.

12. See especially Byers, "Diseases of the Southern Negro," p. 736; McIntosh, "Future of the Negro Race," pp. 186–87; Hecht, "Tabes in the Negro," pp. 705–720; Jones, "Syphilis in the Negro," p. 32; McHatton, "Sexual Status," p. 9; Murrell, "Syphilis and the American Negro," pp. 846–49; and Quillian, "Racial Peculiarities," p. 818. Several authors stressed the high miscarriage rate among syphilitic black women, a tragedy that largely obviated concern about congenital syphilis. Corson, for example, noted in 1893 that "the congenital form [of syphilis] is so virulent that most of the infants do not reach term." He later emphasized the effectiveness of treatment in bringing fetuses to term, but indicated that he had never seen a black adult with congenital syphilis, stating, "I have always explained it by the inability of the negro child to survive the disease sufficiently long." Eugene R. Corson, "The Vital Equation of the Colored Race and Its Future in the United States," in *The Wilder Quarter Century Book* (Ithaca, N.Y., 1893), p. 149; and Corson, "Syphilis in the Negro," p. 245.

13. For a well-developed statement of geographic determinism, see McGuire and Lydston, "Sexual Crimes," pp. 115–16; Rudolph Matas, "The Surgical Peculiarities of the Negro," *Transactions of*

the American Surgical Association (1896), pp. 483–86; Quillian, "Racial Peculiarities" (1906), p. 277; Daniel David Quillian, "Racial Peculiarities as a Cause of the Prevalence of Syphilis in Negroes," Medical Era 20 (1911): 416; or Hazen, "Syphilis in the American Negro," p. 463.

14. Southern physicians wrote the overwhelming majority of articles on black health, a fact that is not surprising since most blacks remained in the South during this period. A few articles by northern writers appeared in the literature in the nineteenth century, and after World War I their number increased, though not dramatically. At no point did the articles by northern physicians differ sharply from those produced by southern physicians in their analysis of the problem. Northern authors generally were concerned with the effects of urban life on blacks and concluded that city living had negative results. Differences in opinion concerning the incidences and the causes of syphilis in blacks did occur, but they were individual differences and in no way reflected sectional views. Perhaps the broad agreement within the medical profession stemmed from northern indebtedness to southern scholarship, for northern physicians consulted and frequently cited the work of their southern colleagues. A more likely explanation, however, is that northern and southern physicians shared the same racial attitudes. For southern claims of responsibility to write on black health, see P. G. DeSaussure, "Is the Colored Race Increasing or Decreasing?" Transactions of the South Carolina Medical Association (1895), p. 119; Matas, "Surgical Peculiarities," p. 486; Miller, "Effects of Emancipation," p. 285; O. C. Wenger, "A Wassermann Survey of the Negroes of a Cotton Plantation," Venereal Disease Information 10 (1929): 286; and Ferdinand Reinhard, "The Venereal Disease Problem in the Colored Population of Baltimore City," American Journal of Syphilis and Neurology 19 (1935): 183–84.

15. Dissenters from the profession's conventional wisdom on black health existed in every period. A few late-nineteenth-century physicians categorically denied that black people were more susceptible to disease than white people due to racial inferiority and explained black health in purely environmental terms, but they remained a distinct minority. See Robert W. Taylor, "On a Peculiarity of the Popular Syphilide of the Negro," American Journal of Syphilography and Dermatology 4 (1873): 107–109; William Powell, "Syphilis in the Negro as Differing from Syphilis in the White Race," Transactions of the Mississippi State Medical Association (1878), pp. 76–78; and M. V. Bell, "Reply to Article by Cun-

ningham, 'The Mortality of the Negro,' " *Medical News* 64 (1894):
389–90.

16. See Sholl, "The Negro and His Death Rate," pp. 340–41; McIntosh, "Future of the Negro Race," pp. 183–84, 187; Russell McWhorter Cunningham, "The Negro as a Convict," *Transactions of the Medical Association of the State of Alabama* (1893), pp. 325–26; McGuire and Lydston, "Sexual Crimes," p. 106; and Quillian, "Racial Peculiarities" (1906), p. 278.

17. Hecht, "Tabes in the Negro," p. 719; Murrell, "Syphilis and the American Negro," p. 847.

18. McGuire and Lydston, "Sexual Crimes," p. 118; Loyd Thompson and Lyle B. Kingery, "Syphilis in the Negro," *American Journal of Syphilis* 3 (1919):386–87.

19. McIntosh, "Future of the Negro Race," p. 186.

20. Quillian, "Racial Peculiarities" (1911), p. 417; Lynch et al., "Concerning Syphilis," p. 452; L. C. Allen, "The Negro Health Problem," *American Journal of Public Health* 5 (1915):199. See also Louis Wender, "The Role of Syphilis in the Insane Negro," *New York Medical Journal* 104 (1916):1287; Thompson and Kingery, "Syphilis in the Negro," p. 387; Belding and Hunter, "Wassermann Test," p. 126; and Douglas, "Difficulties and Superstitions," p. 737.

21. Green, "Psychoses Among Negroes," p. 705; Corson, "Syphilis in the Negro," pp. 241, 244; James E. Paullin, Hal M. Davidson, and R. Hugh Wood, "The Incidence of Syphilitic Infection Among the Negroes in the South, Its Influence in the Causation of Disability, and the Methods Which Are Being Used to Combat this Infection," *Boston Medical and Surgical Journal* 197 (1927):349.

22. McHatton, "Sexual Status," p. 9; Murrell, "Syphilis in the Negro," p. 307; Bruce McVey, "Negro Practice," *New Orleans Medical and Surgical Journal* 20 (1892):332; Murrell, "Syphilis and the American Negro," pp. 847, 848.

23. Wender, "Role of Syphilis,"p. 1287; Hazen, "Syphilis in the American Negro," p. 465. Hazen is an excellent example of the transition in opinion among health officers about black health. In his writings, the most important detriment to treatment was not race, but the poverty of most blacks. See Hazen, "Syphilis in the American Negro," p. 465, and "Personal Observtions upon Skin Diseases in the American Negro," *Journal of Cutaneous Diseases* 32 (1914):712. Note also Keller, "Syphilis and Tuberculosis," pp. 495–98.

24. Baldwin Luche, "Tabes Dorsalis, A Pathological and Clinical Study of 250 Cases," *Journal of Nervous and Mental Disease* 43

(1916): 395; S. S. Hindman, "Syphilis Among Insane Negroes," *American Journal of Public Health* 5 (1915):219.

25. For late-nineteenth-century descriptions of racial differences in the development of syphilis, see Taylor, "On a Peculiarity," pp. 107–109; I. Edmondson Atkinson, "Early Syphilis in the Negro," *Maryland Medical Journal* 1 (1877):135; McVey, "Negro Practice," pp. 331–32; Cunningham, "The Negro as a Convict," pp. 321–22; and Russell McWhorter Cunningham, "The Morbidity and Mortality of Negro Convicts," *Medical News* 64 (1894):113–17. These observations continued in the twentieth century. See Hecht, "Tabes in the Negro," pp. 705–720; Quillian, "Racial Peculiarities" (1906), pp. 277–79, and "Racial Peculiarities" (1911), pp. 416–18; Hazen, "Personal Observations," pp. 705–712; Hazen, "Syphilis in the American Negro," pp. 463–66; H. H. Hazen, "Twenty-five Cases of Extragenital Syphilitic Infection," *Interstate Medical Journal* 23 (1916):661–64; Fox, "Observations," pp. 109–121; Green, "Psychoses Among Negroes," pp. 697–708; Luche, "Tabes Dorsalis," pp. 393–410.

26. Zimmerman, "Comparative Study," pp. 73–88. In 1919 Thompson and Kingery published a review of the literature on syphilis in blacks that merely added to the confusion, for they compiled the contradictory results of clinical studies ("Syphilis in the Negro," pp. 384–97). In the twenties, acceptance of Zimmerman's findings was standard and further clinical studies tended to concentrate on particular studies of syphilis in blacks. For examples of citations of Zimmerman, see Keller, "Syphilis and Tuberculosis," p. 497; L. D. Hubbard, "A Comparative Study of Syphilis in Colored and White Women with Mental Disorders," *Archives of Neurology and Psychology* 12 (1924):201; Howard Fox, "Syphilis in the Negro," *New York State Journal of Medicine* 26 (1926):555. For the more limited studies of the 1920s, see I. I. Lemann, "Diabetes Mellitus, Syphilis and the Negro," *American Journal of Medical Sciences* 162 (1921):226–30; Hubbard, "Comparative Study," pp. 198–205; R. A. Bartholomes, "Syphilis as a Complication of Pregnancy in the Negro," *Journal of the American Medical Association* 83 (1924):172–74; James R. McCord, "Syphilis of the Placenta in the Negro," *American Journal of Obstetrics and Gynecology* 11 (1926): 850–52; Curtice Rosser, "Clinical Variations in Negro Protology," *Journal of the American Medical Association* 87 (1926):2084–85.

In the nineteenth century doctors who thought that syphilis was a milder disease in blacks often believed that treatment should be milder and that in some cases the disease would be spontaneously cured. After the discovery of the spirochete and chemotherapy, however, treatment was standard in both races. See Murrell, "Syphilis and the American Negro," p. 848; Hazen, "Syphilis in the American Negro," p. 465; Frank Cregor and Frank Gastineau, "Stavorsal in the Treatment of Syphilis," *Archives of Dermatology and Syphilology* 15 (1927):45–53; J. R. McCord, "The Results Obtained in Treated and Untreated Cases of Syphilis in Pregnant Negro Women," *American Journal of Obstetrics and Gynecology* 13 (1927):100–103.

Chapter 3. "Disease Germs Are the Most Democratic Creatures in the World"

1. On the Flexner report, see Stephan J. Kunitz, "Professionalism and Social Control in the Progressive Era: The Case of the Flexner Report," *Social Problems* 22 (October 1974): 16–27, and Cableton B. Chapman, *"The Flexner Report* by Abraham Flexner," *Daedalus* 103 (Winter 1974): 105–117. For a more general statement on the increasing elitism of the profession, see Gerald E. Markowitz and David Karl Rosner, "Doctors in Crisis: A Study of the Use of Medical Education to Establish Modern Professional Elitism in Medicine," *American Quarterly* 25 (March 1973): 83–107.

2. Progressivism was fueled by a series of reform movements that sought to adjust the political, economic, and social life of the country to a set of new realities that rapid industrialization and urbanization had visited upon America during the last third of the nineteenth century. Progressive leaders demanded banking reform; a downward revision of the protective tariff; government regulation of big business; the recognition of labor's right to organize and engage in collective bargaining; changes in the machinery of government at the municipal, state, and federal levels; the abolition of child labor; the enfranchisement of women; and a variety of public health measures—to mention only a few areas of concern. Progressives wanted reform to take place within the context of existing institutions and without any fundamental reordering of the basic structure of American society. They advocated limited changes that could be readily incorporated into government's traditional role of limited action on behalf of the general good. Above all, they wished to adjust the relationships among every competing sector, creating a rational society that was both orderly and efficient. For two different interpretations, see Robert H. Wiebe, *The Search for Order, 1877–1920* (New York, 1967), and Richard Hofstader, *The Age of Reform* (New York, 1955).

3. Marion Torchia, "Help Yourself to Health: National Negro Health Week, 1915–1950," unpublished manuscript. See also Rosco C. Brown, "The National Negro Health Week Movement," *Journal of Negro Education* 6 (1937): 553–64, and W. A. Fischer and D. E. Breed, "Negro Health Week in Texas," *Survey* 45 (1920): 100–101.

4. Torchia, "Help Yourself to Health."

5. L. C. Allen, "The Negro Health Problem," *American Journal of Public Health (AJPH)* 5 (1915): 194–203; William Brunner, "The Negro Health Problem in Southern Cities," *AJPH* 5 (1915): 183–91; A. G. Fort, "The Negro Health Problem in Rural Communities," *AJPH* 5 (1915): 191–93; M. L. Graves, "Practical Remedial Measures for the Improvement of Hygienic Conditions of the Negroes in the South," *AJPH* 5 (1915): 212–15; S. S. Hindman, "Syphilis Among Insane Negroes," *AJPH* 5 (1915): 218–24; Lawrence Lee, "The Negro as a Problem in Public Health Charity," *AJPH* 5 (1915): 207–11; and John Trask, "The Significance of the Mortality Rates of the Colored Population of the U.S.," *AJPH* 6 (1916): 251–60.

6. Allen, "Negro Health Problem," p. 199.

7. Brunner, "Negro Health Problem in Southern Cities," pp. 186, 185.

8. Ibid., p. 189.

9. Trask, "Significance of Mortality Rates," p. 254.

10. Ibid., p. 257. Trask also compared the death rates of American blacks with the death rates of white populations in several foreign countries. The black death rate for the registration area of the United States in 1912 was 22.9 per thousand. For the same year, Hungary's was 23.3; Romania's was 22.9; Spain's was 21.8; and Austria's was 20.5. He found the comparisons quite favorable to the American Negro.

11. Ibid., pp. 258–59.

12. Allen, "Negro Health Problem," p. 200; Fort, "Negro Health Problem in Rural Communities," p. 193.

13. Lee, "Negro as a Problem," pp. 211, 209.

14. Fort, "Negro Health Problem in Rural Communities," p. 192.

15. Ibid., pp. 208, 209.

16. Allen, "Negro Health Problem," p. 194; Brunner, "Negro Health Problem in Southern Cities," p. 183; Lee, "Negro as a Problem," p. 211.

17. Brunner, "Negro Health Problem in Southern Cities," p. 188.

18. Fort, "Negro Health Problem in Rural Communities," pp. 191, 193.

19. Brunner, "Negro Health Problem in Southern Cities," p. 188.
20. Graves, "Practical Remedial Measures," p. 214.
21. Ibid., p. 215.
22. Brunner, "Negro Health Problem in Southern Cities," pp. 185, 187.
23. Allen, "Negro Health Problem," p. 194.
24. Ibid.
25. For an overview of public health and social service reforms in the South during the Progressive Era, see George B. Tindall, *The Emergence of the New South, 1913–1945* (Baton Rouge, Louisiana, 1967), pp. 254–84.

Chapter 4. "Holding High Wassermann in the Marketplace"

1. The story of salvarsan is told well in Martha Marquardt, *Paul Ehrlich* (New York, 1951).
2. H. H. Hazen, "Syphilis in the American Negro," *Journal of the American Medical Association* 63 (1914): 465, and "Personal Observations upon Skin Diseases in the American Negro," *Journal of Cutaneous Diseases* 23 (1914): 711.
3. Stewart Welch, "Congenital Syphilis," *Southern Medical Journal* 16 (1923): 420. Several physicians even had the temerity to suggest that the incidence of syphilis (like most other diseases) in any population was a function of social class, not race. H. L. McNeil of the University of Texas Medical School at Galveston released the results of a study showing that the "occurrence of syphilis among white people of the same social class as the negroes would seem to be about the same as that among the negroes." Henry H. Hazen shared the same view. As the author of numerous articles on syphilis in the Negro, he usually took great care to distinguish between lower and upper class blacks. Referring to the latter class, he wrote, "In a considerable experience with these men I am convinced that syphilis is not more prevalent among them than among the whites, although there are no statistics to prove the point." H. L. McNeil, "Syphilis in the Southern Negro," *Journal of the American Medical Association* 67 (1916): 1004, and Hazen, "Syphilis in the American Negro," p. 463.
4. Hazen, "Syphilis in the American Negro," p. 465.
5. For a brief discussion of the social hygiene movement, see John C. Burnham, "The Progressive Revolution in America Toward Sex," *Journal of American History* 59 (March 1973): 885–908. The best

detailed discussion is James F. Gardner, Jr., "Microbes and Morality: The Social Hygiene Crusade in New York City, 1892–1917" (Ph.D. dissertation, Indiana University, 1973).

6. David Pivar, *The Purity Crusade* (New York, 1973) is the standard discussion of the purity forces.

7. Ironically, early in his career Nichols shared many of the attitudes of middle-class whites concerning black sexuality. In 1922, he told a conference of black social workers in Atlanta, Georgia, that "overindulgence of appetites" was a significant cause of the decline in black health. Over the years Nichols changed his position, arguing that the immoral sexual behavior of many lower-class blacks was a product of the black family's "difficult and hazardous history." To underscore the importance of the family, Nichols constructed an explanation of the sexual behavior of lower-class blacks that rested entirely on the damage that slavery had inflicted on the black family. Franklin O. Nichols, "Some Health Problems of the Negro," *Journal of Social Hygiene* 8 (1925): 283, and "Social Hygiene and the Negro," *Journal of Social Hygiene* 15 (1929): 409. For the continuation of Nichols's development of the same themes, see "Social Hygiene in Racial Problems—The Negro," *Journal of Social Hygiene* 18 (1932): 447–51.

8. Thomas Parran, *Shadow on the Land: Syphilis* (New York, 1937), p. 83.

9. D. S. Gill, "How Alabama Meets her Social Hygiene Problems," *Journal of Social Hygiene* 16 (1930): 530–31.

10. Ibid., p. 532.

11. For a discussion of Davis's early career, see Ralph E. Pomeroy, "Michael M. Davis and the Development of the Health Movement, 1900-1928," *Societas* 2 (Winter 1972): 27–41.

12. Cumming to Davis, July 19, 1929, Rosenwald Fund Papers, Fisk University Archives [hereafter, RFP-FUA].

13. Davis to Cumming, July 31, 1929, RFP-FUA.

14. Quoted in Parran, *Shadow on the Land*, p. 161. Wenger was born in St. Louis, Missouri, in 1884. Following graduation from St. Louis University's School of Medicine in 1908, he worked for several years as a diagnostician with the St. Louis Health Department. He then joined the military and from 1912 to 1915 put in a tour of duty with the Phillippine Islands Constabulary. During World War I he served as a captain in the sanitary corps of the American Expeditionary Forces. He continued his military work in World War II when his role as a liaison officer on the staff of the Caribbean Defense Command earned him a personal decoration by King George VI of England.

15. Wenger to Davis, August 13, 1929, RFP-FUA.
16. Ibid.
17. Ibid.
18. Ibid.
19. Ibid.
20. Ibid.; Wenger to Parran, September 4, 1929, RFP-FUA.
21. Ibid.
22. Parran was born in 1892 in St. Leonard, Maryland. He attended St. John's College in Maryland, graduating in 1911. He received his degree from Georgetown University Medical School in 1915. Parran was in charge of health activities at Muscle Shoals in Alabama during World War I and later directed county health programs in Missouri and Illinois. He entered the Public Health Service in 1917 and became the director of its Venereal Diseases Division in 1926. For a brief biographical sketch of Parran's career, see "Editorials—Thomas Parran, M.D. (1892–1968)," *Journal of Public Health* 58 (April 1968): 615, 617.
23. Memorandum enclosed in Parran to Davis, October 9, 1932, RFP-FUA.
24. Ibid.
25. Ibid. In fact Davis was hard pressed to find anything in the proposal to which to object. Taking cognizance of Davis's earlier reservations concerning the Mississippi program, Parran and Clark had tailor-made the demonstration to fit the Fund. They strongly suggested the Fund "consider the advisability of announcing a policy regarding cooperation which shall make clear that the Fund is not to assume responsibility for the control of the veneral diseases in the general population or any group thereof." That task, they agreed, was "the function of official health agencies." They therefore recommended that the Fund limit its activities in this field "to developing and popularizing effective methods by temporary assistance to official health agencies."
26. Taliaferro Clark, *The Control of Syphilis in Southern Rural Areas* (Chicago, 1932), p. 6.
27. Minutes of the Julius Rosenwald Fund Executive Committee meeting, December 18, 1929, Records of the USPHS Veneral Disease Division, Record Group 90, National Archives, Washington National Record Center, Suitland, Maryland [hereafter NA-WNRC].
28. Clark, *Control of Syphilis*, pp. 9–10; Parran, *Shadow on the Land*, pp. 163–64. In announcing the new program, Cumming emphasized that the demonstrations were intended to determine the incidence of syphilis in a representative sample of Negroes; to test the feasibility of mass treatment and measure its effect upon

the incidence of syphilis in the groups treated; to establish whether it was possible to use Negro personnel in these projects in southern areas; to stimulate the state boards and health departments to appoint venereal disease control officers; and to improve the quality of antileutic treatment by providing selected rural physicians with refresher courses in syphilis diagnosis and treatment.

Chapter 5. "The Dr. Ain't Taking Sticks"

1. Thomas Parran, *Shadow on the Land: Syphilis* (New York, 1937), p. 170.
2. Clark to Davis, February 17, 1931, Records of the USPHS Venereal Disease Division, Record Group 90, National Archives, Washington National Record Center, Suitland, Maryland [hereafter NA-WNRC].
3. Ibid.
4. Parran, *Shadow on the Land*, p. 170.
5. Horace Mann Bond, *Negro Education in Alabama: A Study in Cotton and Steel* (New York, 1939), p. 223.
6. In no area was the disparity between the two systems more graphic than the salaries paid to teachers. Per capita expenditures for white teachers' salaries in Macon County in 1932 were $34.21 per student as compared to $3.10 per student for blacks. Horace Mann Bond, *The Education of the Negro in the American Social Order* (New York, 1934), p. 432.
7. Frost Report, November 16, 1931, NA-WNRC.
8. Ibid.
9. Interview, #138, Box 556, Charles Johnson Papers, Fisk University Archives [hereafter CJP-FUA]. Professor Johnson's interviews, numbered in sequence, for *Shadow of the Plantation* (Chicago, 1934) are preserved in the Charles Johnson Papers at Fisk University, Nashville, Tennessee. I have preserved the spelling and punctuation of the original transcriptions.
10. Interview #122, Box 556, CJP-FUA; Interview #231, Box 556, CJP-FUA.
11. Interview #232, Box 556, CJP-FUA. For a discussion of home remedies used in Macon County, see Johnson, *Shadow of the Plantation*, pp. 192–96. For an analysis of the use of marginal medical resources in the deep South, see Julian Roebuck and Robert Quan, "Health-Care Practices in the American Deep South," in Roy Wallis and Peter Morley, eds., *Marginal Medicine* (New York, 1976).

12. Interview #138, Box 556, CJP-FUA.
13. Frost Report, November 16, 1931, NA-WNRC.
14. Graves to Cumming, January 27, 1930, NA-WNRC.
15. Ibid.
16. Clark to Davis, January 28, 1930, NA-WNRC; Davis to Clark, January 31, 1930, NA-WNRC; Minutes of the Rosenwald Fund Executive Committee, February 12, 1930, pp. 243–44, NA-WNRC.
17. Parran, *Shadow on the Land*, p. 166
18. Ibid., p. 167, both quotes.
19. Johnson, *Shadow of the Plantation*, p. 202.
20. Frost Report, November 16, 1931, NA-WNRC.
21. Parran, *Shadow on the Land*, pp. 164–65.
22. Frost Report, November 16, 1931, NA-WNRC.
23. Taliaferro Clark, *The Control of Syphilis in Southern Rural Areas* (Chicago, 1932), p. 64; Parran, *Shadow on the Land*, pp. 164–65.
24. Parran, *Shadow on the Land*, pp. 167–68.
25. Ibid., p. 168
26. Ibid. The problem of how to acquire these specially designed belts on a limited budget was solved by volunteer workers from the local chapter of the Red Cross who made them by the hundreds at a cost of only a few cents each.
27. Ibid., p. 163.
28. Harris to Davis, May 13, 1930, NA-WNRC.
29. Interview #222, Box 556, CJP-FUA; Interview #178, Box 556, CJP-FUA; Johnson, *Shadow of the Plantation*, pp. 202, 203.
30. Frost to Clark, November 16, 1931, NA-WNRC.
31. Johnson, *Shadow of the Plantation*, pp. 201, 202, 196.
32. Ibid., pp. 202, 203.
33. Harris's Memo to Davis, September 22, 1930, Rosenwald Fund Papers, Fisk University Archives.
34. Clark, *Control of Syphilis*, p. 27. The figures for the remaining demonstration sites in descending order were: 26.9 percent in Glynn County, Georgia; 25.9 percent in Tipton County, Tennessee; 23.6 percent in Bolivar County, Mississippi; and 11.8 percent in Pitt County, North Carolina. Ibid., p. 28.
35. Davis to Clark, March 28, 1930, NA-WNRC. Early in March, 1930 (just a few weeks after the program had gotten under way in Macon County), the surgeon general appointed Dr. Clark to head the PHS Division of Venereal Diseases. (The position had become vacant when Dr. Parran left to become commissioner of public health for the state of New York.) Informing Davis of this appointment, Dr. Clark wrote, "It is understood that this detail need not interfere in any way with my relations with the Fund." (Clark to Davis, March 11, 1930, NA-WNRC) The fact that Clark

was therefore in a position to speak as the head of the Venereal Disease Division and the Fund's chief medical adviser on black health gave Davis a doubly good excuse to confront him with what he feared might result from the program.

36. Clark to Davis, March 31, 1930, NA-WNRC.
37. Clark to Wall, March 31, 1930, NA-WNRC; Interview #200, Box 556, CJP-FUA.
38. Clark, *Control of Syphilis*, pp. 53, 28.
39. Ibid., pp. 21–23, 29.
40. Ibid., p. 29, 35; and Wenger to Clark, May 17, 1930, NA-WNRC.
41. Wenger to Clark, May 17, 1930, NA-WNRC.
42. Ibid.
43. Clark, *Control of Syphilis*, p. 17; Parran, *Shadow on the Land*, p. 169.

Chapter 6. "Buying Ear Muffs for the Hottentots"

1. Harris's Memo to Davis, May 13, 1930, Records of the USPHS Venereal Disease Division, Record Group 90, National Archives, Washington National Record Center, Suitland, Maryland [hereafter NA-WNRC].
2. Ibid.
3. Ibid.
4. Interview #494, Box 556, Charles Johnson Papers, Fisk University Archives [hereafter CJP-FUA]; Interview #271, Box 556, CJP-FUA.
5. Harris's Memo to Davis, May 13, 1930, NA-WNRC.
6. Wenger to Clark, May 17, 1930, NA-WNRC.
7. Ibid.
8. Ibid.
9. Ibid. On the whole, Dr. Harris's evaluation of the effects of the conditions on the safety of the therapy was more accurate. Air embolism was a risk; and it was extremely unlikely that no patients had reactions. I wish to thank Dr. William A. Tisdale of the University of Vermont Medical School for sharing his judgment on this topic with me.
10. Ibid.
11. Ibid.
12. Harris's Memo to Davis, September 22, 1930, Rosenwald Fund Papers, Fisk University Archives [hereafter RFP-FUA].
13. Ibid.
14. Harris's Memo to Davis, October 1, 1931, RFP-FUA.

15. Davis to Clark, October 22, 1930, RFP-FUA; Clark to Davis, October 25, 1930, RFP-FUA.
16. Charles Johnson, *Shadow of the Plantation* (Chicago, 1934), pp. 202–207. In March 1931, Professor Johnson and Dr. Wenger met in Nashville and agreed that the study should concentrate on Macon County. Later that month they met again in Macon County and spent several days talking with the families participating in the demonstration. Johnson submitted a preliminary report to the Fund describing the social and economic conditions of these families the following month. Wenger to Davis, March 6, 1931, NA-WNRC; Clark's Memorandum, April 19, 1931, NA-WNRC.
17. Clark to Cumming, January 14, 1931, NA-WNRC; Clark to Davis, January 15, 1931, NA-WNRC; quoted in Davis to Clark, January 13, 1931, NA-WNRC.
18. Clark's Memorandum, April 19, 1931, NA-WNRC.
19. Ibid.; Davis to Clark, May 19, 1932, RFP-FUA.
20. Wenger quoted in Clark to Davis, February 17, 1931, NA-WNRC; Interview #246, Box 556, CJP-FUA.
21. Davis to Rosenwald, September 24, 1931, RFP-FUA.
22. Ibid.
23. Davis's Brief for the Fund's Trustees, November 7, 1931, NA-WNRC.
24. Davis to Clark, November 13, 1931, NA-WNRC.
25. Ibid. Davis cautioned Dr. Clark against calling poor blacks in the demonstrations "indigents," saying, "We should avoid thinking of the problem of syphilis control as relating to 'the indigent'; nor can we assume that any large section of a southern rural community can afford to pay on the usual fee basis for the private treatment of so expensive a disease as syphilis." Davis had done extensive research on the cost of syphilis therapy and estimated that it cost, on average, about $300 per year. Based on these figures, he concluded that fully 80 percent of the entire American public could not afford syphilis therapy on a fee-for-service basis. Davis to Clark, November 2, 1931, NA-WNRC. On the cost of syphilis treatment, see Leon Brombert and Michael M. Davis, "The Cost of Treating Syphilis," *Journal of Social Hygiene* 18 (October 1932): 366–77; and Michael M. Davis, "The Ability of Patients to Pay for the Treatment of Syphilis," *Journal of Social Hygiene* 18 (October 1932): 380–88.
26. Clark to Parran, May 17, 1932, NA-WNRC.
27. Davis to Clark, November 13, 1931, NA-WNRC.
28. Cumming to Davis, August 19, 1932, RFP-FUA.

29. Wenger to Dr. M. O. Bousfield, director of Negro health, Julius Rosenwald Fund, June 12, 1940, RFP-FUA.

Chapter 7. "It will Either Cover Us with Mud or Glory"

1. Clark to O'Leary, September 27, 1932, Records of USPHS Venereal Disease Division, Record Group 90, National Archives, Washington National Record Center, Suitland, Maryland [hereafter NA-WNRC].
2. Ibid.
3. Ibid.
4. Clark to Davis, October 29, 1932, NA-WNRC. For the first published report on the Oslo Study, see E. Bruusgaard, "Über das Schicksal der nicht spezifisch behaldelten Luetiker [The Fate of Syphilitics Who Are not Given Specific Treatment]," *Archive fur Dermatologie und Syphilis* 157 (1929): 309–332. I wish to thank Ruth W. Moskop for translating this article.
5. Ibid.
6. Ibid.
7. For analysis of the concepts used here, see Eliot Freidson, *Profession of Medicine: A Study of the Sociology of Applied Knowledge* (New York, 1972). For historical discussions of the origins of professionalism in medicine, see Joseph F. Kett, *The Formation of the American Medical Profession: The Role of Institutions, 1780-1860* (New Haven, 1968); William G. Rothstein, *American Physicians in the 19th Century: From Sects to Science* (Baltimore, 1972); Rosemary Stevens, *American Medicine and the Public Interest* (New Haven, 1971); James G. Burrow, *Organized Medicine in the Progressive Era: The Move Toward Monopoly* (Baltimore, 1977). For a contrasting view on early nineteenth-century medicine, see Barbara G. Rosenkrantz, "The Search for Professional Order in 19th Century American Medicine," *Proceedings of the XIVth International Congress of the History of Science* (Tokyo and Kyoto, 1974), No. 4, pp. 113–24.
8. For a broad discussion of the role of licensing boards, see Richard H. Shryock, *Medical Licensing in America, 1650–1965* (Baltimore, 1967). See also James G. Burrow, *AMA: Voice of American Medicine* (Baltimore, 1963).
9. There is no full study of the history of medical ethics. For a historical overview of primary documents, see Stanley Joel Reiser, Arthur J. Dyck, and William J. Curran, *Ethics in Medicine: Historical Perspectives and Contemporary Concerns* (Cambridge, Massachusetts, 1977). The best short survey of the history of medical

codes is Donald E. Konold, "Codes of Medical Ethics: History," in *Encyclopedia of Bioethics* (New York, 1978), I: 162–71. His monograph is a longer survey of the same topic: Donald E. Konold, *A History of American Medical Ethics, 1847–1961* (Madison, 1962).

10. See the basic survey by Richard H. Shryock, *American Medical Research: Past and Present* (New York, 1947).

11. The increasing respect given to scientific research was accompanied by the rise of university research centers and the transition from private philanthropic to government support. See George Rosen, "Patterns of Health Research in the United States, 1900–1960," *Bulletin of the History of Medicine* 39 (1965): 201–25.

12. Odin W. Anderson, *The Uneasy Equilibrium: Private and Public Financing of Health Services in the United States, 1875–1965* (New Haven, 1968), contains an overview of medical financing.

13. Clark to Dibble, September 21, 1932, NA-WNRC; Clark to Baker, September 23, 1932, NA-WNRC. Judging from the policy that Dr. Clark's associates actually put into practice after the experiment got under way, the agreement that was reached between Drs. Clark and Baker on treatment must have gone something like this: Syphilitics not included in the study had to be treated immediately after their diagnosis was confirmed, while syphilitics who were brought into the study could have their treatment deferred until after they were examined. Once the examinations were completed, however, they too had to be given treatment.

14. Clark to Davis, October 29, 1932, NA-WNRC.

15. Wenger to Clark, September 16, 1932, NA-WNRC.

16. Wenger also observed that Gill "became more and more enthusiastic" over the proposed demonstration during their conference with Dr. Dibble "and actually offered to furnish as much free neoarsphenamine as he possibly could," a proposal that must have delighted Dr. Clark. Ibid.

17. Dibble to Moton, September 17, 1932, Tuskegee Institute Archives [hereafter TIA].

18. Ibid.

19. Cumming to Moton, September 20, 1932, NA-WNRC.

20. Clark to Dibble, September 20, 1932, NA-WNRC.

21. Clark to Dibble, September 21, 1932, NA-WNRC; Dibble to Clark, September 29, 1932, NA-WNRC.

22. Clark's notes on Baltimore meeting, September 26, 1932, NA-WNRC.

23. Ibid.

24. Ibid.

25. Ibid.

26. Moore to Clark, September 28, 1932, NA-WNRC.
27. Ibid.
28. Ibid.
29. Ibid.
30. Ibid.
31. Wenger to Clark, October 3, 1932, NA-WNRC.
32. Ibid.
33. Ibid.
34. Ibid.
35. Clark's notes on Baltimore meeting, September 26, 1932, NA-WNRC.
36. Gill to Wenger, October 10, 1932, NA-WNRC; see also Clark tò Wenger, October 6, 1932, and Wenger to Gill, October 8, 1932, both NA-WNRC.
37. Clark to Madsen, June 26, 1930, NA-WNRC.
38. Author's Interview, Eunice Rivers Laurie, May 3, 1977.
39. Ibid.
40. Ibid.
41. Ibid.
42. Ibid.
43. Dibble to Moton, September 17, 1932, TIA.
44. Laurie Interview.
45. Clark to Davis, October 29, 1932, NA-WNRC; Wenger to Clark, October 3, 1932, NA-WNRC.

Chapter 8. "Last Chance for Special Free Treatment"

1. Vonderlehr to Clark, October 20, 1932, Records of the USPHS Venereal Disease Division, Record Group 90, National Archives, Washington National Record Center, Suitland, Maryland [hereafter NA-WNRC].
2. Author's Interview, Eunice Rivers Laurie, May 3, 1977.
3. Vonderlehr to Clark, October 26, 1932, NA-WNRC; Clark to Vonderlehr, October 31, 1932, NA-WNRC.
4. Vonderlehr to Clark, November 2, 1932, NA-WNRC; Vonderlehr to Clark, January 7, 1933, NA-WNRC.
5. Clark to Vonderlehr, October 31, 1932, NA-WNRC.
6. Laurie Interview; Vonderlehr to Clark, January 7, 1933.
7. Wenger to Clark, December 25, 1932, NA-WNRC.
8. Wenger to Clark, December 3, 1932, NA-WNRC.
9. Vonderlehr to Clark, November 2, 1932, NA-WNRC.
10. Vonderlehr to Clark, November 28, 1932, NA-WNRC; Vonderlehr to Clark, January 7, and January 22, 1933, NA-WNRC.

11. Clark to Vonderlehr, January 25, 1933, NA-WNRC; Clark to Vonderlehr, January 31, 1933, NA-WNRC.
12. Vonderlehr to Clark, November 18, 1932, NA-WNRC.
13. Vonderlehr to Clark, January 7, 1933, NA-WNRC.
14. Vonderlehr to Clark, January 28, 1933, NA-WNRC.
15. Vonderlehr to Clark, January 22, 1933, NA-WNRC.
16. Vonderlehr to Clark, January 28, 1933, NA-WNRC.
17. Vonderlehr to Clark, January 7, 1933, NA-WNRC.
18. Vonderlehr to Clark, February 6, 1933, NA-WNRC.
19. Vonderlehr to Clark, January 7, 1933, NA-WNRC.
20. Vonderlehr to Clark, February 11, 1933, NA-WNRC; Vonderlehr to Clark, March 6, 1933, NA-WNRC.
21. Vonderlehr to Clark, January 7, 1933, NA-WNRC.
22. Vonderlehr to Clark, December 8, 1932, NA-WNRC; Clark to Vonderlehr, December 10, 1932, NA-WNRC. The trend persisted. Upon completing his eighty-fifth examination. Dr. Vonderlehr was able to reassure Dr. Clark that "the cases continue to present considerable pathology." Vonderlehr to Clark, December 17, 1932, NA-WNRC.
23. Clark to Moore, December 20, 1932, NA-WNRC.
24. Moore to Clark, April 17, 1933, NA-WNRC.
25. O'Leary to Clark, September 20, 1932, NA-WNRC [underscored in source].
26. Vonderlehr to Clark, February 11, 1933, NA-WNRC.
27. Clark to Vonderlehr, February 17, 1933, NA-WNRC.
28. Vonderlehr to Clark, January 12, 1933, NA-WNRC.
29. Clark to Vonderlehr, January 16, 1933, NA-WNRC; Clark to Moore, March 25, 1933, NA-WNRC.
30. Vonderlehr to Clark, January 12, 1933, NA-WNRC. Upon consultation by Dr. Clark, Dr. Moore indicated broad agreement with Dr. Vonderlehr's criteria for determining contraindication, differing only in the opinion that patients suspected of having brain tumors should be excluded as well. Clark to Moore, January 16, 1933, NA-WNRC; Moore to Clark, January 17, 1933, NA-WNRC.
31. Vonderlehr to Clark, April 11, 1933, NA-WNRC.
32. Wenger to Vonderlehr, April 14, 1933, NA-WNRC.
33. Vonderlehr to Clark, April 8, 1933, NA-WNRC; Clark to Vonderlehr, April 12, 1933, NA-WNRC.
34. Vonderlehr to Clark, April 24, 1933, NA-WNRC.
35. Vonderlehr to Clark, April 8, 1933, NA-WNRC.
36. Ibid.
37. Ibid.
38. Clark to Vonderlehr, April 11, 1933, NA-WNRC.

39. Undated letter, appended to Vonderlehr to Clark, April 21, 1933, NA-WNRC. The letter concludes: "There is enclosed a copy of the letter being sent all subjects for spinal punctures. This letter is preceded by a preliminary notice some ten days or so before telling them to watch the mails for this important letter."
40. Ibid.
41. Ibid.
42. Author's Interview, Charles Pollard, May 2, 1977.
43. Vonderlehr to Clark, April 17, 1933, NA-WNRC; Vonderlehr to Clark, May 8, 1933, NA-WNRC; and Wenger to Clark, May 24, 1933, NA-WNRC.
44. Laurie Interview.
45. Ibid.
46. Author's Interview, Carter Howard, May 2, 1977; Pollard Interview; Author's Interview, Bill Williams, May 2, 1977.
47. Laurie Interview.
48. Vonderlehr to Clark, May 4, 1933, NA-WNRC; Wenger to Clark, May 24, 1933, NA-WNRC; Vonderlehr to Clark, May 20, 1933, NA-WNRC; Wenger to Clark, May 24, 1933, NA-WNRC.
49. Rivers to Vonderlehr, June 5, 1933, NA-WNRC.
50. Smith to Vonderlehr, June 26, 1933, NA-WNRC.
51. Rivers to Vonderlehr, June 29, 1933, NA-WNRC.
52. Cumming to Moton, June 2, 1933, NA-WNRC.
53. For a statement of intentions, see Vonderlehr to Clark, December 17, 1932, NA-WNRC.

Chapter 9. "Bringing Them to Autopsy"

1. Vonderlehr to Wenger, July 18, 1933, Records of the USPHS Venereal Disease Division, Record Group 90, National Archives, Washington National Record Center, Suitland, Maryland [hereafter NA-WNRC].
2. Ibid.
3. Ibid.
4. Ibid.
5. Ibid.
6. Wenger to Vonderlehr, July 21, 1933, NA-WNRC.
7. Ibid.
8. Ibid.
9. Ibid.
10. Vonderlehr to Wenger, July 24, 1933, NA-WNRC.
11. Ibid.
12. Ibid.

13. Wenger to Vonderlehr, August 5, 1933, NA-WNRC.
14. Ibid.
15. Vonderlehr to Dibble, July 18, 1933, NA-WNRC.
16. Dibble to Vonderlehr, July 20, 1933, NA-WNRC; Vonderlehr to Dibble, July 25, 1933, NA-WNRC.
17. Cumming to Moton, July 27, 1933, NA-WNRC.
18. Ibid. True to his word, Dr. Dibble supported the surgeon general's request with a letter urging Dr. Moton to agree to the study. Dibble to Moton, August 3, 1933, Tuskegee Institute Archives.
19. Cumming to Baker, July 27, 1933, NA-WNRC; Baker to Cumming, July 29, 1933, NA-WNRC.
20. Vonderlehr to Roberts, July 29, 1933, NA-WNRC.
21. Marvin to Vonderlehr, August 2, 1933, NA-WNRC.
22. "Report of the Reference Committee to the Executive Committee of the American Heart Assocition," October 10, 1933, NA-WNRC.
23. Vonderlehr to Marvin, August 5, 1933, NA-WNRC.
24. Vonderlehr to Dibble, July 28, 1933, NA-WNRC.
25. Vonderlehr to Moore, August 14, 1933, NA-WNRC; Author's Interview, John R. Heller, November 22, 1976.
26. Heller Interview.
27. Memorandum on Conference, October 20, 1933, Tuskegee Institute Archives [hereafter TIA].
28. Dibble to Moton, November 6, 1933, TIA.
29. Vonderlehr to Wenger, October 24, 1933, NA-WNRC.
30. Vonderlehr to Gill, November 17, 1933, NA-WNRC; Gill to Vonderlehr, November 29, 1933, NA-WNRC.
31. Vonderlehr to Dr. A. J. Sanders, president, Macon County Medical Society, and Vonderlehr to Dr. P. M. Lightfoot, chairman, Macon County Board of Health, October 23, 1933, NA-WNRC. Letters containing identical information went out on the same day to the president of the medical society and the chairman of the board of health in each of the contiguous counties.
32. Author's Interview, John R. Heller, April 21, 1977.
33. First Heller Interview.
34. Ibid.
35. Second Heller Interview.
36. Vonderlehr to Dr. Lett, November 20, 1933, NA-WNRC, plus five identical letters to other area physicians of the same date.
37. Heller to Vonderlehr, November 28, 1933, NA-WNRC.
38. Heller to Vonderlehr, November 20, 1933, NA-WNRC.
39. Heller to Vonderlehr, November 28, 1933, NA-WNRC; Heller to Vonderlehr, December 12, 1933, NA-WNRC.

40. Dibble to Vonderlehr, December 18, 1933, NA-WNRC.
41. Vonderlehr to Dibble, December 21, 1933, NA-WNRC; Vonderlehr to Miller, December 21, 1933, NA-WNRC.
42. Heller to Vonderlehr, March 4, 1933, NA-WNRC.
43. Vonderlehr to Dr. D. D. Corrington, February 12, 1934, NA-WNRC; Vonderlehr to Dibble, April 6, 1934, NA-WNRC; Second Heller Interview.

Chapter 10. "The Joy of My Life"

1. Author's Interview, Eunice Rivers Laurie, May 3, 1977.
2. Laurie Interview; Eunice Rivers, Stanley H. Schuman, Lloyd Simpson, and Sidney Olansky, "The Twenty Years of Follow-up Experience in a Long-Range Medical Study," *Public Health Reports* 68 (1953): 394.
3. Laurie Interview.
4. Rivers et al., "Twenty Years," p. 394.
5. Laurie Interview.
6. Ibid.
7. Ibid.
8. Ibid.
9. Ibid.
10. Rivers to Vonderlehr, January 3, 1934, Records of the USPHS, Venereal Disease Division, Record Group 90, National Archives, Washington National Record Center, Suitland, Maryland [hereafter NA-WNRC].
11. Cumming to Davis, October 4, 1934, NA-WNRC.
12. Cumming to Milbank Fund, November 29, 1935, Tuskegee Files, Center for Disease Control, Atlanta, Georgia [hereafter TF-CDC.]. The PHS annual reports to the Milbank Fund provide the best running account of year-to-year fatalities within the experiment.
13. Rivers et al., "Twenty Years," pp. 391–93; Laurie Interview.
14. Laurie Interview; Rivers et al., "Twenty Years," p. 393; Laurie Interview.
15. Laurie Interview.
16. Cumming to Gentlemen [Milbank Memorial Fund], November 29, 1935, TF-CDC.
17. Author's Interview, Carter Howard, May 2, 1977; Rivers et al., "Twenty Years," p. 394
18. Author's Interview, Charles Pollard, May 2, 1977; Laurie Interview.
19. Rivers et al., "Twenty Years," p. 392.
20. Laurie Interview
21. Ibid.

22. Ibid.

23. Author's Interview, John R. Heller, November 22, 1976.

24. Rivers et al., "Twenty Years," p. 393.

25. Ibid., p. 392.

26. Howard Interview; Author's Interview, Frank Douglas Dixon, May 2, 1977.

27. Pollard Interview.

28. Howard Interview; Dixon Interview.

29. Heller Interview.

30. Author's Interview, Herman Shaw, May 2, 1977; Pollard Interview, both quotes.

31. Joseph G. Caldwell to William J. Brown, June 29, 1970, TF-CDC. In this letter, Caldwell was protesting Brown's refusal to honor Mrs. Laurie's authorization of an autopsy expense that was over the $125 then paid by the Milbank Fund. Caldwell was angered that she was almost left personally responsible for the charge and suggested that either the experiment be abandoned or it be pursued more vigorously, accusing Brown of being "penny-wise and pound-foolish." Dr. Caldwell, about to leave the PHS for a job elsewhere, was sharply critical of the VD Division.

32. Laurie Interview.

33. Ibid.

34. Author's Interview, William J. Brown, April 6, 1977; Author's Interview, Sidney Olansky, November 10, 1976.

35. See Vonderlehr to Waller, May 27, 1937, TF-CDC; Bousfield to Vonderlehr, June 1, 1937, TF-CDC [Bousfield was the director of Negro Health for the Rosenwald Fund]; Smith to Vonderlehr, September 27, 1937, TF-CDC, for Smith's concern over treatment of the untreated group; Vonderlehr to Parran, January 15, 1938, TF-CDC, requesting permission to assign Nurse Rivers to Dr. Peters; Parran to Baker, January 18, 1938, TF-CDC, stating that Dr. Perry was fully informed of the experiment and agreed to cooperate; Vonderlehr to Smith, February 24, 1938, TF-CDC, stating Nurse Rivers had been assigned to Dr. Perry not only to assist his work but to integrate with his control work "the measures pertaining to the study of untreated syphilis in the Negro"; Perry to Vonderlehr, June 24, 1938, TF-CDC, letter containing warm praise for Nurse Rivers.

36. Vonderlehr to Walwyn, June 13, 1939, TF-CDC; *New York Times*, August 7, 1972, p. 16. A mobile unit consisted of a tow car with a trailer. At the front of the trailer blood specimens were taken and injections of neoarsphenamine were given. At the rear was a screened-off space for physical examinations and treatment with bismuth. On most units, the professional staff was composed of a

white physician especially trained in the treatment of syphilis
and a white nurse and a black nurse to assist. See Thomas Parran
and R. A. Vonderlehr, *Plain Words About Venereal Disease* (New
York, 1941), p. 171.
37. Pollard Interview.
38. Shaw Interview.
39. Laurie Interview
40. Ibid.
41. Ibid.
42. Ibid.
43. Ibid.
44. Ibid.
45. Ibid.
46. Ibid.
47. Ibid.
48. Ibid.
49. *Washington Post,* April 19, 1958; Laurie Interview.
50. Ibid.
51. Ibid.

Chapter 11. "Even at Risk of Shortening Life"

1. Author's Interview, Sidney Olansky, November 10, 1976.
2. Public health officers, for example, arranged postgraduate training for Dibble and Peters.
3. Author's Interview, William J. Brown, April 6, 1977.
4. Examinations were given in 1938, 1948, 1951–52, 1958, 1963,
   and 1968.
5. Deibert to Vonderlehr, November 28, 1938, Tuskegee File, Center
   for Disease Control, Atlanta, Georgia [hereafter TF-CDC].
6. Vonderlehr to Deibert, December 5, 1938, TF-CDC.
7. Deibert to Vonderlehr, November 28, 1938, TF-CDC.
8. Vonderlehr to Dibble, December 5, 1938, TF-CDC.
9. Deibert to Vonderlehr, February 6, 1939, TF-CDC.
10. Ibid.; Vonderlehr to Deibert, February 8, 1939, TF-CDC.
11. Deibert to Vonderlehr, March 20, 1939, TF-CDC.
12. Deibert to Vonderlehr, March 27, 1939, TF-CDC.
13. Deibert to Vonderlehr, February 6, 1939, TF-CDC; see also Stan-
    ley H. Schuman et. al., "Untreated Syphilis in the Male Negro:
    Background and Current Status of Patients in the Tuskegee
    Study," *Journal of Chronic Diseases* 2 (1955): 543–58; Sidney
    Olansky et al., "Untreated Syphilis in the Male Negro," *A.M.A.
    Archives of Dermatology* 72 (1956): 516–22; and Donald H. Rock

well et al., "The Tuskegee Study of Untreated Syphilis: The 30th Year of Observation," *Archives of Internal Medicine* 114 (1961): 792–98.

14. Deibert to Vonderlehr, May 1, 1939, TF-CDC.
15. Dr. Smith suggested taking names for prospective new cases off the lists of blacks who registered with the Welfare Department for work or relief. He also recommended using the laboratory reports on blacks who were examined for the draft to find new subjects. See Smith to Vonderlehr, September 20, 1939, TF-CDC; and Smith to Vonderlehr, February 14, 1941, TF-CDC. All of the partially treated men were kept in the study, but a few were excluded from the statistical analysis in some of the published reports on the study. See Austin V. Diebert and Martha C. Bruyere, "Untreated Syphilis in the Male Negro: III. Evidence of Cardiovascular Abnormalities and Other Forms of Morbidity," *Journal of Venereal Disease Information* 27 (1946): 303; Pasquale J. Pesare et al., "Untreated Syphilis in the Male Negro," *American Journal of Syphilis, Gonorrhea, and Venereal Diseases* 34 (1950): 4; and Schuman et al., "Untreated Syphilis," p. 544.
16. Smith to Vonderlehr, November 27, 1941, TF-CDC.
17. Ibid.
18. Vonderlehr to Smith, December 2, 1941, TF-CDC.
19. Smith to Vonderlehr, April 27, 1942, TF-CDC.
20. Vonderlehr to Smith, April 30, 1942, TF-CDC; Smith to Vonderlehr, June 8, 1942, TF-CDC. Vonderlehr informed the Alabama State Department of Health of the agreement that had been reached with the Selective Service Board in Tuskegee so that the state health officials would not press for treating the men either. See Gill to Vonderlehr, July 3, 1942, TF-CDC, and Vonderlehr to Gill, July 10, 1942, TF-CDC.
21. For a discussion of the Henderson Act, see Robert T. Daland, *Government and Health: The Alabama Experience* (University, Alabama, 1955) and Thomas D. Clark, *The Emerging South* (New York, 1961), p. 170.
22. Author's Interview, John R. Heller, November 22, 1976.
23. Parran to Miss Catherine A. Doren, November 4, 1943, TF-CDC.
24. Bauer to Doren, November 27, 1951, TF-CDC.
25. Heller Interview. For a discussion of the Nuremberg Code and a text of the ten principles set forth, see Henry K. Beecher, *Research and the Individual* (Boston, 1974), pp. 227–34.
26. Iskrant to Bauer, July 30, 1948, TF-CDC.
27. Heller to Schuman, September 18, 1951, TF-CDC; O. C. Wenger, "Untreated Syphilis in Male Negro," unpublished manuscript, 1950, p. 3, TF-CDC; John C. Cutler to Olansky, October

22, 1951, enclosure entitled "Outline of Problems to be Considered in Tuskegee Study," TF-CDC. Dr. Olansky was pleased by this reasoning. "As pointed out by Dr. O. C. Wenger," he wrote with obvious approval, "we bear a moral obligation for the success of the study, not only to the previous investigators, but also to each member of the patient group who has borne the risks of untreated disease." Olansky to Cutler, November 6, 1951, enclosure entitled "Outline for Tuskegee Study," TF-CDC.

28. Olansky to Cutler, November 6, 1951, enclosure entitled "Outline for Tuskegee Study," TF-CDC.
29. Most of the published articles on the Tuskegee Study admitted that some of the syphilitics had received small amounts of treatment. For especially tortured efforts at denying that treatment injured the experiment, however, see J. K. Shafer et al., "Untreated Syphilis in the Male Negro: A Prospective Study of the Effect on Life Expectancy," *Public Health Reports* 69 (1954): 688; Schuman et al., "Untreated Syphilis," pp. 550–53; Olansky et al., "Untreated Syphilis," pp. 517–18; and Rockwell et al., "The Tuskegee Study," pp. 795, 797.
30. Olansky to Cutler, November 6, 1951, enclosure entitled "Outline for Tuskegee Study," TF-CDC.
31. Schuman et al., "Untreated Syphilis," pp. 544–45; Schuman to Bauer, November 21, 1951, enclosure entitled "Conference with Dr. Gjestland and Dr. Cutler in Atlanta, Georgia, on November 17, 1951," TF-CDC. Despite the interest of the American health officers in linking the two experiments for the purpose of comparisons, no joint article was ever published on the Tuskegee Study and the Oslo Study. Gjestland's reexamination of the Oslo study data was published four years after his visit to Tuskegee. See T. Gjestland, "Oslo Study of Untreated Syphilis: Epidemiologic Investigation of Natural Course of Syphilitic Infection Based upon Restudy of Boeck-Bruusgaard Material," *Acta Dermatovener* (Stockholm) 35, supplement 34 (1955): 1–368.
32. Schuman to James H. Peers, January 14, 1952, TF-CDC. Dr. Peers, a leading pathologist at the National Institutes of Health, did most of the pathology work on the experiment for many years.
33. Ibid.; Schuman to Olansky, January 29, 1952, TF-CDC.
34. J. R. Heller, Jr., and P. T. Bruyere, "Untreated Syphilis in the Male Negro: II. Mortality During 12 Years of Observation," *Journal of Venereal Disease Information* 27 (1946): 39; several years later (1954) another article reported that the syphilitics who were between the ages of twenty-five and fifty when the experi-

ment began had a 17 percent shorter life expectancy than controls in the same age group. Including the forty-five to fifty year age group presumably lowered the shortening of life expectancy from 20 percent to 17 percent. See Shafer et al., "Untreated Syphilis," p. 689. The health officials also stated that the men in the syphilitic group, in addition to having their lives shortened, were in poor health more generally than men in the control group, a discovery that led researchers to warn that the untreated syphilitic "runs a considerable risk of having his life span shortened by other fatal conditions. In addition, he can expect to experience more manifestations of ill health of all kinds than do uninfected persons." See Deibert and Bruyere, "Untreated Syphilis," p. 313.

35. Shafer et al., "Untreated Syphilis," p. 689; Jesse J. Peters et al., "Untreated Syphilis in the Male Negro: Pathologic Findings in Syphilitic and Nonsyphilitic Patients," *Journal of Chronic Diseases* 1 (1955): 129; Rockwell et al., "The Tuskegee Study," p. 795.
36. Peters et al., "Untreated Syphilis," p. 129.
37. Author's Interview, Sidney Olansky, November 10, 1976; Author's Interview, William J. Brown, April 6, 1977.
38. Olansky Interview.
39. Rivers to Brown, April 11, 1960, TF-CDC.
40. Memorandum from Joseph G. Caldwell to Brown entitled "Fifth (final) Report, Tuskegee Study, 1970," June 11, 1970, TF-CDC. The rights of subjects are more likely to be violated when they come from a different background than the investigator. See Hans Jonas, "Philosophical Reflections on Experimentation," *Daedalus* 98 (1969): 234–37.

Chapter 12. "Nothing Learned Will Prevent, Find, or Cure a Single Case"

1. Mark Frankel, "The Politics of Human Experimentation," unpublished manuscript, pp. 150–54.
2. Ibid., pp. 155–59. For an influential article that contributed to the pressure for reform by showing that unethical experiments were widespread in American science, see Henry K. Beecher, "Ethics and Clinical Research," *New England Journal of Medicine* 274 (1966): 1354–60.
3. Frankel, "Politics," pp. 154–59, 355.
4. Irwin J. Schatz to Donald H. Rockwell, June 11, 1965, Tuskegee File, Center for Disease Control, Atlanta, Georgia [hereafter TF-CDC]. Yobs's note is attached to Schatz's letter.
5. Author's Interview, Peter Buxtun, May 23, 1979.

6. So that there would be no doubts about his views, Buxtun enclosed a copy of the paper he had written in which he compared the Tuskegee Study indirectly to the Nazi experiments. Buxtun to Brown, November 6, 1966, TF-CDC.

7. Buxtun Interview; Dr. Brown's draft was dated December 7, 1966. In this response, Dr. Brown insisted that all the men were volunteers and were "completely free to leave the study at any time." He also stated that the men had received all types of accepted therapy over the years and declared: "The participants have been entirely free to seek treatment at any time." Furthermore, he maintained that the men in the study had gotten a great deal of medical care that they would not have received otherwise. Brown to Buxtun, draft, December 7, 1966, TF-CDC.

8. Buxtun Interview.

9. Ibid.

10. Ibid.

11. Buxtun to Brown, November 24, 1968, TF-CDC.

12. Ad Hoc Committee Minutes, undated, TF-CDC.

13. Ibid. Dr. Kiser told the group about a study of executives on the East Coast to learn the incidence of heart disease mortality. Though they received the best medical attention, he stated, most died of the disease. Dr. Kiser expressed amazement at the survival rate in the Tuskegee Study.

14. Ibid.

15. Ibid.

16. Ibid.

17. Ibid.

18. Ibid.

19. Ibid.

20. Author's Interview, David Sencer, November 10, 1976; Author's Interview, Sidney Olansky, November 10, 1976; Author's Interview, William J. Brown, April 6, 1977.

21. Ad Hoc Committee Minutes.

22. Ibid.

23. Ibid.

24. "Minutes of the State Board of Censors," February 19, 1969, TF-CDC; Myers to Brown, March 13, 1969, TF-CDC.

25. Brown Interview. See also Sencer Interview; Brown to Dr. Alexander Robertson, executive director, the Milbank Fund, November 19, 1969, TF-CDC.

26. Memorandum from Dr. Joseph G. Caldwell to Dr. Arnold L. Schroeter, April 9, 1970, TF-CDC; and Memorandum from Caldwell "Third Tuskegee Report," May 8, 1970, TF-CDC.

27. When Nurse Kennebrew's PHS appointment was delayed, Dr. Berrey kindly arranged to pay her at the federal rate for more than a week in September out of state funds. See Berrey to E. C. Kendrick, August 21, 1971, TF-CDC; Don W. Printz to Kennebrew, April 27, 1972, TF-CDC; and Kennebrew to Schroeter, April 24, 1971, TF-CDC. Nurse Rivers came out of retirement to help train her successor. She showed Nurse Kennebrew what to do during the first autopsy in which she participated and accompanied Nurse Kennebrew on her first roundup.

28. Memorandum from Caldwell to Brown, "Report of second week, 1970 survey, Tuskegee Study," May 4, 1970, TF-CDC; "Report of Telephone Call, June 1, 1970," from Andrew Theodore to Caldwell, TF-CDC; and Memorandum, "Tuskegee Study," from Schroeter to Brown, August 5, 1970, TF-CDC. Dr. Caldwell feared that success in locating missing subjects might skew the study. "We are now selecting those patients who were fortunate and somehow managed to live in harmony with syphilis," he wrote, "We will include these as being relatively healthy despite their syphilis, and those 61 [on] whom we have no information whatever will most likely never be allowed to tell their stories." Memorandum from Caldwell to Brown, "Fourth Report, Tuskegee Study, 1970," May 18, 1970, TF-CDC.

29. Memorandum from Caldwell to Brown et al., "Third Tuskegee Report, 1970, May 8, 1970, TF-CDC. Caldwell reported that he had found "five living patients in Macon County who still have significant syphilitic cardiovascular disease." Despite the ad hoc committee's discussion just the previous year of treating subjects who had syphilitic heart disease, Caldwell said nothing of therapy, recommending study instead: "It behooves us, I think, to attempt to record their murmurs as well as their pulse pressure and apex abnormalities now that we are sophisticated enough in medicine to do these measurements."

30. Memorandum from Caldwell to Brown, "Report of second week, 1970 survey, Tuskegee Study," May 4, 1970, TF-CDC.

31. Brown to Harold J. Magnuson, associate dean, School of Public Health, University of Michigan, February 16, 1970, TF-CDC; and Brown to Robertson, November 16, 1969, TF-CDC. The PHS did permit a paper on the Tuskegee Study to be delivered in 1971 at the American Venereal Disease Association's annual meeting in Atlantic City, New Jersey. The paper focused on aortic regurgitation, and, ironically, the authors reported that their research suggested that "specific antimicrobial therapy of late disease may be beneficial." In stark contradiction to the ad hoc committee of

1969, they also asserted that "withholding penicillin treatment from such patients probably cannot be justified by the argument that repair of already existing destruction would be minimal compared to the risk of Jarisch-Herxheimer reactions of fever, angina, or rupture of aneurysms." While admitting that other authorities might disagree, they recommended treatment! See Joseph G. Caldwell et al., "Aortic Regurgitation in a Study of Aged Males with Previous Syphilis," presented, in part, on June 22, 1971, p. 7. The paper was later published under the title, "Aortic Regurgitation in the Tuskegee Study of Untreated Syphilis," *Journal of Chronic Diseases* 26 (1973): 187–94. While the first version of the paper omitted any reference to the Tuskegee Study in its title, the published version (which appeared one year after the experiment was made public and abandoned) contained a specific citation. Obviously, the need for caution had passed, but ethicists will no doubt wish to debate the propriety of the decision by the editor of the *Journal* to print the paper, thus rewarding the authors with a publication for their work on the experiment.

32. Memorandum from Lucas to Brown, "An analysis of the current status of the Tuskegee Study," September 10, 1970, TF-CDC.
33. Ibid.
34. Ibid.
35. Brown to Buxtun, February 27, 1969, TF-CDC; and Buxtun to Brown, March 29, 1969, TF-CDC.
36. Buxtun Interview.
37. Author's Interview, Jean Heller, June 5, 1979.
38. Ibid.

Epilogue

1. *Atlanta Constitution*, July 27, 1972, p. 30A.
2. Ibid.
3. Ibid., July 26, 1972, p. 1A.
4. *Atlanta Daily World*, August 3, 1972, p. 1.
5. Ibid., and *Birmingham News*, July 27, 1972, p. 4.
6. *Birmingham News, July 27, 1972, p. 4.*
7. Ibid.
8. *Montgomery Advertiser*, July 30, 1972, p. 1.
9. Ibid.
10. Ibid. Settler's statement was made a few days after Foster's announcement; however, both statements were released in the same news story.

11. "New Release," August 24, 1972, Office of the Secretary, DHEW, Tuskegee File, Center for Disease Control, Atlanta, Georgia [hereafter TF-CDC]. The other members of the panel were Ronald H. Brown, general counsel of the National Urban League; Dr. Jean L. Harris, executive director of the National Medical Association Foundation, Inc.; Dr. Vernal Cave, director, Bureau of Venereal Disease Control, New York City Health Department; Professor Jay Katz, Yale Law School; the Reverend Seward Hiltner, Princeton Theological Seminary; Fred Speaker, an attorney from Harrisburg, Pennsylvania; Barney H. Weeks, president of the Alabama Labor Council of the AFL-CIO; and Dr. Jeanne C. Sinkford (D.D.S.), associate dean for Graduate Affairs, College of Dentistry, Howard University.

12. *Medical World News*, September 14, 1973, p. 58; for a good general discussion of the experiment, see *Medical World News*, August 18, 1972, pp. 15–17.

13. "News Release," August 24, 1972, Office of the Secretary, DHEW, TF-CDC.

14. One panelist objected publicly to the constraints of the questions. See J. Katz, "Reservations about the Panel Report on Charge 1," in "Final Report of the Tuskegee Syphilis Study Ad Hoc Advisory Panel," Department of Health, Education, and Welfare (Washington, D.C., 1973) [hereafter "Final Report"], pp. 14–15. For a discussion of the limited charges given the ad hoc panel, see Allan M. Brandt, "Racism and Research: The Case of the Tuskegee Study," *Hastings Report* 8 (December 1978): 26–27. While Brandt makes extensive use of archival materials and is a trained historian, his discussion of the Tuskegee Study (which follows a chronological approach) has a wide-eyed and strangely ahistorical tone to it. He is more concerned with proving charges of racism than attempting to understand what happened. For a polemic from another historian who seems intent on seeing little but racism in the Tuskegee Study, see Herbert Aptheker, "Racism and Human Experimentation," *Political Affairs* 53 (February 1974): 46–59.

15. Seward Hiltner, "The Tuskegee Study Under Review," *Christian Century*, November 28, 1973, p. 1175; "Initial Recommendations of the Tuskegee Syphilis Study Ad Hoc Advisory Panel," October 25, 1972, p. 2, TF-CDC.

16. "HEW News," Office of the Secretary, March 5, 1973, TF-CDC. The actual directive came on March 3. See Weinberger to acting assistant secretary for health, March 8, 1973, TF-CDC. The legality of giving treatment as part of the experiment was certified by

the general counsel of DHEW, Wilmot R. Hastings. See the memorandum "USPHS Study of Untreated Syphilis (the Tuskegee Study); Authority to Treat Participants Upon Termination of the Study," from Hastings to the secretary, March 5, 1973, TF-CDC.

17. "Final Report," pp. 7, 23–24. Disagreements within the ad hoc panel had developed early in their deliberations. Dr. Butler, whom several members on the panel suspected of being too sympathetic to the government's defense of the study, angered his colleagues by refusing to open their meetings to the press. Their differences erupted into open warfare when Dr. Butler without warning or advance discussions refused to endorse the panel's final report. In response to this refusal, several panelists held a press conference to defend the report and denounce the chairman. See Hiltner, "Tuskegee Study," p. 1176; and "Report on HEW's Tuskegee Report," *Medical World News*, September 14, 1973, pp. 57–58. For a ringing denunciation of the final report from a medical defender of the experiment, see R. H. Kampmeir, "Final Report on the 'Tuskegee Syphilis Study,' " *Southern Medical Journal* 67 (1974): 1344–53.

18. For an interesting editorial in support of the payment bill, see *Afro-American*, August 19, 1972, p. 4.

19. *Quality of Health Care: Human Experimentation, 1973*, Hearings Before the Subcommittee on Health of the Committee on Labor and Public Welfare, Ninety-third Congress (Washington, D.C., 1973), III:1041.

20. Ibid., p. 1035.

21. Ibid., p. 1042.

22. Mark Frankel, "The Politics of Human Experimentation," unpublished manuscript, pp. 150–59, 355. The national debate over human experimentation led to a special commission to formulate new guidelines. The commission's proceedings may be followed in *National Commission for the Protection of Human Subjects of Biomedical and Behavior Research* (Washington, D.C., 1976).

23. The "Guidelines for Medical Care" were mailed to physicians chosen by the subjects, along with a cover letter. See Donald R. Hopkins to "Dear Doctor," April 13, 1973, TF-CDC. The instructions explicitly recommended treatment for syphilis with penicillin unless the physician "feels there is reasonable suspicion of penicillin allergy or documented proof of prior adequate . . . antibiotic treatment."

24. The CDC began debating whether to treat the wives and children in 1973. A memo written in that year said: "The possibilities are that wives may have contracted the disease directly and that

children may suffer from congenital conditions.'" See Charles M. Gozonsky to William C. Watson, "CDC-Tuskegee Study—Participants—Families—Medical Care," June 6, 1973, TF-CDC. The government estimated that health care for the surviving spouses could cost as much as $12 million, while medical care for the surviving children might cost as much as $127 million. As of May, 1980, approximately fifty surviving wives and twenty surviving children were receiving full medical care because examinations had revealed that they had syphilis that was directly attributable to the government's failure to treat the men.

25. The Tuskegee Files at the Center for Disease Control do not contain a single documented case of harmful drug reactions among the men who received treatment.

26. *Charles W. Pollard, et al. v. United States of America, et al.*, Civil Action No. 4126-N, Northern Division, Middle District of Alabama, District Court of the United States, "Complaint."

27. *Charles W. Pollard, et al. v. United States of America, et al.*, Civil Action No. 4126-N, Northern Division, Middle District of Alabama, District Court of the United States, "Stipulation of Settlement," pp. 1–15.

28. For a critical discussion of Gray's fee, see James J. Cramer, "The $10-Million Giveaway," *American Lawyer*, October 1979, p. 23.

29. Ibid., p. 24.

30. Ibid.

31. Ibid.

32. Author's Interview, Eunice Rivers Laurie, May 3, 1977.

33. Author's Interview, Herman Shaw, May 2, 1977; Author's Interview, Carter Howard, May 2, 1977.

A Note on Sources

BAD Blood is based largely on the official records of the United States Public Health Service's Division of Venereal Diseases. The papers dealing with the origins and first four years of the Tuskegee Study are located in Record Group 90 (1918 – 1936), housed in the Washington National Records Center, Suitland, Maryland. The records of the Tuskegee Study after 1936 are located in the Tuskegee Study Files at the Center for Disease Control in Atlanta, Georgia.

The Julius Rosenwald Fund Papers and the Charles Johnson Papers, both housed in the Fisk University Archives, Nashville, Tennessee, provided essential materials on the Rosenwald Fund's syphilis control demonstrations in the South, undertaken in cooperation with the United States Public Health Service. The raw notes on the field interviews for *Shadow of the Plantation* were especially helpful.

The Archives of the Tuskegee Institute, Tuskegee, Alabama, contain the records of the Institute's long involvement with the Tuskegee Study. With the exception of the first few years of the experiment, most of the letters are fiscal documents of a routine nature.

Copies of some of the documents from the Washington National Record Center, the Center for Disease Control, the Fisk

University Archives, and the Tuskegee Institute Archives are on file in the Tuskegee Study Ad Hoc Advisory Panel Papers in the National Library of Medicine, Bethesda, Maryland. The papers are indexed.

The PHS officers who conducted the Tuskegee Study never published a comprehensive summary of their findings. They did, however, publish thirteen articles over the years, a series of progress reports. As such the following articles represent the best statement of what the researchers thought the Tuskegee Study had to tell science:

1. R. A. VONDERLEHR et al. "Untreated Syphilis in the Male Negro: A Comparative Study of Treated and Untreated Cases." *Venereal Disease Information* 17 (1936): 260–65.
2. J. R. HELLER et al. "Untreated Syphilis in the Male Negro: II. Mortality During 12 Years of Observation." *Venereal Disease Information* 27 (1946): 34–38.
3. A. V. DEIBERT et al. "Untreated Syphilis in the Male Negro: III. Evidence of Cardiovascular Abnormalities and Other Forms of Morbidity." *Journal of Venereal Disease Information* 27 (1946): 301–314.
4. PASQUALE J. PESARE et al. "Untreated Syphilis in the Male Negro: Observation of Abnormalities Over Sixteen Years." *American Journal of Syphilis, Gonorrhea, and Venereal Diseases* 34 (1950): 201–213.
5. EUNICE RIVERS et al. "Twenty Years of Follow-up Experience in a Long-Range Medical Study." *Public Health Reports* 68 (1953): 391–95.
6. J. K. SHAFER et al. "Untreated Syphilis in the Male Negro: A Prospective Study of the Effect on Life Expectancy." *Public Health Reports* 69 (1954): 691–97; and *Milbank Fund Memorial Quarterly* 32 (1954): 261–74.
7. SIDNEY OLANSKY et al. "Environmental Factors in the Tuskegee Study of Untreated Syphilis." *Public Health Reports* 69 (1954): 691–98.
8. JESSE J. PETERS et al. "Untreated Syphilis in the Male Negro: Pathologic Findings in Syphilitic and Nonsyphilitic Patients." *Journal of Chronic Diseases* 1 (1955): 127–48.
9. STANLEY H. SCHUMAN et al. "Untreated Syphilis in the Male Negro: Background and Current Status of Patients in the Tuskegee Study." *Journal of Chronic Diseases* 2 (1955): 543–58.
10. SIDNEY OLANSKY et al. "Untreated Syphilis in the Male Negro: X. Twenty Years of Clincial Observation of Untreated Syphilitic and Presumably Nonsyphilitic Groups." *Journal of Chronic Diseases* 4 (1956): 177–85.

11. SIDNEY OLANSKY et al. "Untreated Syphilis in the Male Negro: Twenty-two Years of Serologic Observation in a Selected Syphilis Study Group." *A.M.A. Archives of Dermatology* 73 (1956): 516-22.

12. DONALD H. ROCKWELL et al. "The Tuskegee Study of Untreated Syphilis: The 30th Year of Observation." *Archives of Internal Medicine* 114 (1961): 792-98.

13. JOSEPH G. CALDWELL et al. "Aortic Regurgitation in the Tuskegee Study of Untreated Syphilis." *Journal of Chronic Diseases* 26 (1973): 187-94.

America's black physicians clearly had a powerful need to settle the question of what was learned from the Tuskegee Study. Acting at the request of the National Medical Association, Dr. McDonald Charles wrote: "The Contribution of the Tuskegee Study to Medical Knowledge," *Journal of the National Medical Association* 66 (1974): 1-7. His assessment was that the Tuskegee Study did make important contributions to the scientific literature on syphilis. He failed to recognize that the small amounts of treatment that the men received completely negated the experiment's value to science.

This work also makes use of oral history. All of the interviews listed below are in the author's possession.

William J. Brown, M.D., April 6, 1977
Peter Buxtun, May 23-24, 1979
Frank Douglas Dixon, May 2, 1977
Jean Heller, June 5, 1979
John R. Heller, M.D., November 22, 1976, and April 21, 1977
Carter Howard, May 2, 1977
Eunice Rivers Laurie, R.N., May 3, 1977
Sidney Olansky, M.D., November 10, 1976
Charles Pollard, May 2, 1977
David Sencer, M.D., November 10, 1976
Herman Shaw, May 2, 1977
Bill Williams, May 2, 1977

For the purpose of this study, two secondary works have been treated as primary documents for understanding the Rosenwald Fund's syphilis control demonstrations in Macon County and the lives of the black patients who participated in the program. Thomas Parran's *Shadow on the Land: Syphilis* (New York, 1937) is invaluable for understanding how PHS officers saw themselves and their black patients. Similarly,

Charles Johnson's classic sociological study, *Shadow of the Plantation* (Chicago, 1934), is quite the best record available for placing the syphilis control work in the larger context of the everyday lives of black sharecroppers in Macon County, Alabama, during the 1930s.

The medical literature on syphilis and blacks in the United States is voluminous. In the last decades of the nineteeth century and continuing through the 1950s, physicians debated alleged differences in racial responses to the disease. Much of the controversy may be traced in medical journals, most notably in the *Southern Medical Journal*, the *Journal of the American Medical Association*, the *Medical News*, the *American Journal of Dermatology and Genito-Urinary Diseases*, and the *American Journal of Public Health*. Less prestigious medical journals at the state and local levels also published articles on blacks and syphilis. No dramatic differences in the tone of the racial views expressed separated the national from the state and local journals. Medical textbooks and monographs on syphilis also included discussions of the alleged racial differences in response to syphilis, though these discussions declined sharply after the 1920s and 1930s.

The racial attitudes of pre–Civil War physicians have been examined in two major studies. Todd L. Savitt's *Medicine and Slavery: The Health Care and Diseases of Blacks in Antebellum Virginia* (Urbana, Ill., 1978) is an important, richly documented examination of racial medicine. A sympathetic treatment of health care afforded to blacks under slavery is offered by William D. Postell's *The Health of Slaves on Southern Plantations* (Baton Rouge, La., 1951). No book-length study has been published on racial medicine after the Civil War.

There is no up-to-date history of the United States Public Health Service, though Ralph Chester Williams's *The United States Public Health Service, 1798–1950* (Washington, D.C., 1951) does provide a helpful overview of the PHS's activities during most of the years covered in this study. Useful state and local studies of public health work include John Duffy's *A History of Public Health in New York City*, 2 vols. (New York: 1968, 1974); Barbara Gutmann Rosenkrantz's *Public Health and the State: Changing Views in Massachusetts, 1842–1936* (Cambridge, Mass., 1972); and Stuart Galishoff's *Safeguarding the Public Health: Newark, 1895–1918* (Westport, Conn., 1975).

Two social histories of particular diseases warrant special attention. Charles E. Rosenberg's *The Cholera Years: The United States in 1832, 1849, and 1866* (Chicago, 1962) is a brilliant study of the interaction between society and medicine. No book does a better job of explaining how social attitudes influence a people's perception of and response to disease. Elizabeth W. Etheridge's *The Butterfly Caste: A Social History of Pellagra in the South* (Westport, Conn., 1972) is an excellent study of the conquest of a mysterious disease. Through her study of pellagra, Etheridge offers an eloquent picture of southern poverty and the politics of both philanthropy and medical research. By centering on the constructive and successful role played by the Public Health Service, focused principally on the quiet leadership of Dr. Joseph Goldberger, Etheridge used the history of disease and health care to create a compelling examination of the moral basis of society. Her book should be read as a counterpoint to this study because she deals with much the same time period and shows the PHS at its best.

There is no satisfactory one-volume history of medicine in the United States. A brave attempt to fill the void is John Duffy's *The Healers: The Rise of the Medical Establishment* (New York, 1976). The best introduction to the field remains Richard Harrison Shryock's *Medicine and Society in America, 1660 – 1860* (New York, 1960). Martin Kaufman's *American Medical Education: The Formative Years, 1765 – 1910* (Westport, Conn., 1976) is a useful survey of medical education until the time of the Flexner Report. The pre – Civil War background of professionalism in American medicine is examined in Joseph F. Kett's *The Formation of the American Medical Association: The Role of Institutions, 1780 – 1860* (New Haven, 1968), and Rosemary Stevens surveys twentieth-century developments in the specialization of medicine in *American Medicine and the Public Interest* (New Haven, 1971). The best sociological study of the medical profession remains Eliot Freidson's *Profession of Medicine: A Study of the Sociology of Applied Knowledge* (New York, 1973). Herbert M. Morais's *The History of the Negro in Medicine* (New York, Washington, and London, 1967) is a broad survey of the admission and contribution of blacks to the medical profession.

The historical literature on the nursing profession is meager. JoAnn Ashley's *Hospitals, Paternalism, and the Role of the Nurse* (New York, 1976) studies the problems confronted by nurses' training schools, and Helen E. Marshall's *Mary Adelaide Nutting: Pioneer of Modern Nursing* (Baltimore, 1972) examines the career of America's first full-time professor of nursing. A good place to begin is Richard H. Shryock's *The History of Nursing: An Interpretation of the Social and Medical Facts Involved* (Philadelphia, 1959).

The attitudes of white people toward blacks in the United States have been studied richly. The most outstanding book in the field is Winthrop Jordan's *White over Black: American Attitudes Toward the Negro, 1550–1812* (Chapel Hill, N.C., 1968). A highly readable study for racial thinking in the first half of the nineteenth century is William Stanton's *The Leopard's Spots: Scientific Attitudes Toward Race in America, 1815–1859* (Chicago, 1960). John S. Haller, Jr., carries the story to the twentieth century in *Outcasts from Evolution: Scientific Attitudes of Racial Inferiority, 1859–1900* (Urbana, Ill., 1971). Also valuable are George M. Fredrickson's *The Black Image in the White Mind: The Debate on Afro-American Character and Destiny, 1817–1914* (New York, 1971), and Thomas F. Gossett's *Race: The History of an Idea in America* (New York, 1965). Finally, Allen Chase offers a detailed chronicle of the residue of racism in twentieth-century American science in *The Legacy of Malthus: The Social Costs of the New Scientific Racism* (New York, 1980).

Dan T. Carter's *Scottsboro: A Tragedy of the American South* (Baton Rouge, La., 1969) is the best study of how racial attitudes influenced a profession in the twentieth century. The book is also incomparable for capturing the tenor of race relations in Alabama. Essentially, Carter told the story of how the American legal profession perpetrated a terrible miscarriage of justice in support of the South's racial system, then had to struggle for years to right the wrong. Because it examines a profession and because it is set in Alabama during the early 1930s, Carter's book offers the best parallel to *Bad Blood*. Useful as background for both books is George B. Tindall's *The Emergence of the New South: 1913–1945* (Baton Rouge, La., 1967), a commanding view of the South's overall development.

Scholarly interest in the field of bioethics has risen sharply in the last fifteen years. The most comprehensive accessible introduction to the full range of topics and arguments is Warren T. Reich's (ed.) *The Encyclopedia of Bioethics* (New York, 1978). Another extremely helpful tool is Paul T. Durbin's (ed.) *A Guide to The Culture of Science, Technology, and Medicine* (New York, 1980). The literature on human experimentation, most of which has been done by philosophers who have been trained in ethics, is especially rich. A helpful introduction to the subject by a distinguished and humane physician is Henry K. Beecher's *Research and the Individual: Human Studies* (Boston, 1970), and an outstanding collection of essays is offered in Paul A. Freund's (ed.) *Experimentation with Human Subjects* (New York, 1970).

Indexes

Name Index

Subject Index